The Ultimate Kaua'i Guidebook

Andrew Doughty
Harriett Friedman

WIZARD
PUBLICATIONS

The Ultimate Kaua'i Guidebook

Published by Wizard Publications
Post Office Box 991
Lihu'e, Hawai'i 96766–0991

ISBN# 0–9639429–0–5
Library of Congress Catalog Card Number 93–61569
Printed in Hong Kong

All photographs taken in 1993 by Andrew Doughty.

Cartography by Andrew Doughty.
All artwork and illustrations by Andrew Doughty and Harriett Friedman.

About the cover:
Photograph of Kaua'i taken by the crew of the Space Shuttle Discovery. The title portion consists of a picture of a sunrise over Lydgate State Park, Kaua'i.

We welcome any comments, questions, criticisms, or contributions you may have. In this way, we can continually enhance the quality of the book in future editions. Please send to:

Wizard Publications
P.O. Box 991
Lihu'e, Hawai'i 96766–0991

Dedicated to Sammie Dollar, who soars on the wind with the white-tailed tropic birds.

CONTENTS

In many ways, this is not a guidebook, it's more of a love story. We first came to Kaua'i as tourists and were immediately smitten. We had no idea that a place like this could exist anywhere in the world. Now as residents of Kaua'i, we marvel at its beauty every day.

We have found many special places that even people born and raised here didn't know about. Whether this your first time on Kaua'i or your tenth, you will find this book as valuable as having a friend living on the island.

Kaua'i is a unique place. People who visit here recognize this immediately. There are plenty of places in the world featuring Sun and sea, but no other place offers the ultimate beauty, lushness, and serenity than does Kaua'i. Living here, we get to see first time visitors driving around with their jaws open, shaking their heads in disbelief at what they see. Without a doubt, you will never see more smiles than during your visit to Kaua'i.

Our objective in writing this book was to assist you in finding the wonder that can accompany a Kaua'i visit. We recognize the effort people go through to visit here, and our goal is to expose you to every option imaginable so you can decide what you want to see and do.

We took great pains to structure this book in such a way that it will be fun, easy reading, loaded with useful information. This book is not a bland regurgitation of the facts arranged in textbook fashion. We feel strongly that guidebooks should present their information so that you don't have to read through every single page every time you want to find something. If you are here on vacation, your time is extremely precious. You don't want to spend all your time flipping through a book looking for what you want. You want to be able to locate what you want, when you want it. You want to be able to access a comprehensive index, a thorough table of contents, and refer to high quality maps that were designed with you in mind. You want to know which Helicopter, Scuba, Boat Tour, or Lu'au is the best on the island. You want to be shown those things that will make this vacation the best of your life.

A quick look at this book will reveal features never before used in a guidebook. Let's start with the maps. They are more detailed than any other maps you will find, and yet omit extraneous information that can sometimes make a chore out of reading a map. We know that people often have difficulty determining where they are on a map, so we included landmarks. Most notable among these are the mile markers, which you will notice on main roads around the island. At every mile on main roads, the Government has erected numbered markers to tell you where you are. We are the first to put these markers on a map so you can use them as reference points. We also took great pains to place north at the top of the page. It can get confusing when you see a compass on a map with south pointing up, or to the right. Only one trail map deviates from this rule. Additionally, we repeatedly drove every inch of every road on the maps. This is important because many of the roads represented on existing maps have been shifted, rerouted, or eliminated. We can't tell you how many times we went to find a beach or other scenic spot using existing maps, only to be frustrated by not finding them. Only by using aerial photography could we determine a method for getting to certain places. We once spent three days trying to find a certain secluded beach using existing maps. When we checked aerial shots, we discovered that *every single map was wrong*. Getting to the beach was a snap...if you knew where to go.

As you read this book, you will also notice that we are very candid in assessing businesses. Unlike some other guidebooks that send out questionnaires asking businesses about themselves (gee, they *all* say they're the best), we have had *personal* contact with the businesses listed in this book. These are *not* advertisements. If we gush over a certain company, it comes from personal experience with the company. If we rail against a business, it is for the same reason. All businesses mentioned in this book are here by *our* choosing. None have had *any* say in what we wrote, and we have not received a single cent from any of them. (In fact, there are some that would probably pay to be left out of this book given our comments.) We always approach businesses as anonymous tourists, and later as guidebook writers. This ensures that we are treated the same as you.

This book brings you independence in exploring Kaua'i. We don't want to waste any of your precious vacation time by giving you bad advice, or bad directions. We want you to experience the best that the island has to offer. In the end, it's probably fair to say that our ultimate objective is to have *you* leave Kaua'i as we did the first time, shaking your head saying, "I never knew a place like this existed."

We hope we succeed.

Andrew Doughty
Harriett Friedman

Kapa'a, Hawai'i

How It Began

The Hawaiian Islands were born of fire thousands of feet below the surface in the icy cold waters on the Pacific Ocean floor. A rupture in the Earth's crust caused a vent to spew forth hot magma which built upon itself as it reached upward. When it began, no one knows exactly, but the first of the existing islands to boil to the surface was Kure. Nothing remains of that island today but its fringing coral reef, called an atoll.

As the vent shifted along the bottom of the sea, more islands were created. Midway, French Frigate Shoals, Necker, Nihoa; all were created and then mostly consumed by the angry ocean. What we call Hawai'i is just the last in a series of islands created by this vent. Someday, these too will be nothing more than atolls, footnotes in the geologic history of the Earth. But this vent isn't finished yet. The Big Island of Hawai'i is still expanding as lava from its active volcano continues to create additional real estate on that island. As we sit here, the future island of Loihi is being created 20 miles southeast of the Big Island. Although still 3,200 feet below the surface of the ocean, in but a geologic moment, the Hawaiian goddess Pele will add yet another piece of paradise to her impressive domain.

These virgin islands were barren at birth. Consisting only of volcanic rock, the first life forms to appreciate these new islands were marine creatures. Fish, mammals, and microscopic animals discovered this new underwater haven and made homes for themselves. Coral polyps attached themselves to the lava and succeeding generations built upon these, creating what would become a coral reef.

Meanwhile on land, seeds carried by the winds were struggling to colonize the rocky land, eking out a living and break-

The walls of Wai'ale'ale, from which the island of Kaua'i burst forth in a fiery cataclysm, now are home to innumerable waterfalls. This part of the Crater is called the Weeping Wall.

ing down the lava rock. Storms brought the occasional bird, hopelessly blown off course. The lucky ones found the islands. The even luckier ones arrived with mates or were pregnant when they got here. Other animals, stranded on a piece of floating debris, washed ashore against all odds and went on to colonize the islands. These introductions of new species were rare events. It took an extraordinary set of circumstances for a new species to actually make it to the islands. Single specimens were destined to live out their lives in lonely solitude. On average, a new species was successfully deposited here only once every twenty thousand years.

As the plants and animals lived out their lives, they broke up the rock, forming soil and organic debris. The ocean, meanwhile, was busily working to reclaim the horizon from these interruptions of land. Waves battered unmercifully against the fragile lava rock. In this battle between titans, there can be but one winner. Whereas the creation of land eventually ceases on an individual island, the ocean never gives up. Wave after wave eventually takes its toll.

In addition to the ocean, rain carves up the islands. As the islands thrust themselves upward into the moisture laden trade winds, their challenge to the rain clouds is accepted. As the air encounters the slopes of these tall islands it rises and cools, causing the air to release its humidity in the form of rain. This rain forms channels which easily carve valleys in the soft lava rock.

So what is the result of all this destruction? Paradise. Absolute par-

Each successive wave helps sculpt the island. Large storms can generate particularly powerful waves such as this one which, over the eons, can have a dramatic effect on an island's coastline.

On rare occasions this ancient Hawaiian petroglyph is exposed in the mouth of the Wailua River.

adise. There are few things more beautiful than Mother Nature reclaiming that which she gave birth to. The older the island, the more beautiful. A Hawaiian island is never more lovely than in its middle age, when the scars of constant environmental battles are carved into its face. Lush landscaped valleys, razorback ridges, long strands of beach; those things we cherish so much are the result of this destructive battle.

Kaua'i consists of 555 square miles of beach, rain forest, desert, mountains, and plains. The island's landscape is as varied as its people. At Wai'ale'ale in the center, it rains every day making it the wettest place on Earth. Just a few miles to the west, rain is rare creating dry, almost arid conditions. The north shore is as lush as any place on the planet. The south shore is a sunny playground. The island's first inhabitants surely must have felt blessed at the discovery of this diversity.

THE FIRST SETTLERS

Sometime around the fourth or fifth century A.D. a large double-hulled voyaging canoe, held together with flexible sennit lashings and propelled by sails made of woven Pandanus, slid onto the sand of a Hawaiian island. These first intrepid adventurers encountered an island chain of unimaginable beauty.

They had left their home in the Marquesas Islands 2,500 miles away for reasons we will never know. Some say it was because of war, overpopulation, drought, or just a sense of adventure. Whatever their reasons, these initial settlers took a big chance, and surely must have been highly motivated. They left their homes and searched for a new world to colonize. Doubtless,

Who Were the Menehune?

Although the legend of Menehune exists throughout the Hawaiian Islands, the folklore is strongest on Kaua'i. Hawaiian legend speaks of a mythical race of people living in the islands before the Polynesians. Called the Menehune, these people are always referred to as being small in stature. Initially referring to their social stature, the legend evolved to mean that they were physically short, and lived in the woods away from the Hawaiians. (The Hawaiians avoided the woods when possible fearing that they held evil spirits, and instead stayed on the coastal plains.) The Menehune were purported to build fabulous structures, always in one night. Their numbers were said to be vast, as much as 500,000. Today, archeologists speculate that a second wave of colonists, probably from Tahiti, may have subdued these initial inhabitants forcing them to live in the woods. It is interesting to note that in a census taken of Kaua'i around 1800, 65 persons from the upper region of the Wainiha Valley identified themselves as Menehune.

Today, Menehune are jokingly blamed for anything that goes wrong. If you lost your wallet, Menehune took it. If your car won't start, Menehune have been tinkering with it. Kaua'i residents greatly cherish their legends of the Menehune.

most of the first groups perished at sea. There was no way for them to know that there were islands in these waters. The Hawaiian Islands are the most isolated island chain in the world. Those that did arrive brought with them food staples from home; taro, breadfruit, pigs, dogs, and several types of fowl. This was a pivotal decision. These first settlers found a land that contained almost no edible plants. With no land mammals other than the Hawaiian bat, the first settlers subsisted on fish until their crops could mature. From then on, they lived on fish and taro. Although we associate throw-net fishing with Hawai'i, this practice was introduced by Japanese immigrants much later. The ancient Hawaiians used fishhooks and spears for the most part, or drove fish into a net already placed into the water. They also had domesticated animals which were used as ritual foods or reserved for chiefs.

As the culture evolved and flourished, it developed into a hierarchical system of order. The society was governed by chiefs, called Ali'i, who established a long list of taboos called kapu. These kapu were designed to keep order, and the penalty for breaking one was usually death by strangulation, club, or fire. If the violation was serious enough, the guilty party's family might be killed. It was kapu, for instance, for your shadow to fall across the shadow of the Ali'i. It was kapu to interrupt the chief if he was speaking. It was kapu to prepare men's food in the same container used for women's food. It was kapu for women to eat pork or bananas. It was kapu for men and women to eat together. It was kapu not to observe the days designated to the gods. Certain areas were kapu for fishing if they became depleted. This allowed the area to replenish itself.

While harsh by our standards today, this system kept the order. Most Ali'i were sensitive to the disturbance their presence caused and often ventured outside only at night, or a scout was sent ahead to warn people that an Ali'i was on his way. All commoners were required to pay tribute to the Ali'i in the form of food and other items.

In January 1778 an event occurred that would forever change Hawai'i.

Captain James Cook, who usually had a genius for predicting where to find islands, stumbled upon Hawai'i. He had not expected islands to be there. He was on his way to Alaska to search for the Northwest Passage linking the Atlantic and Pacific Oceans. As Cook approached the shores of Waimea, Kaua'i on January 19, 1778 the Island's inhabitants thought they were being visited by gods. Rushing aboard to greet their visitors, the Kauaians were fascinated by what they saw: pointy headed beings (the British wore tricornered hats) breathing fire (smoking pipes) and possessing a death-dealing instrument identified as a water squirter (guns). The amount of iron on the ship was incredible. Cook left Kaua'i and briefly explored Ni'ihau before heading north for his mission on February 2, 1778.

The earliest Hawaiians built elaborate terraces to grow taro, used to make poi. This one, in the Limahuli Gardens, is estimated to be 1,000 years old.

Ancient Hawaiians lived off the sea. With reefs teaming with life, Hawaiian waters have always been generous to the people of Hawaii.

When Cook returned to the Big Island of Hawai'i after failing to find the Northwest Passage (there wasn't one), he was killed in a petty skirmish over a stolen rowboat. The Hawaiians were horrified that they had killed a man they presumed to be a god.

About this time, Kamehameha the Great of the Big Island was consolidating his power by conquering the other islands in the chain. Kaua'i, however, presented a unique problem. Cut off from the rest of the chain by the treacherous Kaua'i Channel, Kaua'i's King Kaumuali'i had no intention of submitting himself to Kamehameha. In the spring of 1796 Kamehameha attempted to invade Kaua'i. He and his fleet of 1,200 canoes carrying 10,000 soldiers left O'ahu at midnight hoping to reach Wailua, Kaua'i by daybreak. They were

in the middle of the Kaua'i Channel when the wind and seas picked up. Many of the canoes were swamped. Reluctantly, he ordered a retreat, but too late to stop some of his advance troops who were slaughtered after they arrived at the south shore beach of Maha'ulepu.

In 1804 Kamehameha tried again. He gathered 7,000 men, all heavily armed, and prepared to set sail for Kaua'i. Just before they were to leave, typhoid struck, all but decimating his troops and advisers. Kamehameha himself contracted the disease but managed to pull through. Kaua'i's King must have seen the writing on the wall and agreed to give his Kingdom of Kaua'i over to Kamehameha. In order to solidify his power on Kaua'i, Kamehameha later arranged to kidnap Kaua'i's King Kaumuali'i and forced him to marry his sister. Kaua'i's last king never returned and was eventually buried on Maui.

During the nineteenth century, Hawai'i's character changed dramatically. Businessmen from all over the world came here to exploit Hawai'i's sandalwood, whales, land, and people. Hawai'i's leaders, for their part, actively participated in these ventures and took a piece of much of the action for themselves. Workers were brought from many parts of the world, changing the racial makeup of the islands. Government corruption became the order of the day and everyone seemed to be profiting except the Hawaiian commoner. By the time Queen Lili'uokalani lost her throne to a group of American businessmen in 1893, Hawai'i had become directionless. It

What's it Like in the Wettest Spot on Earth?

Located in the center of the island is Mount Wai'ale'ale, meaning rippling waters. It is here that you will find the rainiest spot on the planet with an average of 440.22 inches of rain per year, and a mean of 432 inches. Rain around the rest of the island is a fraction of this (see chart on page 29). The ancient Hawaiians recognized the importance of this spot and built a temple on the summit which remains there to this day. The only way you will get to see Wai'ale'ale up close and personal is by helicopter.

The top of Mount Wai'ale'ale is somewhat barren. While this might sound strange given its moniker as the wettest spot on Earth, realize that there are no plants on this planet genetically programmed to deal with rain every single day. The bogs on top of the mountain make for a less than well defined soil base. Fungi and lichen flourish in the constant moisture. The result is few trees. Those trees that do survive are stunted by Nature's overgenerous gift of water.

Just below the summit—3,000 feet straight down to be precise—exists the unimaginable lushness one would expect from abundant rain. As the clouds are forced up the walls of Wai'ale'ale Crater, they shed a portion of their moisture. With the majority of the rain falling on the summit, the crater floor is left with just the perfect amount. With volcanically rich soil left over from the fiery eruptions, the Crater floor has become a haven for anything green. Ferns rule the Crater. The ground shakes beneath your feet as your footsteps echo through generations of fallen ferns saturated with water which have created a soft underbelly to what once was a savage, lava-spewing giant.

There is a surprising lack of insect presence. Aside from mosquitoes in the stream beds, we encountered almost no insects in the dense fern growth of the crater. The only exception was a single flightless grasshopper. Some freshwater fish inhabit the streams—which is difficult to understand since we found a fish between two immense waterfalls, neither of which it could have negotiated.

Everywhere one looks, plants have taken root. Every rock has moss, every fallen tree has other plants growing on it, every crevice has growth. Surely, no other place on Earth is as lush as Wai'ale'ale Crater.

barely resembled the Hawai'i Captain Cook had encountered the previous century. The kapu system had been abolished by the Hawaiians shortly after the death of Kamehameha the Great. The "Great Mahele," begun in 1848, had changed the relationship Hawaiians had with the land. Large tracts of land were sold by the Hawaiian Government to royalty, government officials, commoners, and foreigners, effectively stripping many Hawaiians of land they had lived on for generations.

The United States recognized the Republic of Hawai'i in 1894 with Sanford Dole as its President. It was later annexed in 1900. During the nineteenth and twentieth centuries, sugar established itself as king. Pineapple was also heavily grown in the islands, with the island of Lana'i being purchased in its entirety for the purpose of growing pineapples. As the twentieth century rolled on, Hawaiian sugar and pineapple workers found themselves in a lofty position—they became the highest paid workers for these crops in the world. As land prices rose and competition from other parts of the world increased, sugar and pineapple became less and less profitable. Today, these crops no longer hold the position they once had. The island of Lana'i has shifted away from pineapple growing, and is looking toward tourism. Sugar lands are being slowly converted to other purposes and the workers are moving into other vocations, usually tourist-related.

The story of Hawai'i is not a story of good versus evil. Nearly everyone shares in the blame of what happened to the Hawaiian people and their culture. Nevertheless, today Hawai'i is struggling to redefine its identity. The Islands are looking back to the past for guidance. During your stay you will be exposed to a place that is attempting to

The ancient Hawaiians made extensive use of palm trees.

So close, and yet so far. This is as close as most will ever come to the "Forbidden" island of Niʻihau.

recapture its cultural roots. There is more interest in Hawaiian culture and language than ever before. Sometimes it is clumsy, sometimes awkward. There is no common agreement regarding how to do it, but in the end, a reinvigoration of the Hawaiian spirit will no doubt be enjoyed by all.

Niʻihau

No man is an island, or so they say. But in Hawaiʻi, one family can own one. The island of Niʻihau is a dry, somewhat barren island of 46,000 acres located 17 miles to the west of Kauaʻi. When Scottish born Eliza Sinclair was sailing in the Islands with her family in 1863, they were looking for land on which to settle. Having turned downed offers of several tracts on Oʻahu (including what would later become Waikiki), they were about to leave for California when King Kamehameha V offered to sell them Niʻihau. When Eliza's sons went to look at it, they found a green, wet island with abundant grass—perfect for raising cat-

tle. What they were unaware of at the time was that Niʻihau had experienced a rare rainy period and was flourishing as a result. They offered $6,000, the King countered with $10,000 and they took it. This was 1864 and unfortunately for the Sinclairs, the residents of Niʻihau did not respect their ownership and resisted them. They had a further setback when an old Hawaiian showed them a deed indicating ownership to a crucial 50 acre sliver of Niʻihau deeded to the old man by King Kamehameha III. The Sinclairs were in a bind and elicited the aid of Valdemar Knudsen to negotiate the purchase of the remaining 50 acres. He spoke fluent Hawaiian and was well known and respected by the islanders. Knudsen went to Niʻihau and offered $1,000 to the old man by slowly stacking the silver coins on a table while he explained how much better off the old man would be if he sold his land and lived in comfort on Kauaʻi. After repeated refusals from the man, Knudsen went to take the money away when the old

Hawaiian's wife grabbed the money and the deal was consummated on the spot.

When the Sinclairs discovered that the land was actually dry and barren, unsuitable for a cattle ranch at that time, they arranged to buy 21,000 acres of West Kaua'i. (They would continue to buy land, eventually acquiring 97,000 acres, over one fourth of all Kaua'i, which they own to this day.) If you take a helicopter ride, you can see their fabulous estate nestled high in the mountains near Olokele.

Today, Ni'ihau is operated as a cattle and sheep ranch by the Robinsons (the descendants of Eliza Sinclair). The Family and about 250 Hawaiians live there, with the men working the animals and the women making Ni'ihau Shell Leis, worth several hundred dollars each. There is one unpaved road going halfway around the island, no telephones, except for a wireless two way to Kaua'i, and no cable TV (although some residents tell us that they are trying to talk the Robinsons into getting a satellite dish so they can get CNN). Power is supplied by generator.

Ni'ihau's one school houses about 45 students. The sense of family on the island is strong and only Hawaiian is spoken. Ni'ihau residents are a deeply religious people and crime against one another is essentially unknown. They are intensely proud of their community and feel strongly that their people, their heritage, and their way of life are special and are protected by God.

They live in one village called Pu'uwai and receive their mail once a week—the Post Office can deliver only as far as Makaweli on western Kaua'i. They shop for clothes and other durable items on Kaua'i, where most have family.

With a warehouse for staples and gardens for their fruits and vegetables, Ni'ihau Islanders are a happy, relatively content lot who jealously guard their privacy. They are not without their problems, however. No drugs or alcohol are allowed on the island, and recently two families were banished forever from the island for growing pakalolo (marijuana). Their mortality rate is high and nearly all of them receive welfare or food stamps. With no permanent streams on the island, water is sometimes scarce. Although the largest lake in the state is on Ni'ihau, it is usually only a few feet deep, muddy, and generally unpleasant. A drought in 1981 put a scare in the residents and water conservation is encouraged.

Realizing that their relative isolation made them vulnerable to medical emergencies, the Robinsons purchased a twin–engine helicopter. To subsidize its cost, they began **Ni'ihau Helicopters** to fly tours around the island. (See page 123 for more information on this.) They also allow tourists to hunt on the island for $1,200 to assist in ridding the island of unwanted animals. (See page 129 for more information.)

The Robinsons claim that their unique deed to the island gives them ownership to the beaches—directly in conflict with State Law which proclaims that *all* beaches in Hawai'i are public beaches. To date nobody has challenged them in court. If you land on a beach on Ni'ihau, you will be asked to leave. If you refuse, a truly *gargantuan* Hawaiian gentleman will be summoned who will ask you with a bit more firmness. This request is usually sufficient to persuade all but the most determined of individuals.

The bird-of-paradise is a striking flower found all over the island.

GETTING HERE

In order to get to Hawai'i, you've got to fly here. While this may sound *painfully* obvious, many people spend time trying to find an ocean cruise to the Islands. With the advent of jets, the long span of open ocean makes regular cruises here infeasible.

When planning your trip, a travel agent is *strongly* recommended. They are a vastly underutilized resource. They can obtain incredible bargains, cut out the hassle, and their commission is paid directly by the travel industry. If you don't want to, or can't go through a travel agent, there are several large wholesalers that can get you airfare, hotel, and a rental car, often cheaper than you can get airfare on your own. Pleasant Hawaiian Holidays at (800) 242–9244, Suntrips at (800) 786–8747 and Creative Leisure Hawai'i at (800) 426–6367 are all rep-

utable providers of complete package tours. The first two are renowned for their impossibly low rates. We've always been amazed that you can sometimes get round trip airfare from the mainland, a hotel, and car for a week for as low as $600 per person, depending on where you fly from, and where you stay. That's a small price to pay for your little piece of paradise.

If you arrange everything yourself, you can often count on paying top dollar for each facet of you trip. The prices listed in the section on hotels reflect the RACK rates, meaning the price you and I pay if we book direct. Rates *can* be significantly lower if you go through a travel agent.

When you pick your travel agent, shop around—the differences can be dramatic. A diligent agent can make the difference between affording a *one week*

Hey, I Recognize That Place...

When Hollywood wants to convey the impression of beauty and lushness, it's no contest what location they choose. Kaua'i has long been the location of choice for movie directors looking for something special. As you drive around the island, keep an eye out for the locations of scenes from some of these movies: *Jurassic Park, North, Honeymoon in Vegas, Hook, Lord of the Flies, Flight of the Intruder, Throw Mama From the Train, The Thorn Birds, Uncommon Valor, Body Heat, Raiders of the Lost Ark, Fantasy Island, King Kong, Acapulco Gold, Islands in the Stream, The Hawaiians, Lost Flight, Hawai'i, Girls! Girls! Girls!, Donavan's Reef, Blue Hawai'i, South Pacific, Miss Sadie Thompson*, and many more. Hollywood discovered Kaua'i years ago.

vacation, and a *two week* vacation. They don't all check the same sources for bargains, there is an art to it. Look in the Sunday travel section of your local newspaper—the bigger the paper the better.

All flights stop on O'ahu before coming to Kaua'i. When you are coming from the mainland, the seats on the right side of the airplane offer the best view of O'ahu. Sit on the left side going to and from Kaua'i if you can. As you leave O'ahu for the mainland, the right side usually affords a great view of the islands of Moloka'i, Lana'i, Kaho'olawe, and Maui.

Nearly all passengers arriving on Kaua'i come through Lihu'e Airport. Some choose to fly into Princeville Airport on the north shore. If you want to fly directly into Princeville, be aware that they have no agricultural inspection service. This means that luggage must be picked up and inspected on O'ahu. You

can't check your luggage through going either direction. Princeville Airport offers two rental car companies; Avis at 826–9773 and Hertz at 826–7455.

WHAT TO BRING

This list will be of assistance in planning what to bring. Obviously you won't bring everything on the list, but it might make you think of things you may otherwise overlook.

Waterproof sunblock (SPF 15 or higher)
Two bathing suits
Shoes—Thongs, trashable sneakers, reef shoes, hiking shoes
Mask, snorkel, and fins
Camera with lots of film
Beach towels/Straw beach mat
Mosquito repellent for some hikes (100% Deet is best)
Insulated water jug to keep in the car—(Coleman makes a perfect 2

quart jug for this purpose)
Shorts and other cool cotton clothing
Fanny pack—also called waist pack, to
carry all your various vacation
accouterments
Cheap, simple backpack—you don't
need to go backpacking to use
one; a ten minute trek down to a
secluded beach is much easier if
you bring a simple pack
Light windbreaker jacket for trip to
Kalalau Lookout or helicopter trip
Hat or cap for Sun protection
Walkman
Long pants (sweats) for hiking if you
are going through jungle country

GETTING AROUND

Rental Cars

The rental car prices in Hawai'i are cheaper than almost anywhere else in the Country, and the competition is ferocious. Nearly every visitor to Kaua'i gets around in a rental car, and for good reason. The island's towns are separated by distances sufficient to discourage walking. Many of Kaua'i's best sights can only be reached if you have your own independent transportation.

At Lihu'e Airport, rental cars can easily be obtained from the booths across the street from the Main Terminal. It's usually a good idea to reserve your car in advance since companies can run out of cars during peak times.

Listed below are the companies currently operating on Kaua'i. Local numbers are in the 808 Area Code.

Alamo Rent A Car
(800) 327–9633 or
246–0645 at Lihu'e Airport

Avis Rent A Car
(800) 831–8000 or
245–3512 at Lihu'e Airport
826–9773 at Princeville Airport
742–1627 at Po'ipu Hyatt

Budget Rent A Car
(800) 527–0700 or
245–1901 at Lihu'e Airport

Dollar Rent A Car
(800) 800–4000 or
245–3651 at Lihu'e Airport

Hertz Rent A Car
(800) 654–3131 or
245–3356 at Lihu'e Airport
826–7455 at Princeville Airport

National Car Rental
(800) 227–7368 or
245–5636 at Lihu'e Airport

If you are between the ages of 21 and 25, only Alamo will rent to you at the current time, and expect to pay $15 more *per day* for your vehicle. *Occasionally*, tour packages can bypass this restriction. If you are under 21, see **Buses**, or bring a bike.

Here are a few tips to keep in mind when you rent a car.

• The nearby Hanama'ulu Shell Station usually has the cheapest gas on the island. Don't allow the rental company to fill you tank when you return it; their gas rates are usually very high and are meant to dissuade you from returning the car empty.

• Many gold credit cards cover the Collision Damage Waiver (CDW) if you charge your rental car with them.

Large banyan trees, such as this one near the Waimea Plantation Cottages, are found throughout the islands. Note the person standing underneath. The largest banyan tree in the world takes ten minutes to walk around. (It's in India.)

Their coverage, however, is usually far less comprehensive than rental car CDWs and offers less protection. In addition, settling claims with them can be a very long process.

- Many CDWs will not cover the vehicle on unpaved roads. Consider this when driving on dirt cane roads.

- Seat belt use is required by law and police will stop you for this alone.

Car break-ins can be a problem anywhere. Although the problem is less severe on Kaua'i than on other islands, we are not immune to it. There seems to be more frequent reports in the summer due to school vacations. The places usually hit are those that require you to leave your car in a secluded place for an extended period of time. Contrary to popular belief, locals are targeted just as often as tourists. (In fact Waipahe'e Slippery Slide, which is used almost exclusively by locals who ignore the fact that it is closed, is a place often hit.) To protect yourself, don't leave anything valuable in the car. At secluded spots that have recently been robbed, locals will often leave their doors unlocked and the windows partially open to prevent having their windows smashed. If you park in a secluded spot and notice several piles of glass on the ground, leave your windows rolled down—this is evidence that some juvenile has a new hobby. Don't kid yourself by believing that trunks are safe—they are often easier to open than doors. One place thieves rarely look is under the hood. But don't put something there after you arrive at your destination since someone might be watching.

All of this is not meant to convey the impression that car break-ins are rampant. In fact, the opposite is true. You could probably spend your entire life here and never experience it. But if you lose you brand new $1,000 auto–everything SLR camera because you were one of the few…well, won't *you* be sick?

Four Wheel Drive JEEPs

With its many rugged roads, one of the best ways to see Kaua'i is by four wheel drive. Unfortunately, these are sometimes difficult to come by. Liability insurance is forcing many companies to curtail renting 4WD vehicles. Sometimes, when you are able to rent them, they will have the 4WD mechanism disabled. If you use a gold credit card for the automatic insurance, check with the card carrier to see if you are covered when you're on unpaved roads. Another tip is to avoid deep, soft sand. Even 4WD vehicles can get stuck in it if they have the wrong tires. If you must drive on sand, let much of the air out of the tires to get more sand traction. (I'll leave it up to you how to get the air back in.) On occasion, Dollar Rent A Car carries 4WD vehicles, usually trucks but sometimes JEEPs. Westside U–Drive at 332–8644 carries JEEPs at times. Expect to pay up to $50 per day for the privilege of cheating the road builders.

Buses

Kaua'i now has a bus system called the Kaua'i Bus (clever, eh?). It has been temporarily subsidized by Federal money and is *free*. They don't expect to start charging until 1995 (but that may change, you never know when it comes

to politics), so until then, feel free to take advantage of it. It goes all around the island and up Kuamo'o Road in Wailua. They have stops all over the place but they aren't always marked as well as they should be. For a bus schedule or more information, call them at 241–6410.

Tours

If you want to leave the driving to someone else, you can always take a tour bus. Seeing Kaua'i this way has its disadvantages, of course. The buses only go to selected areas. And no *large* bus is allowed to go past Princeville due to the limited capacity of the Hanalei Bridge. But if you want a guide and don't mind the limitations, you have several companies to choose from. Polynesian Adventure Tours at 246–0122 uses buses small enough to go all the way to Ha'ena. Roberts Hawai'i at 245–9558, Gray Line at 245–3344 and Trans Hawaiian Kaua'i at 245–5108 all have similar tours.

For the more adventurous, Kaua'i Mountain Tours at 245–7224 provides 4WD tours in the Koke'e area. For $78 they pick you up at your hotel, provide a continental breakfast and box lunch, and drive you around the Koke'e wilderness area. The vans are heavy duty and have air conditioning.

Taxis

If you want to tour the island by taxi, then you have entirely too much money to burn. For those that need an occasional taxi service, you will find these available: North Shore Cab at 826–6189, ABC Taxi at 822–7641 on the east shore, or Kaua'i Cab at 742–8640 on the south shore.

Even a beach with no sand can have something to offer. Queen's Bath on the north shore is an example.

GETTING MARRIED ON KAUA'I

If you're looking to get married in paradise, there are several full service companies on Kaua'i that offer wedding services. Contact them to discuss your wedding plans, whether for a conventional wedding or something a little bit different. You may also want to consider a renewal of your vows. Either way, these companies will be able to help.

Island Weddings
(808) 828–1548 or 800–998–1548
Mohala Wedding Services
(808) 823–0522 or 800–800–8489
Wedding in Paradise
(808) 246–2779 or 800–733–7431
Coconut Coast Weddings
(808) 826–5557 or 800–585–5595
Weddings on the Beach
(808) 335–3327 or 800–758–1999

Major resort hotels can also be contacted about their wedding services. The Hyatt in Po'ipu can arrange to have a Hawaiian bridal gown made for you. The Princeville Hotel and the Embassy Suites/Hanalei Bay Resort in Princeville each have wedding coordinators that can arrange the perfect wedding at any of the scenic spots on their properties.

Obtaining a License

The bride and groom must apply for their marriage license *in person* here in Kaua'i. They need proof of age. There is a $16 charge and the license is valid for 30 days. All brides of childbearing age must be tested for German measles (rubella) and present proof of testing signed by a physician. No other health testing is required. There is no residency requirement and no waiting period.

WEATHER

"I've heard it always rains in Kaua'i." I heard this many times before I came here for the first time. The reality of Kaua'i is that they get more rain here than the other Hawaiian Islands. In fact, the rainiest spot on Earth is right smack dab in the middle of the island. Mount Wai'ale'ale is the undisputed rain magnet, receiving an average of 440.22 inches per year (that's more than 36 *feet*), and a median of 432 inches per year. The mountain is shaped like a funnel pointing directly into the moisture laden trade winds which are forced to drop their precious cargo on their march up the slopes. The summit of Wai'ale'ale is other–worldly, with plants stunted and dwarfed by the constant inundation of rain. Moss, fungi and lichen flourish in the swamp just west of the actual peak. Alaka'i Swamp contains flora and fauna found nowhere else in the world. On the opposite side of the mountain, the spent clouds can do no more than drift by, making the west side of the island rather arid. What rain they do get comes from the sporadic Kona winds. (Throughout the islands, Kona wind refers to winds which come from the southwest, and are often associated with inclement weather.)

All that said, the odds are overwhelming that rain will *not* ruin your Kaua'i vacation. The coast gets far less rain than the waterlogged central interior, and throughout Kaua'i the lion's share of rain falls at night. When it does rain during the day, it is usually quite short lived, often lasting a matter of a few minutes. One of the things that takes a little getting used to is the fleeting nature of the weather here. In many parts of the Country, rain or sunshine are words used *by themselves* to describe the day's weather. On Kaua'i, a warm passing shower is to be expected and rarely signifies that a long period of rain is to follow. If you call the local telephone number for the National Weather Service (see below), you will probably hear something like this. "Today—mostly sunny, with a few passing windward and mauka (mountain) showers. Tonight—mostly fair with a few passing windward and mauka showers. Tomorrow—mostly sunny, with a few passing windward and mauka showers." So don't get bummed if it suddenly looks ominous in the sky, it'll probably pass within a few minutes leaving happy plants in its wake.

If your decision of when to visit and where to stay takes rainfall amounts into account, the graph on the facing page should be of interest.

If you want to know whether to take the top down on the convertible, look windward and you'll be able to see the weather coming. Dark clouds drop rain—the darker the cloud, the harder the rain. It's as simple as that and you will often see locals looking windward if they feel a drop on their head. If you're inland, you will often be able to hear the rain approaching. When you hear the sound of a rushing river but there isn't one around, take cover until it passes. (Mango trees are ideal for this purpose and have ancillary benefits as well.)

In planning your daily activities, a good rule of thumb is that if it is going to be a rainy day, the south shore will probably be sunny, and the west shore will almost certainly be sunny. The exception is during Kona winds when the weather is opposite of normal.

As far as temperatures are concerned, Kaua'i is incredibly temperate. The average *high* during January is 78°, whereas our hottest month August has an average *high* of 85°. With humidity percentages usually in the 60s and low 70s, Kaua'i is almost always pleasant. The exception is the extreme west side which is about 3 degrees hotter. (That might not sound like much but you sure do notice it.)

Kaua'i's surface water temperatures range from a low of 73.4° in February to a high of 80° in October. Most people find this to be an ideal temperature range.

To get current weather or ocean information call:

245–6001—National Weather Service; Weather Forecast
245–3564—National Weather Service; Hawaiian Waters Forecast
335–3611—KUAI Surf Report

GEOGRAPHY

Kaua'i is located in the tropics at 22° latitude, meaning that it receives direct sunlight twice each year near the summer solstice. (No part of the mainland United States ever receives direct sunshine due to its northern location.) The island is 555 square miles, with 50 of its 113 miles of shoreline being sand beaches. Compared to the other Hawaiian Islands, Kaua'i has by far the highest proportion of sand beach shoreline. You might read in brochures about "white sand beaches." Actually, they are *golden* sand beaches, unlike the truly white sand beaches found in other parts of the world. Kaua'i is too old to have any black sand beaches.

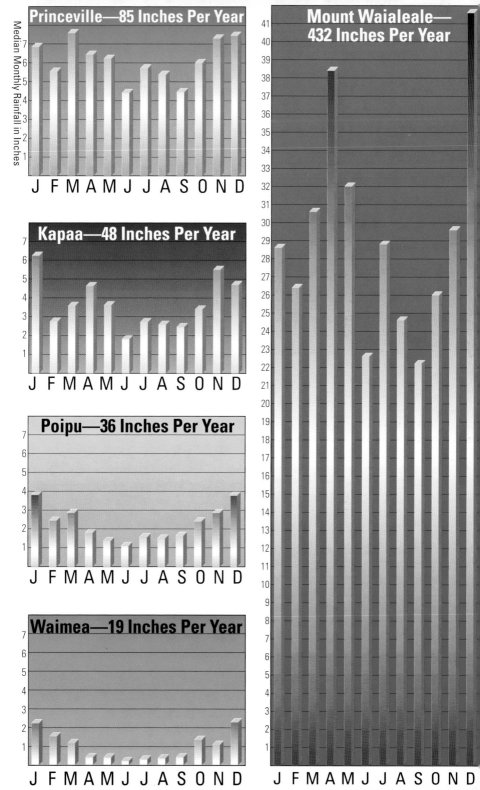

Kaua'i's interior is mountainous, with deeply eroded valleys and large plains around most of the coastal areas. Its rainfall is more varied than any place in the world. (See Rain Graphs above.) The northern and eastern parts of the island (called the windward side) receive the majority of the rain with the southern and western section (leeward side) being considerably drier.

Looking at the map on the back flap, you will notice that a road stretches *almost* all the way around the island. This means that Ke'e is as far as you can go on the north shore, and Polihale or the top of Waimea Canyon Road is as far as you can go on the west side. An attempt to link the two a few years back ended with almost comic results. (See page 89.)

The maps in this book are unique in that they show the mile markers. These correspond to the little green signs you will see along the main roads of Kaua'i. This will give you a perspective regarding distances beyond the map scales. Another feature of our maps is that north always points up. We have found that many people get confused when they try to use a map where south is pointing to where east should be, etc. The only exception we made is the Kalalau Trail Map where this wasn't possible.

In getting around, distances are usually measured in time, rather than miles. Traffic can sometimes be a problem in Lihu'e and Kapa'a, so be prepared to wait.

From Lihu'e, the average driving time (barring traffic) is:

Ha'ena	65 minutes
Hanalei	50 minutes
Kapa'a	10 minutes
Po'ipu	25 minutes
Waimea Canyon	70 minutes

HAZARDS

The Sun

The hazard that affects by far the most people is the Sun. Kaua'i, at 22° latitude, receives more direct sunlight than anywhere on the mainland. If you want to enjoy your *entire* vacation, make sure that you wear a strong sunblock. We recommend a waterproof sunblock with at least a SPF of 15. Try to avoid the Sun between 11 a.m. and 2 p.m. since the Sun's rays are particularly strong during this time. If you are fairskinned or unaccustomed to the Sun and want to lay out, 15-20 minutes per side is all you should consider the first day. You can increase it a bit each day. *Beware of the fact that Kaua'i's ever constant trade winds will hide the symptoms of a burn until it's too late.* You might find that trying to get your tan as golden as possible isn't worth it; tropical suntans are notoriously short lived, whereas you are sure to remember a bad burn far longer.

Water Hazards

The most serious water hazard is the surf. During the winter, many beaches

Watch where you choose to take a nap.

are not swimmable. Eastern and northern beaches are especially dangerous, and the sad fact is that more people drown in Hawai'i each year than anywhere else in the Country. This isn't said to keep you from enjoying the ocean, but rather to instill in you a healthy respect for Hawaiian waters. See **Beaches** for more information on this.

Ocean Critters

Hawaiian marine life, for the most part, is quite friendly. There are, however, a few notable exceptions. Below is a list of those that you should be aware of. This is not mentioned to frighten you out of the water. The odds are overwhelming that you won't have any trouble with any of the beasties listed below. But should you encounter one, this information should be of some help.

Sharks

Kaua'i does have sharks. They are mostly white-tipped reef sharks and the occasional hammerhead or tiger shark. Contrary to what most people think, sharks are in every ocean and don't pose the level of danger people attribute to them. In the past 25 years there have been a total of eight documented shark attacks off Kaua'i. Considering the number of people who swam in our waters during that time, you are more likely to choke to death on a bone at a lu'au than be attacked by a shark. If you do happen to come upon a shark however, swim away slowly. This kind of movement disinterests them. *Don't* splash about rapidly. By doing this you are imitating a fish in distress, and you don't want to do that. The one kind of water you want to avoid is murky water, such as that found in the mouth of the Waimea River on the west side, which is not interesting to swim in anyway. Most shark attacks occur in murky water since sharks are basically cowards who like to sneak up on their prey. In general, don't go around worrying about sharks. *Any* animal can be threatening. (Remember when President Carter was attacked by a rabbit?)

Stone Fish

These are very rare here but they have been seen. They will lay on the bottom and blend in with their surroundings and can be difficult to detect even when you are looking directly at them. The number of people who have been stung is quite small. The stonefish will not attack you. If you manage to step on one and get stung, the pain is excruciating. The best treatment is to immediately apply very hot water and see a physician at once.

Sea Urchins

These are like living pin cushions. If you step on one, or accidentally grab one, remove as much of the spine as possible with tweezers. See a physician if necessary.

Cone Shells

People tend to forget that shells are created by organisms to serve as housing. Most of these creatures are capable of protecting themselves by the use of a long stinger called a proboscis, which can inject venom. You might hear that it's safer to pick up a shell by the large end. You should be aware that many shells have stingers that can reach any part of the shell and can penetrate most gloves. Therefore, it is recommended

Ahhhhh…

that you do not pick up live shells. If you do find yourself stung, immediately apply hot water, as it breaks down protein venoms.

Portuguese Man-of-War

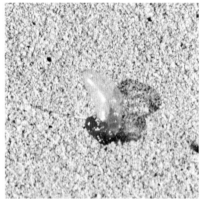

These creatures are related to jellyfish but are unable to swim. They are instead propelled by a small sail and are at the mercy of the wind. Though small, they are capable of inflicting a painful sting. This occurs when the long trailing appendages are touched, triggering the spring loaded stinger, called a nematocyst, which injects poison. The resulting burning sensation is usually very unpleasant but not fatal. Fortunately, the Portuguese Man-of-War is not a common visitor to Kaua'i. On the rare occasions that they do come ashore, they usually do so in great numbers, jostled by a strong storm offshore. If you see them on the beach, don't go in the water. If you do get stung, immediately remove the stinger and as much of the venom as possible with a cloth or sand. Be careful not to stimulate any inactivated nematocyst on your skin or you'll be stung some more. Remove them carefully or use white vinegar to destroy them. Then apply baking soda, diluted ammonia, or alcohol and see a physician. The folk cure is urine but you might look pretty silly.

Coral

Coral is very sharp, and since it is made up of millions of individual living organisms, a scrape can leave proteinaceous matter in the wound causing infection. This is why coral cuts are notoriously slow to heal. Immediate cleaning and disinfecting of coral cuts should speed up healing time. The one type of coral you should be especially wary of is fire coral. It's very rare here and has stingers similar to anemones and should be treated in the same way.

Sea Anemones

Related to the jellyfish, these also have stingers and are usually found attached to rocks or coral. It's best not to touch them with your bare hands. Treatment for a sting is similar to that of a Portuguese Man-of-War.

Bugs

The Hawaiian Islands have less of a bug problem than most tropical locations, but that doesn't mean we're without our pests. Mosquitoes were unknown in the islands until the first stowaways arrived in Maui on the *Wellington* in 1826. Since then they have thrived. A good mosquito repellent containing DEET will come in handy, especially if you plan to go hiking. Forget the guidebooks that tell you to take vitamin B12 to keep mosquitoes away, it just gives the little critters a healthier diet. If you find one dive bombing you at night in your room, turn on your overhead fan to help keep them away.

Bees are more common on the drier west side of the island. Usually, the only way you'll get stung is if you run into one. If you rent a scooter, beware; one of us received his first bee sting while singing *Come Sail Away* on a motorcycle. A bee sting in the mouth can definitely ruin one of your precious vacation days.

Regarding cockroaches, there's good news and bad news. The bad news is that here, some are bigger than your thumb and can fly. The good news is that you probably won't see one. One of their predators is the gecko. This small, lizard-like creature makes a surprisingly loud chirp at night. They are cute and considered good luck in the islands, (probably because they eat mosquitoes and roaches).

The only bug on the island that is poisonous is the centipede. You'll almost certainly never encounter one. They hang out on the underside of leaves in wet forest areas. If you do happen to get stung, you won't die (but you might wish you had). Their bite is extremely painful and can last for several days. Some local doctors even advise that the only treatment for a centipede bite is to stay drunk for three days.

One thing nearly all visitors have heard is there are no snakes in Hawai'i. There is concern lately that the brown tree snake might have made its way onto the islands from Guam. Although *completely harmless* to humans, these snakes can spell extinction to native birds. Guam has lost nearly all of its birds due to this egg-eating curse. Once they are fertilized, they can reproduce for life from a single specimen. If there are any on Kaua'i (and this has not been confirmed) it would be a disaster. Government officials aren't allowed to tell you this, but we will: If you ever see one anywhere in Hawai'i, please *kill it* and contact the Department of Land and Natural Resources at 241–3326. At the very least, call the DLNR immediately. The entire bird population of Hawai'i will be grateful.

The Albatross is protected on Kaua'i.

Road Hazards

There are a couple things you should know about driving around Kauaʻi. The speed limits here are probably slower than what you are used to, and Kauaʻi police do have a few places where they regularly catch people (read that speed traps). Also be aware that we have something here called Contra Flow. That means that during commute hours, cones are placed on the lane divisions forcing you to drive on the wrong side of the road. The stretch between Lihuʻe and Wailua is an example of Contra Flow and it can be a bit unnerving for the uninitiated. Wearing seat belts is required by law and police will pull you over for this alone. You should know that the Kauaʻi Police Department recently received funds to expand their seat beat violation enforcement, speeding enforcement, and their sobriety checkpoints. So don't even think about violating these laws or you will likely get stung.

Dirt

Dirt? Yes dirt. Kauaʻi's notorious red dirt has ruined many new pairs of Reeboks in its time. If you are driving on a cane road on the west side and have your window rolled down, you will eat a lot of it. It's always best to bring some trashable sneakers if you plan to do any hiking. And leave your silk argyle socks at home. If you get some of our dirt ground into your expensive clothes, just do what the locals do—wear it anyway or get a new one.

TRAVELING WITH CHILDREN

If you are looking for baby sitters, nearly every lodging on the island has lists of professional services, as well as employees that baby-sit. Some hotels, such as the Hyatt, offer rather elaborate services. Their Camp Hyatt is a rug rat's dream. If you are staying at a place that has no front desk, contact your rental agent for an up-to-date list of sitters.

As far as swimming in the ocean with your little one, Lydgate State Park in Wailua has a boulder enclosed keiki pond that is wildly popular. Salt Pond Beach Park in Hanapepe is also similarly used. Poʻipu Beach Park in Poʻipu is popular with local parents as well as visitors. These are considered ideal for children except during periods of high surf. I'm sure I don't need to tell you that surf and keikis don't go well together.

During calm summer surf, Kalihiwai Beach can be a pleasant place to bring kids. While not as protected as Lydgate or Salt Pond, it is picturesque and your kids will make many new local friends there.

With its strange colored sugar mill equipment everywhere, Coconut Marketplace in Wailua is usually a hit with kids, and a decent place to shop for grownups. Mustard's Last Stand in Lawaʻi has a *very* small mini golf course for your youngin's edification, as well as several interesting diversions and good hot dogs. Wally World near Kukui Grove Shopping Center in Lihuʻe has an 18 hole miniature golf course and they are in the process of installing bumper boats and batting cages.

DISABLED PERSONS

Those with physical disabilities will find resorts with wheelchair accessible rooms under **Where To Stay**. Just look for the ♿ at the bottom of the various descriptions. For those who are certified paratransit eligible under the Americans with Disabilities Act, the Kauaʻi Bus provides special transportation services. Call them at 241–6410 for more information.

Monthly Calendar of Local Events

Each month the *Kaua'i Museum* at 245–6931 and the *Koke'e Museum* at 335–9975 sponsor events. Call them for exhibits and activities during your visit.

January

Brown Bags to Stardom, Kaua'i War Memorial Convention Hall, Lihu'e, 241–6623.

February

Miss Garden Island Pageant, Kaua'i War Memorial Convention Hall, Lihu'e 241–6623; second week of February.

Waimea Town Celebration, Waimea; third week in February. Call the Hawai'i Visitors Bureau at 245–3971.

March

Prince Kuhio Festival. Island-wide activities occur near the State Holiday on 3/26. Contact the Hawai'i Visitors Bureau at 245–3971.

April

Spring Craft Fair, Kaua'i Museum, Lihu'e, 245-6931.

Polo Season, 'Anini Field, Sundays at 3:00 p.m. Admission Fee.

May

May Day by the Bay, Hanalei. Contact Hawai'i Visitors Bureau at 245–3971.

May Day is Lei Day, Kaua'i Museum, Lihu'e, 245–6931.

Pacific Missile Range Facility Open House, Barking Sands. Contact the Public Affairs Office at PMRF.

Annual Kaua'i Chili Cookoff, Kaua'i Village, Kapa'a, 822–4904.

Taste of Hawai'i, end of May, sponsored by Rotary of Kapa'a.

Queen Emma Festival, end of May, Koke'e State Park, 335–9975.

Polo Season, 'Anini Field, Sundays at 3:00 p.m. Admission Fee.

June

Tahiti Fete, third week of June (Sometimes held in August). Call the Hawai'i Visitors Bureau at 245–3971.

Hula Show, Thursdays at 6:00 p.m., *Entertainment* Fridays at 7:00p.m. and Saturdays at Noon, Kukui Grove Shopping Center, Lihu'e, 245–7784.

Polo Season, 'Anini Field, Sundays at 3:00 p.m. Admission Fee.

King Kamehameha Day, second Friday in June (State Holiday), Lihu'e. Contact the Hawai'i Visitors Bureau at 245–3971.

July

O-Bon Season (July and August); weekends at various Hongwanji missions around Kaua'i. Floating lantern ceremony on Sunday evenings near the mission.

Fourth of July, Vidinha Stadium, Lihu'e.

Hula Exhibition, Kaua'i War Memorial Convention Hall, Lihu'e. 241–6623.

Koloa Plantation Days, Old Koloa Town, mid to late July. Call the Hawai'i

Visitor's Bureau at 245–3971

Hula Show Thursdays at 6:00 p.m., *Entertainment* Fridays at 7:00p.m. and Saturdays at Noon, Kukui Grove Shopping Center, Lihu'e, 245–7784.

Methley Plum Harvest, Koke'e State Park, permit required. 335–9975.

Na Holo Kai Canoe Race, from O'ahu to Kalapaki Bay, Kaua'i (mid-July or August). Contact the Hawai'i Visitors Bureau at 245–3971.

Polo Season, 'Anini Field, Sundays at 3:00 p.m. Admission Fee.

August

Summer Craft Fair, Kaua'i Museum, Lihu'e, first Saturday, 245–6931.

O-Bon Season (July and August); weekends at various Hongwanji missions around Kaua'i. Floating lantern ceremony on Sunday evenings near the mission.

Polo Season, 'Anini Field, Sundays at 3:00 p.m. Admission Fee.

Hula Show Thursdays at 6:00 p.m., *Entertainment* Fridays at 7:00 p.m. and Saturdays at Noon, Kukui Grove Shopping Center, Lihu'e, 245–7784.

Admission Day, August 21st; State Holiday.

Tahiti Fete (if not held in June). Contact the Hawai'i Visitors Bureau at 245–3971.

September

Kaua'i County Farm Fair, Kaua'i War Memorial Convention Hall; first week of September, Lihu'e, 241–6623.

Banana Poka Festival, Koke'e State Park, first week of September, 335–9975.

Mokihana Festival; mid to late September. Contact the Hawai'i Visitors Bureau at 245–3971.

Polo Season, 'Anini Field, Sundays at 3:00 p.m. Admission Fee.

October

Aloha Festival, third week of October. Contact the Hawai'i Visitors Bureau, 245–3971.

November

Santa's Arrival, 500 Keiki Puppeteers, day after Thanksgiving, Kukui Grove Shopping Center, Lihu'e, 245–7784.

December

PowerMan Kaua'i Duathlon, first week of December. 332–9201.

Craft Fair, first Saturday of December at Kilohana, 245–5608

Christmas Craft Fair, first Saturday of December, Kaua'i Museum, Lihu'e, 245–6931.

Hawai'i International Film Festival; film screenings will be free on a first-come, first-serve basis at various sites around the Island. Contact the Hawai'i Visitors Bureau at 245–3971.

Holiday Hula Show, early December. Kaua'i War Memorial Convention Center, Lihu'e. 241–6623.

Holiday Entertainment, Kukui Grove Shopping Center, Lihu'e, 245–7784.

THE PEOPLE

The people of Kaua'i are the friendliest people in the entire Country. "Oh, come on!" you might say. But this is not the admittedly biased opinion of someone who lives here. This conclusion was reached by the participants in the *Condé Nast Readers' Choice Awards.* This is a sophisticated and savvy lot. *Condé Nast* is the magazine of choice for world travelers. When asked in 1993 to name the friendliest place in the U.S., Kaua'i was the clear winner. A distant second was Maui, followed by Seattle, Lana'i, Moloka'i, San Antonio, and Santa Fe.

In this same poll, Kaua'i was number two *in the world* in terms of environment and ambiance. (Victoria, Canada was number one.) While we're at it, two of Kaua'i's resorts were named in the list of top ten tropical resorts in the world (the Princeville Hotel and the Hyatt).

What does all this mean? Well, you will notice that people smile here more than other places. Drivers wave at complete strangers (without any particular fingers leading the way). If you try to analyze the reason, it probably comes down to a matter of happiness. People are happy here, and happy people are friendly people. It's just that simple. Some people compare a trip to Kaua'i with a trip back in time, when smiles weren't rare, and politeness was the order of the day.

Some Terms

If you are confused regarding terms in Hawai'i, this should help. A person of Hawaiian blood is Hawaiian. Only people of this race are called by this term. They are also called Kanaka Maoli; but only another Hawaiian can use this term. Anybody who was born here, regardless of race (except whites) is called a local. If you were born elsewhere but have lived here a long time, you might be called a kama'aina. If you are white, you are a haole. It doesn't matter if you have been here a day or your family has been here for over a century, you will always be a haole. The term comes from the time when westerners first encountered these islands. Its precise meaning has been lost but it is thought to refer to people with no background (since westerners could not chant the kanaenae of their ancestors).

The continental United States is called the mainland. If you are here and are returning, you are not "going back to the states" (we *are* a state). When somebody leaves the island, they are off-Island.

Ethnic Breakdown

Kaua'i has an ethnic mix that is as diversified as any you will find. Here, *everyone* is a minority, there are no majorities. The 1990 Census revealed the ethnic make up below.

White	17,712
Filipino	12,709
Japanese	10,242
Hawaiian	7,736
Chinese	810
Black	211
Korean	204
American Indian	157
Other	1,396
Total	51,177

Hawaiian Time

One aspect of Hawaiian culture you may have heard of is Hawaiian Time. The stereotype is that everyone in

Hawai'i moves just a little bit slower than on the mainland. That we are more laid back and don't let things get to us as easily as people on the mainland. This is the stereotype...OK, it's not a stereotype. It's real. Hopefully, during your visit, you will notice that this feeling infects *you* as well. You might find yourself letting another driver cut in front of you in circumstances that would incur your wrath back home. You might find yourself willing to wait for a red light without feeling like you're going to explode. The whole reason for coming to Hawai'i is to experience beauty and a sense of peace, so let it happen. If someone else is moving a bit slower than you would like, just go with it.

THE HAWAIIAN LANGUAGE

The Hawaiian language is a beautiful, gentle, and melodic language which flows smoothly off the tongue. Just the sounds of the words conjure up trees gently blowing in the breeze and the sound of the surf. Most Polynesian languages share the same roots, and many have common words. Today, Hawaiian is spoken *as an everyday language* only on the privately owned island of Ni'ihau, 17 miles off the coast of Kaua'i (see **Introduction**). Visitors are often intimidated by Hawaiian. With a few ground rules you will come to realize that pronunciation is not as hard as you might think.

When missionaries discovered that the Hawaiians had no written language, they sat down and created an alphabet. This Hawaiian alphabet has only 12 letters. Five vowels; A, E, I, O, and U as well as seven consonants; H, K, L, M, N, P, and W.

The consonants are pronounced just as they are in English with the exception of W. It is often pronounced as a V if it is in the middle of a word and comes after an E or I. Vowels are pronounced as follows:

A—pronounced as in Ah if stressed, or above if not stressed.
E—pronounced as in say if stressed, or dent if not stressed.
I—pronounced as in bee.
O—pronounced as in nose.
U—pronounced as in stew.

If you examine long Hawaiian words, you will see that most have repeating syllables making it easier to remember and pronounce.

One thing you will notice in this book are glottal stops. These are represented by an upside-down apostrophe ' and are meant to convey a hard stop in the pronunciation. So if we are talking about the a type of lava called 'a'a, it is pronounced as two separate As.

Another feature you will encounter are diphthongs, where two letters glide together. They are ae, ai, ao, au, ei, eu, oi, and ou. Unlike many English diphthongs, the second vowel is always pronounced. One word you will read in this book, referring to Hawaiian temples, is heiau (hey-ee-ow). The e and i flow together as a single sound, then the a and u flow together as a single sound. The ee sound binds the two sounds making the whole word flow together.

Let's take a word that might seem impossible to pronounce. When you see how easy this word is, the rest will seem like a snap. The Hawaiian State Fish is the Humuhumunukunukuapua'a. At first glance it seems like a nightmare. But if you read the word slowly, it is pronounced just like it looks and isn't nearly as horrifying as it appears. Try it. Humu (hoo-moo) is pronounced twice. Nuku (noo-koo) is pronounced twice. A (ah) is pronounced once. Pu (poo) is pronounced once. A'a (ah-ah) is the ah sound pronounced twice, the glottal stop indicating a hard stop between sounds. Now try it again. Humuhumunukunukuapua'a. Now, wasn't that easy? OK, so it's not easy, but it's not impossible either.

Below are some words that you might hear during your visit.

'Aina (eye-nah)—Land.

Ali'i (ah-LEE-ee)—A Hawaiian chief; a member of the chiefly class.

Aloha (ah-LOW-ha)—Hello, goodbye, or a feeling or the spirit of love, affection, or kindness.

Hala (hah-la)—Pandanus tree.

Hale (hah-leh)—House or building.

Hana (ha-nah)—Work.

Hana hou (ha-nah-HO)—To do again.

Haole (how-leh)—Originally foreigner, now means Caucasian.

Heiau (hey-ee-ow)—Hawaiian temple.

Hula (hoo-lah)—The story telling dance of Hawai'i.

Imu (ee-moo)—An underground oven.

'Iniki (ee-nee-key)—Sharp and piercing wind (as in Hurricane 'Iniki).

Kahuna (kah-HOO-na)—A priest or minister; someone who is an expert in a profession.

Kai (kigh)—The sea.

Kalua (KAH-loo-ah)—Cooking food underground.

Kama'aina (kah-ma-EYE-na)—Long time Hawaiian resident.

Kane (kah-neh)—Boy or man.

Kapu (kah-poo)—Forbidden, taboo; keep out.

Keiki (kay-key)—Child or children.

Kokua (koh-koo-ah)—Help.

Kona (koh-NAH)—Leeward side of the island; wind blowing from the south, southwest direction.

Lanai (lah-NIGH)—Porch, veranda, patio.

Lani (lah-nee)—Sky or heaven.

Lei (lay)—Necklace of flowers, shells, or feathers. The mokihana berry lei is the lei of Kaua'i.

Liliko'i (lee-lee-koi)—Passion fruit.

Limu (lee-moo)—Edible seaweed.

Lomi (low-mee)—To rub or massage; lomi salmon is raw salmon rubbed with salt and spices.

Lu'au (loo-ow)—Hawaiian feast; literally means taro leaves.

Mahalo (mah-hah-low)—Thank you.

Makai (mah-kigh)—Toward the sea.

Malihini (mah-lee-hee-nee)—A newcomer, visitor, or guest.

Mauka (mow-ka)—Toward the mountain.

Moana (moh-ah-nah)—Ocean.

Mo'o (moh-oh)—Lizard.

Nani (nah-nee)—Beautiful, pretty.

Nui (new-ee)—Big, important, great.

'Ohana (oh-hah-nah)—Family.

'Ono (oh-no)—Delicious, the best.

'Okole (oh-koh-leh)—Derrière.

Pakalolo (pah-kah-low-low)—Marijuana.

Pali (pah-lee)—A cliff.

Paniolo (pah-nee-OH-low)—Hawaiian cowboy.

Pau (pow)—Finish, end, i.e. pau hana means quitting time from work.

Poi (poy)—Pounded kalo (taro) root that forms a paste.

Pono (poh-no)—Goodness, excellence, correct, proper.

Pua (poo-ah)—Flower

Pupu (poo-poo)—Appetizer, snacks, or finger food.

Wahine (wah-hee-ney)—Woman.
Wai (why)—Fresh water.
Wikiwiki (wee-kee-wee-kee)—To hurry up, very quick.

Quick Pidgin Lesson

Hawaiian Pidgin is fun to listen to. It's like ear candy. It is colorful, rhythmic, and sways in the wind. Below is a list of some of the words and phrases you might hear on your visit. It's tempting to read some of these and try to use them. If you do, the odds are you will simply look foolish. These words and phrases are used in certain ways and with certain inflections. People who have spent years living in the islands still feel uncomfortable using them. Thick pidgin can be incomprehensible to the untrained ear (that's the idea). If you are someplace and hear two people engaged in a discussion in pidgin, stop and eavesdrop for a bit. You won't forget it.

An' den—And then? So?
Any kine—Anything; any kind.
Ass right—That's right.
Ass wy—That's why.
Beef—Fight.
Brah—Short for bradah; friend; brother.
Buggah—That's the one; it is difficult.
Bumbye—By and by; after awhile.
Bummahs—Bummer; too bad.
Broke da mouf—Delicious.
Chicken skin kine—So good it will give you goose bumps.
Cockaroach—Steal; rip off.
Cool head main ting—Stay cool; relax.
Cornbeef eye—Same as stink eye.
Da kine—A noun or verb used in place of whatever the speaker wishes. Heard constantly.
Geevum—Go for it! Give 'em hell!

Grind—To eat.
Grinds—Food.
How you figga?—How do you figure that? It makes no sense.
Howzit?—How is it going? How are you? Also, Howzit o wot?
Lesgo—Let's go; let's do it.
Make house—Make yourself at home.
Mek ass—Make a fool of yourself.
Mo' bettah—This is better.
No can—Cannot; I cannot do it.
No, yeah?—No, or is "no" correct?
Okole squeezer—Something that suddenly frightens you (okole meaning derrière).
O wot?—Or what?
Poi dog—A mutt.
Shahkbait—Shark bait, meaning pale, untanned people.
Shaka—Great! All right!
Sleepahs—Flip flops, thongs, zoris.
Stink eye—Dirty looks; facial expression denoting displeasure.
Talk story—Shooting the breeze; to rap.
Tanks eh?—Thank you.
To da max—All the way; the most you can get.
Waddascopps?—What's the scoop? What's happening?
Yeah?—Used at the end of most sentences.

MUSIC

Hawaiian music is far more diverse than most people think. Many often picture Hawaiian music as someone twanging away on a ukulele and letting their voice slip and slide all over the place. In reality, the music here can be outstanding. There is the melodic sound of the more traditional music. There are young local bands putting out modern music with a Hawaiian beat. There is even Hawaiian reggae. If you get a chance, stop by Ruby Tuesday in the Waipouli Town Center in Kapaʻa. They have a good selection of Hawaiian music and they will let you hear it first before you buy it.

THE HULA

The hula evolved as a means of worship, later becoming a forum for telling a story with chants (called mele), hands and body movement. It can be fascinating to watch. When most people think of the hula, they picture a woman in a grass skirt swinging her hips to the beat of a ukulele. But in reality there are two types of hula. The modern hula, or hula ʻauana, uses musical instruments and vocals to augment the dancer. It came about after westerners first encountered the islands. Missionaries found the hula distasteful and the old style was driven underground. The modern type came about as a form of entertainment and was practiced in places where missionaries had no influence. Ancient Hawaiians didn't even use grass skirts. They were later brought by Gilbert Islanders.

The old style of hula is called hulaʻolapa or hula kahiko. It consists of chants and is accompanied by percussion only. It can be exciting to watch as performers work together in a synchronous harmony. Both men and women participate with women's hula being softer (though no less disciplined) and men's hula being more active. This type of hula is physically demanding requiring strong concentration. Keiki (children's) hula can be charming to watch as well.

Kauaʻi was the home of the most prestigious hula school in all the islands. People came from every part of the chain to learn the hula from the Ka-ulu-a-Paoa. Great discipline was required and the teachers could be very strict. The remains of this school are still evident as a heiau near Keʻe Beach.

The calendar of events lists many of the festivals which have demonstrations. The two luʻaus in Kapaʻa usually have entertaining hula shows, though not as "authentic" as some of the festival demonstrations.

MISCELLANEOUS INFORMATION

Kauaʻi has no distinct visitor season. People come here year round to enjoy the island's blessings. However, certain times of the year are more popular than others. Christmas is always a particularly busy time and you may have trouble getting a room if you are set on staying at a particular resort. The graph below illustrates visitor distribution in 1991 (1992 numbers were obviously skewed). The island is never crowded the way other destinations can get. This might sound surprising given poll results. When pollsters ask people where they would like to go, Kauaʻi is always in the top ten.

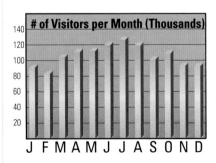

# of Visitors per Month (Thousands)

Traveler's checks are usually accepted but you should be aware that some merchants might look at you like you just tried to offer them Mongolian money. You should also know that the

American Express Card seems to be less welcome here than other destinations. *Many* places will not accept it.

If you are planning to see either of the National Tropical Botanical Gardens or the Grove Farm Museum, make your reservations before you get here to assure admittance. Campers should also obtain their permits before they arrive. See **Camping** under **Activities**.

It is customary on Kaua'i for *everyone* to remove their shoes upon entering someone's house (sometimes their office). Kaua'i's red dirt can be particularly pernicious and nobody wants to spend their day cleaning floors.

If you are going to spend any time at the beach (and you really should), woven bamboo beach mats can be found all over the island for one to two dollars. Some roll up, some can be folded. The sand comes off these easier than it comes off towels.

Another tip is to take an insulated water jug with you in the car. People exploring Kaua'i for the first time often get so caught up in the moment that they dehydrate. Our weather is almost certainly different than what you left behind at home and you will probably find yourself thirstier that usual. Just fill it before you leave in the morning and use it all day.

THE HURRICANE

No book on Kaua'i would be complete without a discussion of "The Hurricane." As you may be aware, Kaua'i was struck by a major hurricane on September 11, 1992. Media attention was intense for about a week, but when the media lost interest in the story people on the mainland were left without any information other than the initial images. As a consequence, many inaccurate impressions have been generated. Let's set the record straight.

Hurricane 'Iniki slammed into Kaua'i only weeks after Hurricane Andrew had ravaged Florida. In one of those ironies of life, it is little known that 'Iniki and Andrew were more like twins than distant cousins—both born around the same time off the coast of Western Africa. But while Andrew made the relatively short journey toward Florida, what would later be called 'Iniki (Hawaiian for piercing wind) took a more leisurely route, across the Atlantic, over the isthmus of Panama and into the Pacific, where it would eventually develop sustained winds of 165 mph and gusts up to 200 mph. (The Navy's Makaha Ridge Radar Station on the edge of Na Pali recorded a gust of 227 mph before it blew down). Kaua'i had had hurricanes before; 'Iwa had been here in 1982 with its eye passing between Kaua'i and Ni'ihau. But 'Iniki was in a different category altogether—category 4 to be precise. While 'Iwa had been bad, 'Iniki was catastrophic. Thousands of homes were destroyed or damaged, 35% of the power poles were knocked down and three lives were lost. In some areas, water would be off for weeks, power for months. Kaua'i had suffered like it had never suffered before. The worst Hawaiian hurricane in modern history had passed directly over Kaua'i, leaving a battered island in its wake.

But Kaua'i had two things going for it that Florida did not: a community that would band together to rebuild, and an island environment so fertile that a broomstick left stuck in the ground will grow into a mop. (OK, maybe not that

fertile.) While some residents of Florida preyed on each other, Kaua'i residents prayed *for* each other. Neighbor helped neighbor. The Aloha Spirit was palpable. The result is a faster recovery than anyone could have imagined. Although five of the big resorts have stalled in their reopening efforts—for the most part by choice or because of insurance woes—most of the rest of the island has rebuilt and is ready for business. During your stay, the only areas where you are likely to notice any rebuilding is in parts of the south and west shore areas, a little bit in Princeville, and the Coco Palms Resort in Wailua. The storm surge in Po'ipu was intense, and businesses are rethinking their ideas about how close to the ocean they should build. This should not dissuade you from staying in Po'ipu; the Hyatt and nearly all the smaller Po'ipu accommodations are open. The Waimea area is not frequented as much by tourists except as part of the drive to the Waimea Canyon. Consequently, this area hasn't received the same attention,

and lacks sufficient resources or motivation to rebuild as quickly.

Mother Nature needed no assistance to return to her pre–hurricane lushness. The young vigorous growth is greener and more vibrant than ever before. After the Hurricane, locals will tell you that barely a leaf could be found on a tree. Now, practically the only *natural* evidence you will find that there was a hurricane here are larger beaches, a few broken or uprooted trees which will be consumed by nature in time, and partially bare albizzia and Norfolk Island pines, which are slow recovering trees. Nature's recovery has astonished even long time locals.

If your only concern about a vacation in Kaua'i is "but what about the Hurricane?", fear not. Aside from some *minor* inconvenience in the Po'ipu area and a few lingering buildings being renovated, you won't be distracted by 'Iniki's legacy. Although some already weak businesses are gone, most have been replaced by new ones. While sad, this is as much a part of nature as a hurricane.

A father swims with his daughter in Queen's Bath, an undiscovered north shore gem.

Kaua'i's north shore, where lushness takes on a whole new meaning. Every shade of green imaginable is represented in the myriad of plant life. Its beaches are exquisitely beautiful, and its mountains are unmatched in terms of sheer majesty. After a heavy rain, you will literally be unable to count the number of waterfalls etched into the sides of north shore mountains.

For the sake of clarity, we will identify the north shore as everything north of Kapa'a. (Look at the back flap to orient yourself.) While this description includes Anahola (which some may consider east shore), it is easier to remember this way, and anyone driving north of Kapa'a is usually going to the north shore any way. The main highway, which stretches around the island occasionally changing its name, has mile markers every mile. These little green signs can be a big help in knowing where you are at any given time. Therefore, we have placed them on the maps represented as a number inside a small box 16. We will often describe a certain feature or unmarked road as being, ".4 miles past the 22 mile mark." We hope this helps.

On Kaua'i, everything is either on the *mauka* side of the highway (meaning toward the mountains) or *makai* (toward the ocean). Since people sometimes get these confused, we will refer to them as *mauka side* or *ocean side*.

All beaches we mention are described in detail in the section on **Beaches**.

Driving north of Kapa'a, you see Kealia Beach on your right, just past the 10 mile mark. This is a popular boogie boarding beach. Left, up Kealia Road is Spalding Monument which isn't much to see but it is on most maps. Farther up Kealia Road is the Waipahe'e Slippery

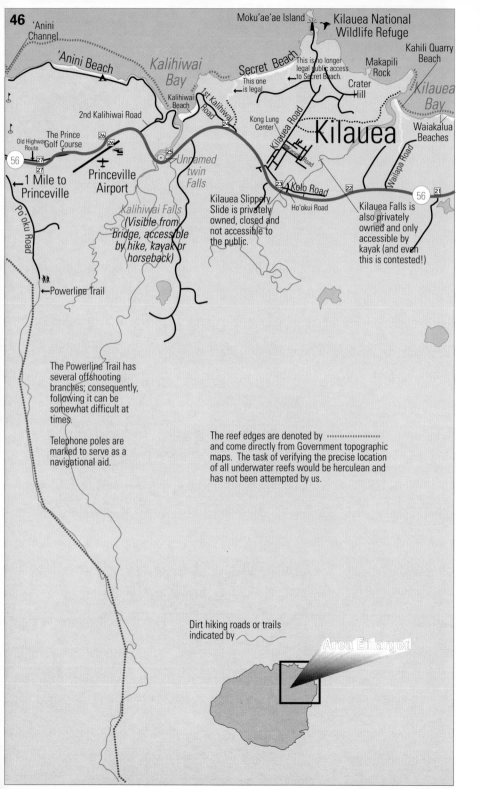

Moku'ae'ae Island

Kilauea National Wildlife Refuge

'Anini Channel

'Anini Beach

Kalihiwai Bay

Secret Beach

This is no longer legal public access to Secret Beach.

This one is legal

Makapili Rock

Kahili Quarry Beach

Kilauea Bay

Kalihiwai Beach

2nd Kalihiwai Road

1st Kalihiwai Road

24

Kong Lung Center

Kilauea Road

Kilauea

Crater Hill

Waiakalua Beaches

The Prince Golf Course

26

26

25

Keneke Road

Wailapa Road

Old Highway Route

56

27

27

Unnamed twin Falls

23

Kolo Road

22

56

21

1 Mile to Princeville

Princeville Airport

Ho'okui Road

Kalihiwai Falls (Visible from bridge, accessible by hike, kayak or horseback)

Kilauea Slippery Slide is privately owned, closed and not accessible to the public.

Kilauea Falls is also privately owned and only accessible by kayak (and even this is contested!)

Pō'oku Road

← Powerline Trail

The Powerline Trail has several offshooting branches; consequently, following it can be somewhat difficult at times.

Telephone poles are marked to serve as a navigational aid.

The reef edges are denoted by ·········· and come directly from Government topographic maps. The task of verifying the precise location of all underwater reefs would be herculean and has not been attempted by us.

Dirt hiking roads or trails indicated by

Area Enlarged

Map #2—Northern Kapa'a to 'Anini

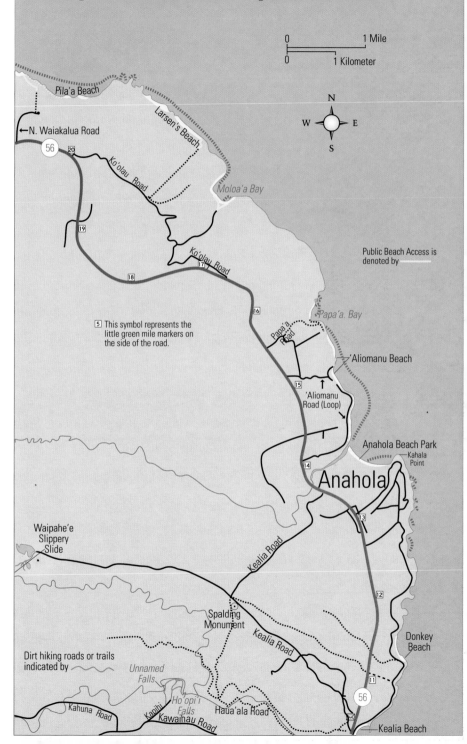

0   1 Mile
0   1 Kilometer

N
W   E
S

Pila'a Beach

Larsen's Beach

← N. Waiakalua Road

56   20

Ko'olau Road

Moloa'a Bay

19

Ko'olau Road

18   17

16

Public Beach Access is denoted by ——

5 This symbol represents the little green mile markers on the side of the road.

Papa'a. Bay

Papa'a Road

'Aliomanu Beach

15

'Aliomanu Road (Loop)

Anahola Beach Park
Kahala Point

14

Anahola

13

Waipahe'e Slippery Slide

Kealia Road

12

Spalding Monument

Kealia Road

Donkey Beach

Dirt hiking roads or trails indicated by ·······

Unnamed Falls

11

Ho'opi'i Falls

Kahuna Road

Kapini

Kawaihau Road

Haua'ala Road

56

Kealia Beach

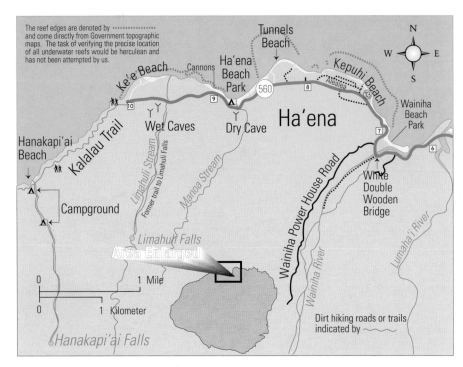

The reef edges are denoted by •••••••••••• and come directly from Government topographic maps. The task of verifying the precise location of all underwater reefs would be herculean and has not been attempted by us.

Tunnels Beach

Ke'e Beach

Cannons

Ha'ena Beach Park

560

8

Ke'e Beach

Kepuhi Beach

Atelea

13

Wainiha Beach Park

10

Wet Caves

Dry Cave

Ha'ena

7

N
W   E
S

Hanakapi'ai Beach

Kalalau Trail

Limahuli Stream

Former trail to Limahuli Falls

Manoa Stream

White Double Wooden Bridge

Wainiha Power House Road

Wainiha River

Lumaha'i River

6

Campground

Limahuli Falls

Area Enlarged

0   1 Mile

0   1 Kilometer

Dirt hiking roads or trails indicated by ～～

Hanakapi'ai Falls

Slide. This is a marvelous natural slide/waterfall where users ride into a deep pool below. It was closed a decade ago for liability reasons since people had drowned when the stream flow was heavy, and the rocks can be slippery. Although still used heavily by locals on weekends, their presence constitutes trespassing. If LPCO (who administers the land) reopens it, take Kealia Road up until you come to a reservoir. Past the fence, take the right trail until you see an old handrail on your left made out of train track. The trail from there to the bottom is only about five minutes. Don't go if the stream is flowing too hard. Check with Lihu'e Plantation Company for their current policy. We mention all this so you will know why all those cars are parked at the area up Kealia Road.

Back on the highway you might notice cars parked on the side of the road past the 11 mile mark. They are at Donkey Beach, a popular surfing and nudist beach. (Nude Surfing on the next Geraldo.)

ANAHOLA

Next, comes the town of Anahola. This area is designated Hawaiian Homelands, meaning it is available to individuals of Hawaiian descent. The spike shaped mountain you see on the mauka side is Kalalea Mountain, sometimes called King Kong's Profile. As you drive north of Anahola, look back and you will see the striking resemblance to King Kong (fitting, since the remake was filmed here in 1976). To the right of the profile is a small hole in the mountain called (this is clever) Hole-in-the-Mountain. It used to be bigger but a

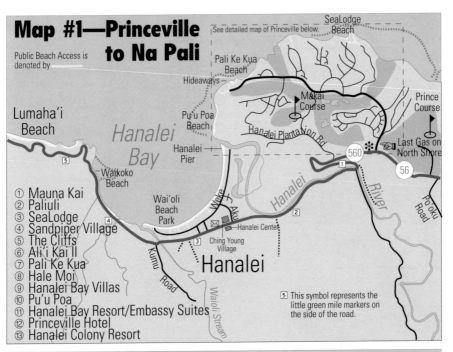

Map #1—Princeville to Na Pali

See detailed map of Princeville below.

Public Beach Access is denoted by

Lumaha'i Beach

Hanalei Bay

SeaLodge Beach

Pali Ke Kua Beach

Hideaways

Pu'u Poa Beach

Makai Course

Prince Course

Hanalei Plantation Rd.

Last Gas on North Shore

560

56

Hanalei Pier

Waikoko Beach

Po'oku Road

Hanalei River

① Mauna Kai
② Paliuli
③ SeaLodge
④ Sandpiper Village
⑤ The Cliffs
⑥ Ali'i Kai II
⑦ Pali Ke Kua
⑧ Hale Moi
⑨ Hanalei Bay Villas
⑩ Pu'u Poa
⑪ Hanalei Bay Resort/Embassy Suites
⑫ Princeville Hotel
⑬ Hanalei Colony Resort

Weke
Aku
Wai'oli Beach Park

Kumu Road

Waioli Stream

Hanalei Center

Ching Young Village

Hanalei

⑤ This symbol represents the little green mile markers on the side of the road.

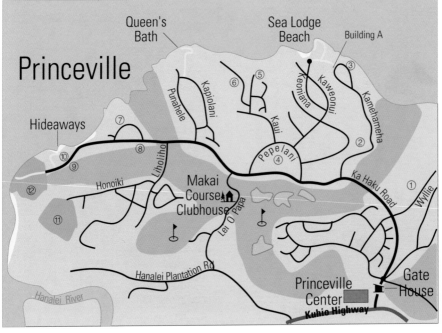

Princeville

Queen's Bath

Sea Lodge Beach

Building A

Hideaways

Punahele

Kapiolani

Keoniana

Kaweonui

Kamehameha

Kaui

Pepelani
④

Liholiho

Honoiki

Makai Course Clubhouse

Lei O Papa

Ka Haku Road

Wyllie

①

Hanalei Plantation Rd

Hanalei River

Princeville Center

Gate House

Kuhio Highway

landslide in the early 1980s closed off most of it. You can see it best between the 15 and 16 mile mark. There are several legends of how it happened. One says that a supernatural bird named Hulu pecked the hole in order to see Anahola on the other side.

Duane's Ono-Char Burger is in Anahola. This is a great place for burgers if you are hungry.

The part of the highway between Anahola and Kilauea is one of the longer stretches of road with relatively few sights to see. There are several secluded beaches along here which require walks of various lengths. See map on previous page, and the section on **Beaches**.

KILAUEA

The former plantation town of Kilauea is just past the 23 mile mark and accessible off Kolo Road. It is famous for the Kilauea Lighthouse. This is a postcard perfect landmark perched on a bluff and represents the northernmost point of the main Hawaiian Islands. When it was built in 1913 it had the largest clamshell lens in existence and was used until the mid '70s when it was replaced by a beacon. Directly offshore is Moku'ae'ae Island, a bird sanctuary. Limited tours of the lighthouse are available now. Take Kilauea Road. It is run by the Federal Government, which explains why they have been *ridiculously* slow in putting their visitor's center back up after it was whacked by the Hurricane. Figure 1995 before they get their act completely together. Until then, you can see it on a limited basis. Call them at (808) 828–1413. It's worth your time.

While you are in Kilauea, stop by the

The Kilauea Lighthouse stands as a silent sentry over the vast Pacific Ocean.

Kong Lung store. They have an eclectic assortment of upscale merchandise and it's definitely worth a peek.

Just north of Kilauea, Banana Joe's on the *mauka* side is one of the better places on the island to get fresh fruit without paying a fortune. They grow much of it themselves and the selection is usually excellent.

KALIHIWAI

After Kilauea you will notice two Kalihiwai Roads on the map. It used to be a loop connected at the bottom via a bridge. The bridge was removed by the tsunami of 1957 and residents are not looking to replace it. The first Kalihiwai Road leads to a beautiful little bay, Kalihiwai Bay. This is a good place to stretch your legs and enjoy the scenery.

Back on the highway, pull over at the turnout just past the 25 mile mark. You just passed an unnamed falls to the left which is often used to rinse off saltwater by people coming from Secret Beach. The stream flows under the road and falls again into the valley. The long bridge before you has a narrow walkway. Visible on the *mauka* side is Kalihiwai Falls, a gorgeous two tiered falls accessible by hike, kayak, or horseback. (See **Adventures** for more information on the hike.) The cars on this bridge *seem* to go by at 110 mph so be careful.

As you continue, the second Kalihiwai Road leads to ʻAnini Beach, where many of the rich and famous (such as Sylvester Stallone) chose to build their homes. This is the safest place on the north shore to swim and is protected by a long fringing reef. If you saw *Honeymoon in Vegas*, this is where the house scenes were filmed.

PRINCEVILLE

Continuing on Highway 56, the resort area of Princeville beckons. It was named after Prince Albert, the two year old son of King Kamehameha IV. Although the young lad died two years later, the name stuck. The resort is renowned for its ocean bluff condominiums and its golf. In fact, the best course on the island (some say the best in all Hawaiʻi) is The Prince Course located on your right after the 26 mile mark. This is the sort of course that makes the non-golfer want to learn.

Past the 27 mile mark is Poʻoku Road. The end of this road is the beginning of the Powerline Trail; nine miles of outstanding views. The trail has lots of offshoots and is only for the dedicated granola eater.

Princeville's cliffs lead many to think that it has no beaches to offer. *Au contraire*, beaches don't get much better than Hideaways. During the summer, this is a very pleasant little pocket of course sand. The catch is that you need to hike down to it. Another unknown

A Real Gem

gem is Queen's Bath. This is a natural pool located on a lava shelf. See **Beaches**. The Princeville Hotel is a good place to dine, shop, or just gawk.

As you leave Princeville, note that the highway changes names again and the mile markers start at 0. The gas station here is the last place to get gas on the north shore (and they have the prices to prove it). Across the street is the Hanalei Lookout. Many postcards have been sold featuring this view. This valley is where most of the taro in Hawaiʻi is grown. Taro corm (the root

The Hanalei Lookout is a postcard waiting to happen...

portion) are pounded to make poi. This is the stuff that everyone told you not to eat when you came to Hawai'i. If you go to a lu'au, try it anyway. Then you can badmouth it with authority. The Hanalei Lookout always makes for a great photo opportunity.

HANALEI

Going down the road, you come to the Hanalei Bridge. Look to your right and you may see buffalo. This is where several restaurants around the island get their buffalo burgers. (Actually, it's quite good; leaner and usually not as densely packed as regular hamburger.) This is a good time to tell you about Kaua'i's one lane bridge etiquette. *All* vehicles on one side proceed, so if the car directly in front of you goes, you go. Otherwise, stop and wait for the other side to go first. All bridges from here on have one lane. The Hanalei Bridge has a 15 ton weight limit so you won't see big tour buses past this point.

Hanalei (meaning wreath shaped or crescent shaped) Bay is a pretty little community. The surfing is famous throughout the islands for its challenging nature during the winter. The entire bay is ringed by beach. A wide assortment of people live in Hanalei representing long time locals, itinerant surfers, new age types, celebrities, and every other imaginable type of individual. Tahiti Nui is a good place to enjoy the local flavor. Or just pick up some good, inexpensive Mexican food from Tropical Taco, the green truck parked on the ocean side of the road at lunchtime.

While in Hanalei, stop by the Wishing Well Shave Ice for some world class shave ice.

After Hanalei, you ascend the road to a turnout overlooking Lumaha'i Beach. This is a fantastic looking beach made famous when Mitzi Gaynor washed that man right out of her hair in *South Pacific* in 1957. The eastern portion is the best but requires a hike down. Otherwise, you can walk right onto it just before the Lumaha'i Stream.

Notice how lush everything looks from here on? This part of the island gets the perfect amount of rain and sunshine making anything green very happy.

HA'ENA

Wainiha Beach Park, past the 6 mile mark, is often a great place to beachcomb, but the swimming is no good.

One of the best snorkel and SCUBA spots on the island, Tunnels Beach, is past the 8 mile mark. See **Beaches**. Before you get to the 9 mile mark, the road dips at Manoa Stream. The stream flows over the road and is always creating potholes. It often creates a hole big and deep enough to pop your tire, so look for it as you cross. You are now at Ha'ena Beach Park. Camping is allowed with County permit and the beach is lovely year round (but the *swimming* isn't always lovely; see **Beaches**). Across the street is the Manini-holo Dry Cave. Manini-holo was the chief fisherman for the Menehune. He and other Menehune dug the cave looking for the supernatural beasts called akua who had been stealing their fish.

Past the 9 mile mark you will come to Limahuli Stream. Many people use this stream to rinse off saltwater after their day at Ke'e Beach which is still ahead.

Above Limahuli Stream is the Limahuli Gardens at (808) 826–5547. They are part of the National Tropical Botanical Gardens. The garden is run by a delightful fellow named Charles "Chipper" Wichman. His grandmother, Juliet Rice Wichman, was a powerful presence on Kaua'i. She made the garden available to the NTBG in 1976. Until now, the only way to see the garden was to join the NTBG. But as we went to press, they were in the final

Shave Ice: An Island Delicacy

One treat everyone should try is shave ice. Lest you be confused, shave ice is *not* a snow cone. Snow cones are made from crushed ice with a little fruit syrup sprinkled on. True shave ice (that's *shave*, not *shaved*) uses a sharp blade to literally "shave" a large block of ice, creating an infinitely fine powder. Add to this copious amounts of exotic fruit flavors and put it all on top of a big scoop of ice cream and you have an island delight that is truly "broke da mouf". In our constant quest to provide as thorough a review as possible, we have unselfishly tried nearly every combination of shave ice. The result: We recommend the rainbow shave ice with macadamia nut ice cream. But by all means, engage in research of your own to see if you can come up with a better combination. The best places to get shave ice on the island are *Wishing Well Shave Ice* in Hanalei, *Halo Halo Shave Ice* in Lihu'e, and *Ritchie's Ono Saimin and Bento Shop* in Kekaha. *Wishing Well* is described above. The others can be found in the section called **Dining**.

process of getting a permit to make the gardens available to the general public. Starting in early 1994, they will have self guided tours for up to 120 people per day. As the year progresses, they will even open up a trail to beautiful Limahuli Falls. At a leisurely pace through the lush rain forest, the hike will take as much as six hours round trip to the 800 foot falls. The garden tour itself is strongly recommended and features native Hawaiian plants, an area for plants brought by the first settlers, and several other types. A real treat is the ancient terrace, crafted by some of the earliest Hawaiians, estimated to be 1,000 years old and in fantastic condition. Expect to pay $10–$20 per person, or join the NTBG for $65 which allows entrance for up to three persons. Make reservations well in advance.

A Real Gem

Just past the Limahuli Stream are the Wet Caves, called Waikapala'e Cave (reachable by a short trail) and Waikanaloa Cave (right there on the road). These are ancient lava tubes now filled with fresh water. SCUBA divers who have braved the bitter cold water (especially toward the bottom) report that there is not much to see, but the dive looks good on a diving resume. Legend has it they were dug by the fire goddess Pele. She dug them for her lover but left them when they became filled with water.

At the 10 mile mark, you have gone as far as you can go by car. This is Ke'e Beach, marked by a fabulous lagoon which offers great swimming and snorkeling when it's calm. This beach usually has a lifeguard present. The well-known Kalalau Trail begins here. Eleven miles of hills and switchbacks culminating in a glorious beach setting, complete with waterfall. The first leg of the hike leads to Hanakapi'ai Beach with a side trip to Hanakapi'ai Falls. For more

The eastern portion of Lumaha'i is the best part of the beach.

Walk a bit past Ke'e Beach for a great view of Na Pali.

on the Kalalau Trail, see **Adventures** on page 149.

Ke'e is where the Na Pali Coast begins. You can see its edges from here. Part of *The Thornbirds* was filmed at this location. If you walk past Ke'e Beach on the rocks you'll get an enticing look at the rugged Na Pali coastline. Look up toward the mountains and you see Bali Hai, Hawaiian name Makana Peak. Clever photography turned the peak into the mystical island of Bali Hai in the movie *South Pacific*. As you stare at this peak with its incredibly steep sides, picture the following scene which took place in ancient times.

Men would climb the 1,600 foot peak carrying special spears made of hau and papala. The trail was so difficult in spots that they had to cling to the side of the mountain for dear life. When it got dark, they would light the spears and hurl them toward the ocean below. The spears were designed to leave a fire trail behind and the light show was as good as any you could see in modern times.

Just east of Ke'e is where the infamous Taylor Camp used to be. This is where Howard Taylor, brother of Elizabeth Taylor owned a piece of land in the 1960s and encouraged other "hippies" to come and live off the land. The camp swelled to over 100 people who mostly ended up living off residents or the government. Before the State condemned the property in 1977, camp residents began what would become the national *puka shell* craze when one of the residents fashioned a necklace of shells and gave it to Howard, who in turn gave it to his famous sister Liz.

If you want to park at Ke'e and find the lot full, take the dirt road next to the rest rooms and stay to the left. There are many places to park here and it usually goes unnoticed.

NORTH SHORE SHOPPING

If you want to do a little shopping while you're on the north shore, these shops stood out from the rest in our opinion.

Kong Lung Co. in Kilauea has a beautiful collection of gifts, cards, clothing, and home decorating items. One of our favorite places to shop on the island.

At Princeville Shopping Center in Princeville check out SanDudes which has very high quality T–shirts, shorts, and the like. Kaua'i Kite & Hobby Company has kites, frisbees, art supplies, and games. Stunt kites start at under $20.

The Princeville Hotel has a couple of shops worth a peek if you are nearby.

At Ching Young Village in Hanalei is Inside Out. They offer a nice selection of women's clothing, shoes, and jewelry. At Village Variety check for good prices on souvenirs, casual clothing, fishing and snorkeling supplies. Hot Rockets has distinctive and colorful men's and women's clothing.

Across the street from Ching Young Village is the Old Hanalei School/ Hanalei Center. There, you might want to check out the Hanalei Surf Company, a surf shop with a good selection and surprisingly reasonable prices. Nice selection of casual clothing. They also rent a full line of beach equipment.

NORTH SHORE BEST BETS

Best Beach—Ke'e or Hideaways
Best Snorkeling—Tunnels or Hideaways
Best Treat—Wishing Well Shave Ice
Best Fast Food—Tropical Taco
Best Hidden Gem—Queen's Bath
Best Secluded Beach—Waiakalua
Best Store—Kong Lung
Best Swimming When Calm—Ke'e
Best SCUBA—Tunnels Beach
Best Beachcombing—Wainiha Beach
Best Golf—The Prince Course
Best Horseback Ride—Kalihiwai Falls
Best View—Sunset from Ke'e
   overlooking Na Pali

Kaua'i's north shore is where the majority of the State's taro is grown. This field, in the Hanalei Valley, was planted with rice to look like Vietnam in the movie Uncommon Valor.

Kaua'i's east shore is where the majority of the population resides. The Kings of yesteryear chose the Wailua River area to live, making it forever royal ground. All members of royalty were born in this area. Kuamo'o Road, designated as 580 on the maps is also called the King's Highway. In ancient times, only the king could walk along the spine of this ridge. (In fact, Kuamo'o means the lizard's spine.)

Today, the east shore is often referred to as the Coconut Coast. One drive through Wailua and you will quickly see why. Thousands of coconut trees planted a century ago by an idealistic young German immigrant who dreamed of overseeing a giant copra (dried coconut) empire. Unfortunately for him, the coconut plantation was not economically successful but his legacy lives on in the form of a gigantic coconut grove.

For our description, the east shore means the Wailua/Kapa'a area and the Lihu'e area. (Take a look at the back flap to orient yourself.) Both are heavily populated (this is a relative term, together they have about 15,000 residents).

The main highway, which stretches around the island occasionally changing its name, has mile markers every mile. These little green signs can be a big help in knowing where you are at any given time. Therefore, we have placed them on the maps represented as a number inside a small box 16. We will often describe a certain feature or unmarked road as being, ".3 miles past the 8 mile mark." We hope this helps. Many County roads have mile markers as well but some are missing. Since the County has informed us that they will not be replacing these, we have left them off the map if they are not there.

On Kaua'i, everything is either on the *mauka* side of the highway (meaning toward the mountains) or *makai* (meaning toward the ocean). Since people

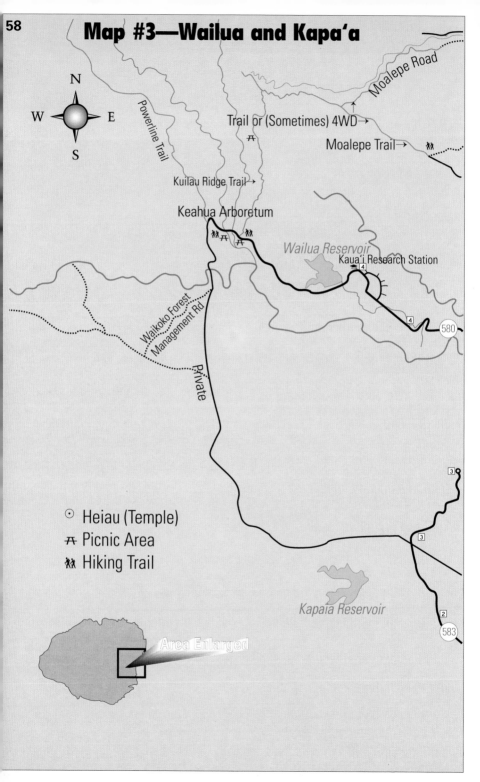

Map #3—Wailua and Kapa'a

N
W E
S

Moalepe Road

Powerline Trail

Trail or (Sometimes) 4WD →

Moalepe Trail →

Kuilau Ridge Trail →

Keahua Arboretum

Wailua Reservoir

Kaua'i Research Station

Waikoko Forest Management Rd

Private

580

3

3

Heiau (Temple)
Picnic Area
Hiking Trail

2

583

Kapaia Reservoir

Area Enlarged

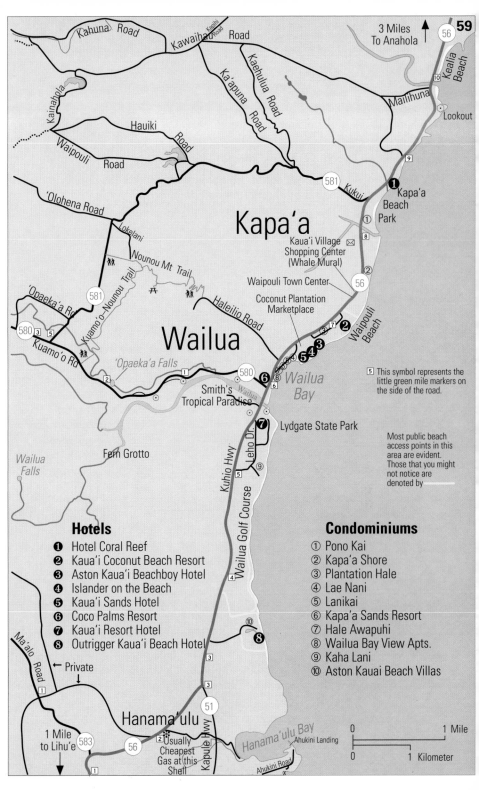

Hotels

❶ Hotel Coral Reef
❷ Kaua'i Coconut Beach Resort
❸ Aston Kaua'i Beachboy Hotel
❹ Islander on the Beach
❺ Kaua'i Sands Hotel
❻ Coco Palms Resort
❼ Kaua'i Resort Hotel
❽ Outrigger Kaua'i Beach Hotel

Condominiums

① Pono Kai
② Kapa'a Shore
③ Plantation Hale
④ Lae Nani
⑤ Lanikai
⑥ Kapa'a Sands Resort
⑦ Hale Awapuhi
⑧ Wailua Bay View Apts.
⑨ Kaha Lani
⑩ Aston Kauai Beach Villas

⑤ This symbol represents the little green mile markers on the side of the road.

Most public beach access points in this area are evident. Those that you might not notice are denoted by ——

3 Miles To Anahola

1 Mile to Lihu'e

Usually Cheapest Gas at this Shell

sometimes get these confused, we will refer to them as *mauka side* or *ocean side*.

All beaches we mention are described in detail in the section on **Beaches**.

Unlike other areas of the island where a single road dominates your tour, this area has many significant sights located off the main road. Therefore, we will describe them in a more scattershot manner and generally work our way from north to south.

WAILUA/KAPA'A

In the extreme northern part of Kapa'a is a delightful waterfall called Ho'opi'i Falls which is nearly always deserted during the week. If you want to spend an hour or two and have a picnic, this is a good place to do it. Mosquito repellent for the ten minute hike down is recommended. The trail is located at the end of the .2 mile dirt extension of Kapihi Road. (See maps on pages 47 and 59.) The trail is fairly well worn from weekend users and goes through a pleasant forest canopy. There are several forks leading down to the stream. Stay on the main one generally to the right. Remember where the trail encounters the stream for your return journey. All told it's less than .5 miles. The falls are located about 100 feet downstream from the end of the trail depending on which fork you end up on. The longer but easier-to-follow way is to take the dirt road/trail forking off to the left about halfway down Kapihi Road. When it encounters the stream, go to the right. After one minute, you will hear a thunderous unnamed waterfall. Stop here or continue another 10–15 minutes. The trail generally fol-lows the stream. Either route goes through beautiful forest and necessitates crossing the stream 100 feet *upstream* of Ho'opi'i Falls. It is shallow except during extraordinary rains. At the falls, there is even a staircase constructed to assist you to the base. The expected natural hazards such as slippery rocks, mud, and occasionally confusing trail intersections can apply here.

While we are up the road off the main highway, there are several hikes in this area that provide excellent views. The Nounou Mountain Trail (also called the Sleeping Giant), the Kuilau Ridge Trail, and the Moalepe Trail, all are located up the road and all worthy of consideration. (See **Hiking** under **Activities** for more information.)

One aspect of ancient Hawaiian culture that can be seen to this day is the heiau, a structure carefully built out of lava rocks and used for religious purposes. There are seven heiaus stretching for the mouth of the Wailua River to the top of Mount Wai'ale'ale. All except the Wai'ale'ale heiau are located on Map #3. The mouth of the Wailua River was well known, not only throughout the Hawaiian Islands, but also in parts of central Polynesia as well. Ancient Polynesians are thought to have come all the way from Tahiti to visit it.

The first heiau, near the mouth of the Wailua River on the southern side, is called Hauola, City of Refuge. It is part of what was a larger structure called Hikina A Ka La, the Rising Sun. If a person committed an offense worthy of execution (such as allowing his shadow to touch the shadow of a chief, or interrupting an important person), he would attempt to elude his executioners by coming here. By staying at the site and performing certain rites prescribed by the priest, he would earn the right to leave without harm. There's a plaque here identifying Hauola, City of Refuge.

The second temple is on that large forested mound on the mauka side of the highway between the north end of Leho Road and the road to Smith's Tropical Paradise. It's in the middle of a Lihu'e Plantation cane field and difficult to reach. This is called Malae and at 273 X 324 feet, it is the largest heiau on Kaua'i. Legend states that it was built by Menehune. Although there is not a lot to see, the view from there is interesting. If you decide to visit it, be wary of your footing. The twigs and leaves cover gaps and holes between the rocks.

The third heiau is just up Kuamo'o Road (580) on the left side. This area had several names and several functions. The first portion that you see is called Holoholo-ku. Some archeologists say that this area was used for human sacrifice. Most of the time those sacrificed were prisoners of war. If none could be found, however, the Kahuna would select a commoner and have the executioner strangle him secretly at night. Some archeologists find this interpretation of Hawaiian history in spiritual bad taste, given its very close

Please do not disturb offerings at heiaus.

proximity to the Birthstones, described below, and assume that the area was used for animal sacrifices. Regardless, most archeologists maintain that the heiau was later purposely desecrated and used as a pigpen by the wife of the last king of Kaua'i, who did so as a signal that the ancient religious ways should be abandoned in favor of Christianity.

Just a few dozen feet up the road from Holoholo-ku is the Birthstone. It was essential that all kings of Kaua'i be born here, even if they were not of chiefly origin. One of the two stones supported the back of the woman while the other is where she placed her legs while giving birth. The outline of stones near here was where a grass shack once stood. It was in this dwelling that the pregnant mother stayed until it was time to give birth. The flat slab of stone that you see on the ground covered the remains of a sacrificed dog, indicating that the place was kapu, or forbidden to commoners. The giant crack in the rock wall was where the umbilical cord of the newborn was placed. If a rat came and took the cord, it was a sign that the child would grow up to be a thief, otherwise all was well.

Lacy 'Opaeka'a Falls is a Wailua landmark.

Continuing up 580, a short way past the 1 mile mark is a dirt road angling back toward the ocean. This leads to the Bellstone. Located at the end of the road are two large boulders. If you walk down the path about 100 feet past the guardrail you will see several large stones. One of them, if thwacked properly, can produce a metallic clank (not the gong we have come to expect from western metal bells). This sound supposedly carried throughout the entire Wailua Valley. The stone was struck in ancient times to signal the birth of what would be a new chief.

Just before you get to the 'Opaeka'a Falls turnout is the last heiau you will see. Called Poli'ahu, this is a rather mysterious heiau. Legend states that it was built by Menehune, the legendary people of small stature and was devoted to the interests and activities of the

gods, demigods, and high Ali'i.

The actual final heiau in this chain rests atop the rain-soaked plateau of Wai'ale'ale. The remnants of this most sacred heiau are still visible today. Called Ka'awako, the altar itself stood 2 feet high, 5 feet wide, and 7 feet long. Toward the rear, standing on one end was a phallic stone. It is located on the wettest spot in the entire world. According to the USGS, this spot receives 440.22 inches of rain per year. (You read a lot of numbers about the annual rainfall on Wai'ale'ale—this number comes straight from the people who read the rain gauges.)

While on Kuamo'o Road, stop by the 'Opaeka'a Falls Look-out. These lacy falls flow year round. There is a crude trail

NOT TO BE MISSED!

between the end of the guardrail and the 2 mile mark leading to a spot several hundred feet upstream of the falls. One could walk in the stream to the edge of the falls if they wished. Needless to say, the top of the falls can be very dangerous, so use your best judgment. There is a Wailua River Lookout across from the ʻOpaekaʻa Lookout and an even better one just a few hundred feet back down the road.

Continuing up Kuamoʻo Road you will pass the Wailua Reservoir just past the second 4 mile mark. (When you see a second mile mark with the same number, it denotes the end of a County or State road.) Wailua Reservoir is a good place to freshwater fish.

The road gets pretty bumpy from here and crosses several streams. Don't cross if a stream is flowing over the road, it might get even higher. This area is very lush. Several trailheads are in this region. The Keahua Arboretum is located near here but has not been spectacular for a few years.

If you take the road past the point where it is paved, you are on Waikoko Forest Management Road. This can take you to a pleasant place to have a picnic if you take the right fork (see map) to a stream, or it can take you to a marvelous short jungle hike. (See **Jungle Hike** on page 126.)

Back on the main highway, you'll find Kapaʻa loaded with places to shop. (See **Shopping** at the end of this section.) If you are there on a Saturday, stop by the Roxy Swap Meet on the corner of Kukui Street and the main highway. Look for the big tents. This is the best place on the island to pick up souvenirs and the like at great prices. There is also a farmers market on

Wednesdays at 3:00 called the Sunshine Market. It is just up 581 on your right on the other side of the tennis courts. Arrive at 2:45 to get the best selection, the local fruit sold here goes fast.

One of Kapaʻa's notable views is the Sleeping Giant. The best angle is across the street from the Chevron Station (on the main highway) near the little parking lot. Look mauka and you will see the outline of a giant (this is your *ink blot test* for the day). According to legend, the giant you see (you *do* see it, don't you?) was a friendly sort who flattened areas where he sat. Local villagers liked this and also planted bananas in his footsteps. One day the chief ordered a heiau to be built. Villagers were too busy so the giant volunteered. It took two weeks and he did a great job. Villagers threw a party to celebrate and the giant ate a bit too much. He fell asleep and has not been roused since, but is expected to wake up any time (maybe during your visit).

Local folklore says that if Kauaʻi's people learned of an attempt to invade their island, they would light fires behind the Sleeping Giant in order to illuminate his profile at night. This would frighten invading warriors into thinking that Kauaʻi had some really big dudes and should not be a candidate for invasion.

While you are in Wailua, riverboat trips up the Wailua River can take you to the Fern Grotto for $10 per person. This is a natural amphitheater filled with ferns and is a popular place to hold weddings. See **River Trips** under **Activities**. The Wailua River is usually called the only navigable river in all Hawaiʻi, but that depends on your definition of navigable. The mouth of the river has several stones with ancient petroglyphs carved in them. After heavy rains, the river sometimes washes away large amounts of sand revealing these stones for a short period of time. The mouth itself is always changing and watching it wash over its banks after a heavy rain can be wild. The river can go from not flowing at all to carving up the mouth in a matter of hours.

There is a beachside walking path behind the Kaua'i Coconut Beach Hotel which makes for a pleasant stroll. A good place to take a long beach walk is from Lydgate State Park south as far as the Outrigger Hotel. The sand is almost continuous the whole way.

Lydgate State Park is the best place on the island to learn snorkeling. It has a boulder enclosed pond that allows water and fish in, but keeps out the ocean's force. See **Snorkeling** on page 138 and **Beaches** on page 102. There is even a keiki (kid) pond which is shallower. Add to this showers and rest rooms and you have a nice little park for a picnic.

On the southern side of the Wailua River is Smith's Tropical Paradise. Here you will find a lovely garden in which to stroll, filled with tropical plants and peacocks. Entrance is $5 per person. They also hold a nice lu'au here, see **Dining** for more information.

As you pass the Wailua Golf Course going south toward Lihu'e, realize that the entire coast fronting the course is sand beach. Called Nukoli'i Beach, there are rarely more than a handful of people here.

LIHU'E

Coming from Kapa'a and just before you enter Lihu'e from Highway 56, you see Ma'alo Road (583). This leads to Wailua Falls. If you ever saw the television show *Fantasy Island*, these are the falls featured in the opening credits (just before Tattoo shouts about da plane, da plane). In ancient (and occasionally modern) times, men would jump off the top of the 80 foot falls to prove their manhood. This test was often fatal. There is a trail leading down to the top of the falls. Down there you find an old cane bridge straddling the valley. The top of the falls is flat with the river having carved several channels into the rock. If you take the trail, beware that a fall from

NOT TO BE MISSED!

These petroglyphs are usually submerged in the mouth of the Wailua River, but can appear after heavy rains.

Wailua Falls, made famous in the TV show Fantasy Island, *is always a nice place to stop.*

the ledge has proven fatal many times over. Just down the road from the turnout there is an overgrown trail leading down to the pools below. You might see people splashing about in the pool but the trail to the bottom is unbelievably steep and slippery.

As you reenter the highway you will pass Kapaia Stitchery. They have a large inventory of beautiful Hawaiian fabrics that can be made up for you in selected styles and mailed to you on the mainland. High quality clothing for all family members at reasonable prices make this a good place to check out. We mention it here instead of in the section on shopping because it's there by itself and is easy to overlook.

In Lihu'e, one place worth stopping for is the Kaua'i Museum (245–6931) on Rice Street. They have an interesting display of old Hawaiian artifacts and a permanent display called *The Story of Kaua'i.* Numerous local events take place year-round. Their gift shop is well stocked with books, maps, and assorted items. If you are looking for topographic maps of the various areas (serious hikers prefer these as traveling companions) or just an obscure book on Kaua'i or Hawai'i, this is a good place to stop. Admission is $3 per person unless you are going to the gift shop which is free.

If you need any camping permits or other County or State items, their buildings are behind the museum on Eiwa Street.

While you are in the area, there is a dumpy little place on Kress Street called Halo Halo Shave Ice that serves outstanding shave ice. Have them put ice cream on the bottom for a real treat.

A Real Gem

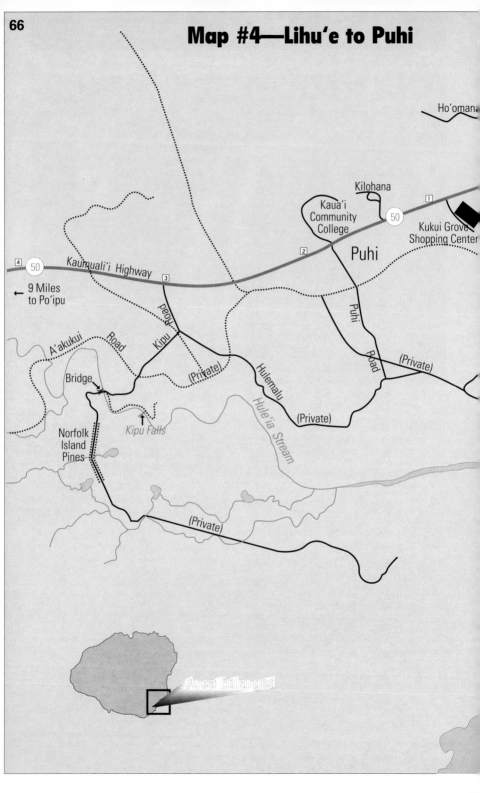

Ho'oman

Kilohana

Kaua'i
Community
College

50

1

Kukui Grove
Shopping Center

2

Puhi

4 50

Kaumuali'i Highway

3

← 9 Miles
to Po'ipu

A'akukui   Road

Kipu   Road

(Private)

Puhi   Road

(Private)

Bridge

Hulemalu

(Private)

Hule'ia Stream

↑
Kipu Falls

Norfolk
Island
Pines

(Private)

Area Enlarged

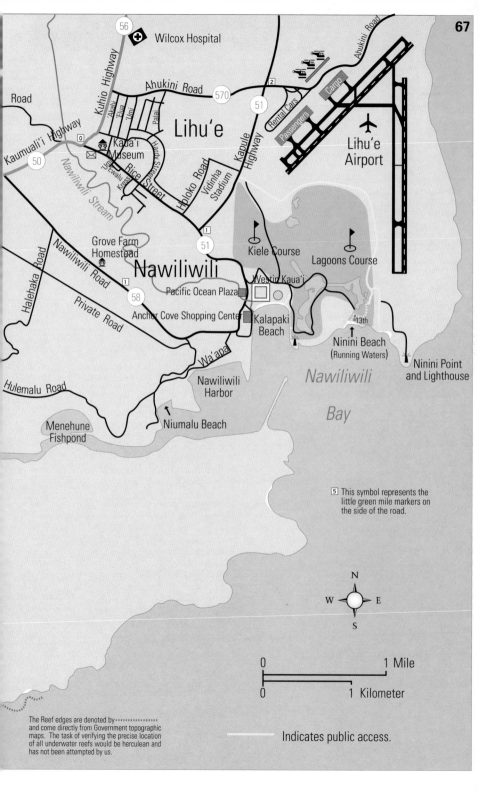

56 ✚ Wilcox Hospital

Kuhio Highway

Ahukini Road 570

51

Ahukini Road

Cargo

Rental Cars

Passengers

✈ Lihu'e Airport

Lihu'e

Kaua'i Museum

✉

Kaumuali'i Highway

50

Road

0

Nawiliwili Stream

Rice Street

Hardy Street

Holoko Road

Vidinha Stadium

Kapule Highway

Kress Street

Eiwalu Street

Akahi

Eiwa

Umi

Palai

1

51

Grove Farm Homestead

Nawiliwili

1

58

Kiele Course

🚩

Lagoons Course

🚩

Pacific Ocean Plaza

Anchor Cove Shopping Center

Westin Kaua'i

Kalapaki Beach

13th

Ninini Beach (Running Waters)

Ninini Point and Lighthouse

Wa'apa

Nawiliwili Harbor

Halehaka Road

Nawiliwili Road

Private Road

Niumalu Beach

Nawiliwili Bay

Hulemalu Road

Menehune Fishpond

5 This symbol represents the little green mile markers on the side of the road.

N
W ⊕ E
S

0   1 Mile
0   1 Kilometer

Indicates public access.

The Reef edges are denoted by ••••••••••••
and come directly from Government topographic
maps. The task of verifying the precise location
of all underwater reefs would be herculean and
has not been attempted by us.

Taking Rice Street leads you to Nawiliwili Harbor. There are two shopping centers here called Pacific Ocean Plaza and Anchor Cove Shopping Center. Kalapaki Beach, behind Anchor Cove, is a good place to watch sailboats come ashore in addition to the beach's other attributes.

On Rice Street, you will pass one of the entrances to the now closed Westin. Its other entrance is off Kapule Highway (51) and leads through the Westin to either Running Waters Beach or the Ninini Lighthouse. If there is a maintenance person at the lighthouse, ask him if you can go to the top. The view from the 100 foot lighthouse is superb. If you happen to be on top when a jet comes in for a landing, you'd swear you could reach up and touch it. To get to the lighthouse, you pass by two golf courses. The Kiele is definitely the better of the two.

Rice Street loops around and becomes Nawiliwili Road. It is here that you will find Grove Farm Homestead Museum at (808) 245–3202. This was the private home of George N. Wilcox and his nieces. It was turned into a museum by Mabel Wilcox shortly before her death in 1978. With 80 acres and several buildings to browse through, it is quite popular. They had extensive hurricane damage and were scheduled to reopen shortly after we went to press. The reason we listed the area code is because you *must* make reservations well before you arrive on Kaua'i or you won't be admitted.

Off Nawiliwili Road is Wa'apa Road. Take this road to Hulemalu Road and you will come to an overlook for the Menehune (Alekoko) Fishpond. This is a large, impressive fishpond adjacent to the Hule'ia Stream. According to legend, it was built in one night by the Menehune as a gift for a princess and her brother. Estimates of its age range as high as 1,000 years. Today, it is privately owned and has fallen into disrepair as a fishpond. Nonetheless, it is a remarkable landmark that is worth a look.

Back on the main highway (which has changed its name to Highway 50, the Kaumuali'i Highway), we find ourselves heading south. Before the 1 mile mark is Kukui Grove Shopping Center, the biggest shopping center on the island. Behind the center is Wally World (245–5252). This is a good place to bring the kids as they have miniature golf, and are installing batting cages and bumper boats.

Past the 1 mile mark you will see Kilohana (245–5608) on your right. This was the home of Gaylord and Ethel Wilcox and has been lovingly restored to its former glory. Gaylord was manager of Grove Farm Plantation. Walk through the door of this 16,000 square foot mansion and you get a sense of Kaua'i in days past. The furniture, fittings, and motif all harken back to a simpler day when sugar was king. Inside is Gaylord's Restaurant and several shops. One shop called Grande's Gems and Gallery has particularly fine jewelry and is worth a stop. Kilohana's also offers carriage rides around the grounds pulled by Clydesdale horses at a cost of $7. They also have sugar cane carriage rides for $18 per person. For these latter rides, call 246–9529.

Also located on the grounds is Paradise River Rentals at 245–9580. This is a particularly good place to rent all sorts of goodies from boats to golf clubs to kites.

Across from the 3 mile mark on the main highway is Kipu Road. Located off this road is a glorious little secret place you might find enchanting. If you go, do it during the week and you will probably have it all to yourself. It is a small waterfall called Kipu Falls pouring into a deep pool. It is ringed half way around by a 20 foot cliff. On the far side is a rope swing with a ladder leading up the side. Get out of the pond via thick tree roots and swing all over again. The entire setting is wonderful. Obviously, you need to evaluate the condition

A Real Gem

of the rope and pond yourself to determine if it is safe. People use it all the time (including us) but we won't vouch for its safety. To get there take the dirt road just before the bridge on Kipu Road (see map). If it is muddy, park at the top and walk down or your car might get stuck. Just before the road begins to ascend, there is a very short (but sometimes slippery) trail down to the top of the falls. You're on your own from here.

If you were to continue on Kipu Road you would quickly come to a magnificent strand of Norfolk Island pines. These trees were highly valued as ships masts in the Age of Discovery. This entire area is called Kipu and is currently owned and administered by the Rice family and the Waterhouse Trust. William Hyde Rice was a cattle rancher and a monument to him was erected here by his Japanese workers. Behind the mountain is the fabulous beach called Kipu Kai. This long crescent of sand is a beachgoers dream. Unfortunately, the only way to reach it is by boat or over the private road owned by the Waterhouse Trust. Naturally this road is closed to the public. However, John T. Waterhouse deeded the 1,096 acres of land to the State effective at the time of death of the last of his four nieces and one nephew. So if you want to see it, either go on one of the boat trips listed under **Ocean Tours**, or put the year 2050 on your calendar of things to do.

EAST SHORE SHOPPING

These are some places you might want to keep an eye out for during your travels. Stores change, owners change. These are *not* paid advertisements. We simply visited every store and shop on the island and these are the ones that caught our attention. We've already mentioned a few in the tour above, so we won't repeat ourselves.

Starting in northern Kapa'a, the Privilege Collection at the fork of Lehua and Kuhio Highway offers some unique jewelry pieces. Behind them on Lehua Street is a tiny yellow house called Kii Hale that sells dolls, handicrafts, and gifts.

Park your car in downtown Kapa'a, as all of the following are an easy walk to each other. Starting at the New Pacific House, there are three shops you shouldn't miss. The Yellowfish Trading Co. and Rainbow Ducks downstairs are very special. At the former they have a wonderful selection of new and antique jewelry, furniture, and home decorating items carefully selected and displayed. Next door at Rainbow Ducks you will find perfect gifts of clothing and toys for the children in your life. Upstairs, the Tin Can Mailman is a different kind of bookstore for those with interest in South Sea topics.

Next to the ABC Store, stop by the Kauaʻi Arts and Crafts Market under the big tents for good buys, and try some island treats while you're there.

Down the street in Kapaʻa, stop by Tropical Tantrum, specializing in hand-painted ladies clothing.

Heading north again, Nightengayles sells beautiful ladies clothing, including lingerie and bridal wear.

Next door, still going north is Jim Saylor Jewelers—custom designed and crafted jewelry by its namesake.

North are Bo-ku-ma-rue and Earth Beads. The former has a good selection of Polynesian inspired clothing; the latter is a good place for unique gifts and jewelry.

Behind American Savings Bank near the 8 mile mark is Cost-U-Less. This is a warehouse type store good for discounts on Keoki or Macadamia Liqueur and multiple film roll packs.

At Waipouli Plaza you'll find Waipouli Variety. They sell all kinds of outdoor activity gear, souvenirs, and tabis. The Shell Factory is also worth a stop for their shell collection and jewelry.

At the Kauaʻi Village, under the clock tower, is Art to Wear featuring women's handpainted clothing and a large selection of jewelry. The Baskin-Robbins here seems to have more generous scoops for the ice cream lovers.

Just down the road across from the Waipouli Town Center are two small shops. Buddies sells casual ladies clothing. Marta's Boat carries enchanting children's clothes.

If you are a dedicated shopper, set aside a few hours to browse Coconut Marketplace. It will be on your left going south. Children can play in the courtyard while you shop the variety of mer-chandise offered here.

Always worth a stop is Hilo Hattie, located at the corner of Kuhio Highway and Ahukini Road (570) in Lihuʻe. They have a large selection of aloha wear and souvenirs sold in a fun atmosphere.

Just down the highway on your right is East West Imports Wholesale Jewelry and Hobby Beads with a vast assortment of beads, jewelry, shells, and craft material.

Among the many Kukui Grove Shopping Center stores, check out Liberty House, The Penthouse, and Indo-Pacific Trading Co. and Espresso Cafe All offer something worth seeing.

In Nawiliwili be sure to stop at Anchor Cove Shopping Center. A good variety of merchandise is offered here. Don't miss the view of Kalapaki Bay from the back of the Center.

East Shore Best Bets

Best Beach Walk—Lydgate State Park to Outrigger Hotel

Best View—From the top of Sleeping Giant for hikers, sunrise over Lydgate for non-hikers

Best Place for Novice Snorkelers, Fish Feeding, or to Let Children Swim—Lydgate State Park

Best Treat—Halo Halo Shave Ice

Best Fast Food—Buffalo Burger at Kalapaki Beach Burgers in Nawiliwili

Best Hidden Gem—Kipu Falls

Best Uncrowded Beach—In front of Wailua Golf Course

Best Boogie Boarding—Kealia Beach

Best Restaurant View—Al and Don's for breakfast, window seat at Bull Shed for dinner

Best Evening Stroll—Paved beach path beginning in front of Kauaʻi Coconut Beach Resort (interrupted in parts)

Best Luʻau—Smith's Tropical Paradise

Normally calm, Brennecke Beach is spectacular when the surf's really up.

The sunny south shore. Here, rainfall is less frequent and sunshine is abundant. Many people prefer the sunnier aspect of the south shore to the lushness of the north shore. Fortunately, you can have it all.

For the sake of this discussion, we will consider the south shore everything from Kipu to Kalaheo. (Look at the map on the back flap to orient yourself.) Past Kalaheo, the character of the island changes again and we will cover that under **West Shore Sights**.

The same descriptive ground rules that we discussed at the beginning of **North Shore Sights** apply here.

All beaches we mention are described in detail in the section on **Beaches**.

Driving to Po'ipu from Lihu'e along the main highway you will pass through the Knudsen Gap between the 6 and 8 mile marks. A century ago, this was the scariest part of the island. The small gap between the mountains was the only route you could take and was a perfect place for an ambush. Even Sheriff Wilcox always dreaded going through the Knudsen Gap.

Past the 6 mile mark you will come to 520, or Maluhia Road. This road to Koloa and Po'ipu is referred the Tree Tunnel. When Walter Duncan McBryde was landscaping his home in the early part of this century he found that he had over 500 eucalyptus trees *left over*. He donated these trees, called swamp mahogany to the County. Many residents showed up to help plant the trees. The result is the Tree Tunnel. Today, it should more aptly be called the "tree corridor." Though still beautiful, the trees don't intermesh at the top the way they did before either Hurricane 'Iwa in 1982 or 'Iniki in 1992.

Map #5—Koloa to Kalaheo

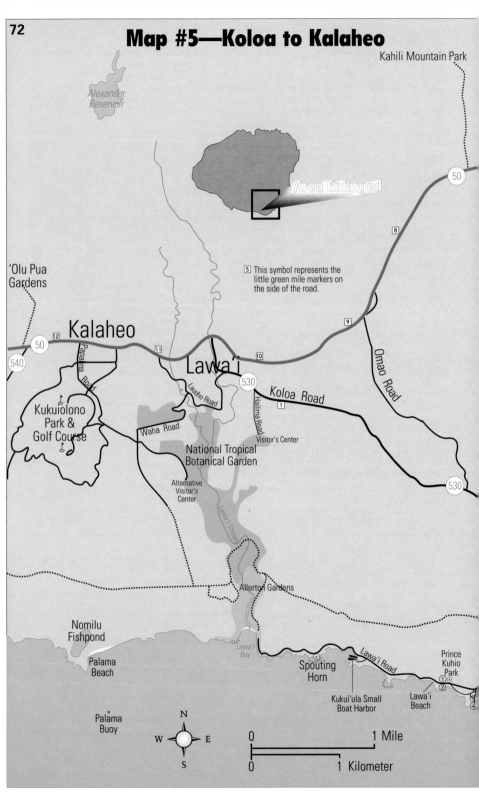

Kahili Mountain Park

Alexander Reservoir

Area Enlarged

50

8

'Olu Pua Gardens

⑤ This symbol represents the little green mile markers on the side of the road.

9

Omao Road

12

Kalaheo

50

540

Papalina Road

11

Lawa'i

10

530

Koloa Road

1

Laudho Road

Kukuiolono Park & Golf Course

Waha Road

Hailima Road

Visitor's Center

530

National Tropical Botanical Garden

Alternative Visitor's Center

Lawa'i Stream

Allerton Gardens

Nomilu Fishpond

Lawa'i Bay

Palama Beach

Spouting Horn

Lawa'i Road

Prince Kuhio Park

1
2

Kukui'ula Small Boat Harbor

Lawa'i Beach

4

Palama Buoy

N
W E
S

0   1 Mile

0   1 Kilometer

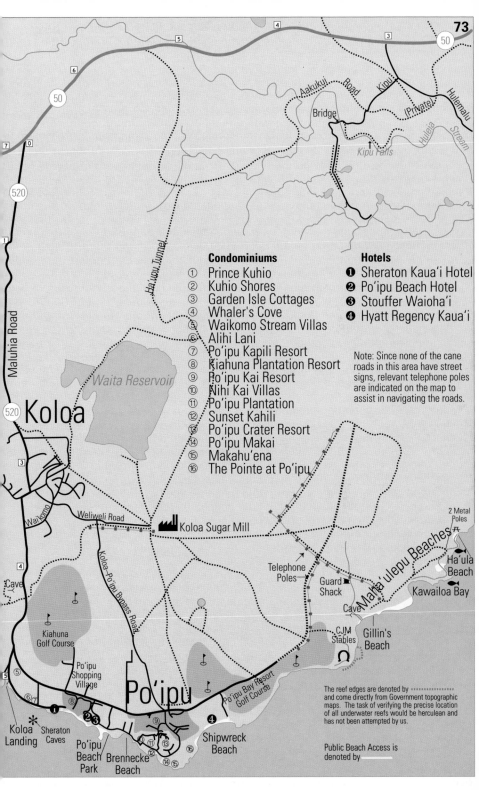

Condominiums

① Prince Kuhio
② Kuhio Shores
③ Garden Isle Cottages
④ Whaler's Cove
⑤ Waikomo Stream Villas
⑥ Alihi Lani
⑦ Po'ipu Kapili Resort
⑧ Kiahuna Plantation Resort
⑨ Po'ipu Kai Resort
⑩ Nihi Kai Villas
⑪ Po'ipu Plantation
⑫ Sunset Kahili
⑬ Po'ipu Crater Resort
⑭ Po'ipu Makai
⑮ Makahu'ena
⑯ The Pointe at Po'ipu

Hotels

❶ Sheraton Kaua'i Hotel
❷ Po'ipu Beach Hotel
❸ Stouffer Waioha'i
❹ Hyatt Regency Kaua'i

Note: Since none of the cane roads in this area have street signs, relevant telephone poles are indicated on the map to assist in navigating the roads.

The reef edges are denoted by ••••••••••••••••• and come directly from Government topographic maps. The task of verifying the precise location of all underwater reefs would be herculean and has not been attempted by us.

Public Beach Access is denoted by ——————

KOLOA

Driving down 520 you come to the town of Koloa, sometimes called Old Koloa Town. This became the first sugar plantation town in all the islands when Kamehameha III leased the land to Ladd and Company in 1835. The town has much charm and is worth a stop. There is a marvelous monkey pod tree next to the Crazy Shirts whose branches seem to meander forever. While in Koloa, stop for an ice cream at Lappert's. They make it here on Kaua'i; it's delicious and extra fattening. (Hey, you're on vacation, right?)

Across the street (catty-corner) from the shops are the remnants of an old sugar mill built 150 years ago. There you will also find a plaque dedicated to the sugar plantation workers.

Looking at the map, you will see a dirt road leading to Waita Reservoir. This huge reservoir (the biggest in the State) is used by local fishermen. Past it is the Ha'upu Range Tunnel, a half mile long tunnel blasted through the mountain to bring sugar cane to the Koloa Mill. The Tunnel is decidedly spooky, completely dirt lined all the way around, unlit, and only wide enough for one vehicle. McBryde Sugar doesn't like tourists driving through it since a cane truck coming the other way could definitely ruin your day.

PO'IPU

Continuing to Po'ipu on 520 and doglegging onto Po'ipu Road, watch your speed. This is sometimes a speed trap and the limit is 25 mph (15 mph near the school). Past the 4 mile mark is a wide haul cane road. Off this road is another dirt road (see map) leading to a *vague* trail to a cave. The cave is an

Sugar cane played an important part in Koloa's history.

Spouting Horn as dusk approaches.

Congress until the early 1920s. In this park you will also find the Ho'ai Heiau, impressive in its perfection and almost chiseled appearance. The entrance is toward the rear on the left side.

Continuing on Lawa'i Road, you will come to Spouting Horn Beach Park. This wonderful delight is a small lava shelf where water from waves is thrust through an opening causing water and air to squirt out a horizontal blowhole. This particular site distinguishes itself from other blowholes around Hawai'i in that it has an additional

old lava tube and can be difficult to find. If you are determined, it is near the tallest tree in the area. This hole in the ground has a few tunnels in it. There is a ladder leading down into the cave; trust it at your own risk.

Past the 4 mile mark as you approach Po'ipu, the road forks. If you take the right fork you come to Prince Kuhio Park. There you will find a monument to Prince Kuhio who was the last royally designated heir to the Hawaiian throne. He went on to become a delegate to

hole which blows only air, causing a loud moaning and gasping sound. Legend has it that the entire coastline in this area was once guarded by a giant female lizard called a mo'o. She would eat anyone who tried to swim or fish in the area. One day a man named Liko went fishing. The mo'o went to attack Liko who threw a spear into the mo'o's mouth.

NOT TO BE MISSED!

The angry mo‘o chased Liko into the lava tube. Liko escaped but the mo‘o became trapped in what we now call Spouting Horn where its cries of hunger and pain can be heard to this day.

The view from the guardrails is quite interesting. Many people walk down and view the Horn and some of the other delightful offerings from the lava area itself. The power and forces in this area can only be experienced from this vantage point. Be forewarned, however, that while the experience is far more rewarding than the view from the guardrails, it can be dangerous. There have been incidents where people have been swept to their deaths into the Horn. Unexpectedly large waves can even wash over the entire shelf, dragging you into the hole or over the edge into the open ocean. There should be signs warning you not to go down. If you ignore them, you do so at your own risk. In any event, NEVER stand between the hole and the ocean. A very large wave would have no difficulty dragging you in. On July 14, 1993, two visitors from San Francisco were knocked in while they stood between the hole and the ocean. One was *on crutches* at the time. They were lucky— rather than being crushed inside the hole, they were immediately sucked out of the blowhole and into the open ocean. With marginal swimming abilities, they would have surely drowned but for the heroics of some GTE workers on their lunch break who braved (and I do mean braved) the choppy waters to bring them back in.

Going back the way you came just before the fork is a road leading to Koloa Landing. This is a

These lithified sand dunes of Maha‘ulepu are a stunning testament to the power of the ocean.

popular SCUBA shore dive. Until this century this was Kaua'i's main port. Whaling ships used to winter here and all goods brought to Kaua'i came through either Koloa Landing or Waimea.

Going to the fork again, take the left (eastern) fork (or, as Yogi Berra used to say, "If you come to a fork in the road, take it.") All along Po'ipu is turtle country. Look out at the water for any reasonable length of time and you will see sea turtles swimming nearby. This area was developed in the '70s and '80s and has become a much sought after visitor destination. Swanky hotels and condominium resorts line the road. (See **Where To Stay** for more information.) The beaches in this area are fantastic, with the best of the best located past the resorts at a place called Maha'ulepu. This beach (see **Beaches**) sports lots of places to walk and even a large natural

A Real Gem

amphitheater. The cane roads around here can be good places to ride mountain bikes. Horseback rides, windsurfing, snorkeling, fishing and more are all available in this area. See **Activities** for more information.

On your way back to the main highway(50), you will pass by the best bargain on the island as far as food is concerned. A little hole-in-the-wall called Taqueria Nortenos (see **Dining**) serves good and very inexpensive Mexican food in gigantic proportions.

LAWA'I

Continuing on Highway 50 you come to Lawa'i, most notable for the National Tropical Botanical Gardens at 332–7361. This incredibly beautiful garden consists of 186 acres of the National Tropical Botanical Garden and 100 acres called the Allerton Gardens. Even if you normally wouldn't visit a garden, you'll probably like this one. Rich and lush with remarkably varied plants and abundant birds, tours are guided and last about two hours. The fee for the tour is $20 per person. However, if

Watch your step around these ficus roots at the National Tropical Botanical Garden in Lawa'i.

you want to join the NTBG system, entrance is free and also allows you to tour the Limahuli Gardens on the north shore in Ha'ena. Family Membership is $65 and allows entrance for up to three people.

Another Lawa'i feature is Mustard's Last Stand. If you have kids, they will enjoy coming here and playing on the small miniature golf course (that might sound redundant but it *really* is small). Inside the shop they sell excellent merchandise at mostly reasonable prices. Their Ni'ihau Shell Lei selection is the best on the island.

KALAHEO

After Lawa'i comes Kalaheo. This small town is over represented when it comes to good restaurants (see **Dining**). One of Kalaheo's lesser known gems is the Kukuiolono Park and Golf Course (see **Golf**). This is the private course and garden donated by Walter D. McBryde to the people of Kaua'i. If you want to try your hand at golf, this is the place to learn. The price is $5 *per day*. The small Japanese garden located on the course was Mr. McBryde's pride and joy. This is where he chose to be buried, near the 8th tee.

If you haven't had your fill of gardens yet, the 'Olu Pua Gardens at 332–8182 are lovely gardens in a lush tropical setting. This is actually one of the private homes of the Irvine family (as in Irvine, California) and was originally the home of the Alexander family (as in Alexander & Baldwin). It has now been opened for tours to the general public (as in you). Impeccably groomed grounds with an amazing diversity of flora. Guided 45 minute tours daily. Admission $10 for adults, and $5 for children 5 - 12.

Located just past Kalaheo going west across from entrance to Highway 540.

Just after the 14 mile mark you will come to the Hanapepe Valley Lookout. As you gaze over the peaceful vista, it's hard to believe that this was the scene of the bloodiest and most savage battle known to have taken place on Kaua'i. The embittered son of Kaua'i's last king started a revolt against government rule. Remember that Kaua'i had never been conquered by Kamehameha the Great. Both of his invasion attempts had been costly in terms of men and neither had even reached Kaua'i. Even though Kaua'i's last king voluntarily accepted Kamehameha's rule, it forever stuck in the royal craw that Kaua'i had not been *forced* into submission. So when this revolt occurred, it was a perfect excuse to go over and show those Kauaians who's boss. Government troops sent to put down the revolt were unimaginably brutal and their methods were reviled even among their supporters. Men, women, and children where needlessly slaughtered and the wanton killing continued for ten days.

SOUTH SHORE SHOPPING

While in Koloa check out Crazy Shirts and Progressive Expressions. The former has several outlets around the island specializing in silkscreened T-shirts. Their selection is usually pretty good. Progressive Expressions is a

Ni'ihau Shell Leis

The women of Ni'ihau carry on a tradition dating back centuries. With indescribable patience, they collect tiny Ni'ihau shells, clean, drill, string and pack them with fiber creating fabulous leis. This is no easy task. An entire day's labor often reaps only 4 or 5 useable shells. And it requires thousands of shells to make a lei. Some women only search for shells at night believing that the sunlight dulls the shell's luster. While costing from several hundred to several thousand dollars each, this is a relative bargain given the amount of labor that goes into one. It commonly takes several years to complete one lei. The result is a perfect, hand-crafted and tightly packed lei representing one of the last truly Hawaiian art forms. There are less and less people on Ni'ihau that are willing to participate in this process, and many consider it a matter of time before this art form will be lost.

If you purchase one, the best selection on the island is at the Hawaiian Trading Post on the corner of Highways 50 and 530 (Koloa Road) in Lawa'i.

One last caveat; if you buy one, do it for yourself. It would be crushing to spend all that money only to show your lei to someone and have them say, "Oh yeah, I got one for free at Hilo Hattie's." While Ni'ihau Shell Leis are infinitely more beautiful, some might not appreciate the difference.

good surf shop with a nice selection of beach wear and street clothing, boogie boards, and sunglasses. Discount Variety on Weliweli has a good selection of inexpensive souvenirs, fishing gear, beach supplies, camping gear, snorkel gear, boogie boards, and T–shirts. Treasures Shared is on Po'ipu Road. They have beach sand on the floor and a nice selection of women's clothing.

The Po'ipu Shopping Village in Po'ipu is a large shopping center with several upscale gift and clothing shops. The Hyatt has lots of shops that are thoughtfully stocked and definitely worth a stop.

Lawa'i has The Hawaiian Trading Post, discussed previously in this chapter. They have several shops at their location and are one of the better places to shop on the south shore.

SOUTH SHORE BEST BETS

Best Strolling Beach—Maha'ulepu

Best Sunset View—Corner window table at Brennecke's (in Winter) or through Spouting Horn

Best Snorkeling—Around the tombolo at Po'ipu Beach Park

Best Treat—Lappert's Ice Cream Koloa

Best Fast Food—Taqueria Nortenos

Best Place To Watch Fools Jump Off A Cliff—Shipwreck Beach in front of the Hyatt Po'ipu

Best Secluded Beach—Ha'ula Beach

Best Swimming—Po'ipu Beach Park

Best Pizza—Brick Oven Pizza

Best Beachcombing—Kawailoa Bay

Best Golf—Po'ipu Bay Resort

Best Hotel Grounds—Hyatt

Best Seafood Selection—House of Seafood

Best Romantic Restaurant—Tidepools at the Hyatt

Hanapepe Valley Lookout often provides rainbows for its audience. No matter where you are, rainbows can only be seen when the Sun is behind you, never in front of you.

Polihale is where the Na Pali coastline gives way to seventeen miles of uninterrupted sand beach.

If the south shore is referred to as the sunny south shore, western Kaua'i should be called the *very* sunny west shore. That's because rain is very scant indeed and the temperature is 3-4 degrees hotter than most of the rest of the island. The first two things visitors notice on this side of the island is the relative aridity of the land, and the deep red color of the soil. Trade winds coming from the northeast lose the bulk of their rain on Mount Wai'ale'ale, creating a rain shadow on the west side. Unless there are Kona winds (meaning from the south or west) you can pretty much be assured that it will be dry and sunny on the west side.

This part of the island is dominated by two attractions; the 17 mile long sand beach stretching from Kekaha to Polihale, and the incredible Waimea Canyon in the interior.

The same descriptive ground rules that we discussed at the beginning of **North Shore Sights** apply here. All beaches we mention are described in detail in the section on **Beaches**.

On Kaua'i, everything is either on the *mauka* side of the highway (meaning toward the mountains) or *makai* (meaning toward the ocean). Since people sometimes get these confused, we will refer to them as *mauka side* or *ocean side.*

HANAPEPE

As you drive along the main highway leaving Kalaheo you will come to the Hanapepe Valley Lookout, described under **South Shore Sights**. After you go through 'Ele'ele you come to Hanapepe. Called Kaua'i's "Biggest Little Town," Hanapepe is but a shad-

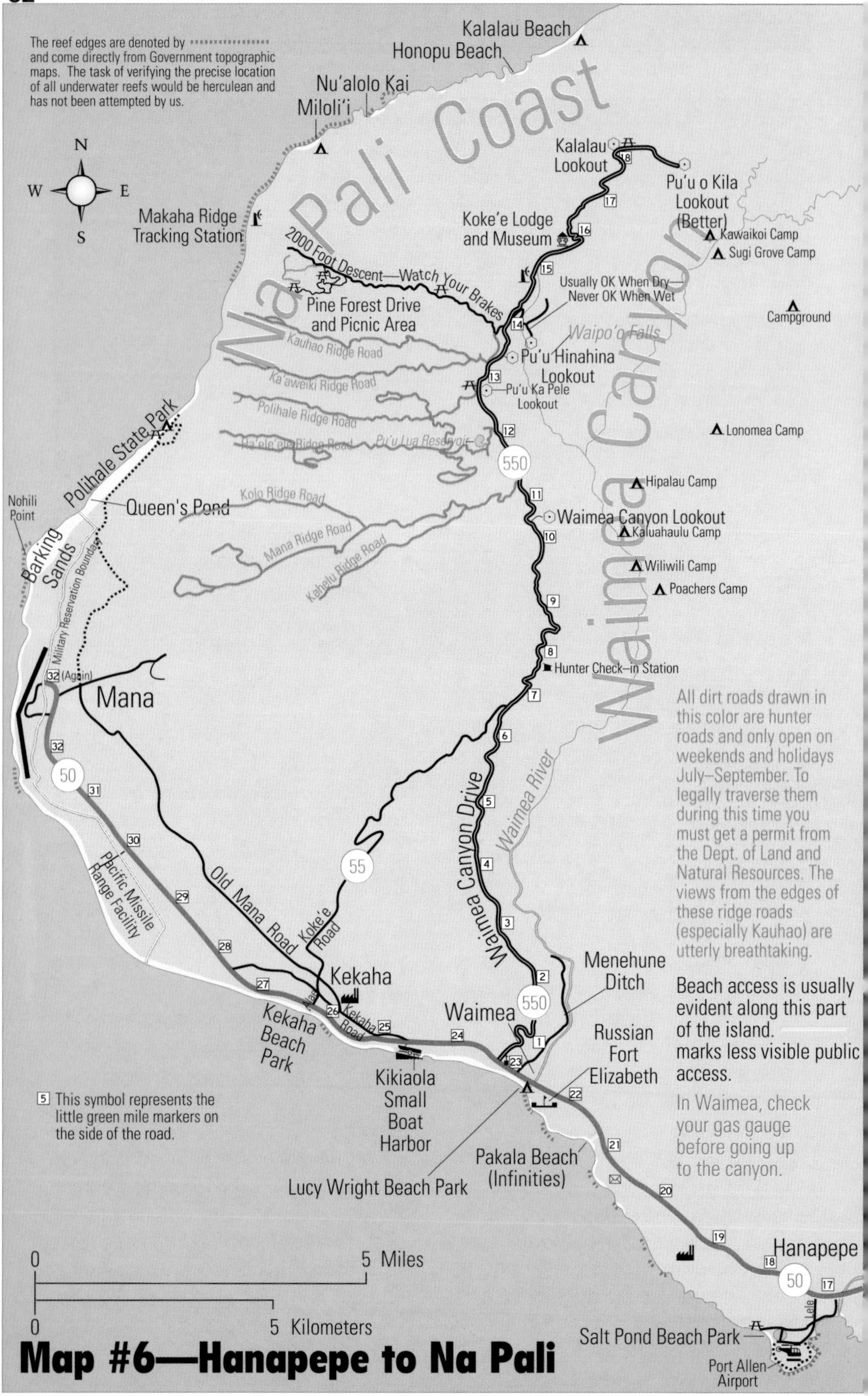

The reef edges are denoted by •••••••••••••••••••
and come directly from Government topographic
maps. The task of verifying the precise location
of all underwater reefs would be herculean and
has not been attempted by us.

Na Pali Coast

N
W E
S

Kalalau Beach
Honopu Beach
Nu'alolo Kai
Miloli'i

Kalalau
Lookout

Pu'u o Kila
Lookout
(Better)

Kawaikoi Camp
Sugi Grove Camp

Makaha Ridge
Tracking Station

Koke'e Lodge
and Museum

2000 Foot Descent—Watch Your Brakes

Pine Forest Drive
and Picnic Area

Kauhao Ridge Road

Ka'aweiki Ridge Road

Polihale Ridge Road

Na'ele'ele Ridge Road

Pu'u Lua Reservoir

Usually OK When Dry
Never OK When Wet

Waipo'o Falls

Campground

Pu'u Hinahina
Lookout

Pu'u Ka Pele
Lookout

Lonomea Camp

550

Polihale State Park

Queen's Pond

Kolo Ridge Road

Mana Ridge Road

Kahelu Ridge Road

Hipalau Camp

Waimea Canyon Lookout
Kaluahaulu Camp

Wiliwili Camp

Poachers Camp

Waimea Canyon

Nohili
Point

Barking
Sands

Military Reservation Boundary

Hunter Check–in Station

All dirt roads drawn in
this color are hunter
roads and only open on
weekends and holidays
July–September. To
legally traverse them
during this time you
must get a permit from
the Dept. of Land and
Natural Resources. The
views from the edges of
these ridge roads
(especially Kauhao) are
utterly breathtaking.

32 (Again)

Mana

Waimea River

50
32
31

Old Mana Road

Koke'e Road

55

Waimea Canyon Drive

Beach access is usually
evident along this part
of the island.
marks less visible public
access.

In Waimea, check
your gas gauge
before going up
to the canyon.

Pacific Missile
Range Facility

30

29

28

27

Kekaha

Kekaha
Beach
Park

Kekaha Road

Menehune
Ditch

Russian
Fort
Elizabeth

26
25
24
23
22
21
20

Waimea

550

5 This symbol represents the
little green mile markers on
the side of the road.

Kikiaola
Small
Boat
Harbor

Lucy Wright Beach Park

Pakala Beach
(Infinities)

19
18

Hanapepe

50
17

0   5 Miles

0   5 Kilometers

Salt Pond Beach Park

Port Allen
Airport

Map #6—Hanapepe to Na Pali

Throw-net fishing was introduced to Hawai'i by Japanese immigrants. The native Hawaiians quickly embraced this method and today it is considered an island tradition.

ow of its former self. It was founded by Chinese rice farmers in the mid to late 1800s. They were opium smoking bachelors and underground opium shops could be found there as recently as the 1930s. Hanapepe was the only non plantation town on the island and it quickly gained a reputation as Kaua'i's wildest spot. In 1924 they had a riot that killed 16 Filipino workers and 4 police officers. This was a violent and flamboyant town that had as many bars as churches. It began to decline in the late '70s and early '80s. The opening of Kukui Grove Shopping Center in 1982, marked the end of an era for Hanapepe's business community.

A good analogy for Hanapepe today is that of an old chair. Whereas some people look at an old stick of furniture and see a priceless antique, others see it as an old used item to be replaced by a newer one. Depending on your outlook, you will either find Hanapepe alluring or run down. Either way you look at it, it's worth your time to drive through and observe its historic buildings. The town also has several shops and galleries worth exploring. There used to be a swinging bridge over the Hanapepe River but it was a victim of 'Iniki. Out on the main highway, stop by Giorgio's Gallery and check out their handpainted coconuts and surfboards.

If you take Lele Road (543) you will come to Salt Pond Beach Park. This is where they continue to make salt out of seawater (see **Beaches**). This park usually offers very safe swimming.

Before you get to Waimea you will see a road to Fort Elizabeth just past the 22 mile mark. Here are the remains of a Russian fort built in 1816 by George Scheffer.

Scheffer was a German born doctor working for a Russian company. A difficult, quarrelsome, and conceited man, he had a habit of eventually alienating most people he met. He did make a good first impression, however, and managed to sufficiently impress a Russian official, who sent Scheffer to Hawai'i to ingratiate himself to King Kamehameha and recover a lost ship's cargo. When Kamehameha eventually became suspicious of Scheffer, the German went to Kaua'i. There he found a receptive King Kaumuali'i who, although he had officially given his kingdom to Kamehameha, still resisted offshore rule. Kaua'i's king-in-name-only saw a chance to get the Russians involved and perhaps restore his island to him. The two men realized how much they could help each other, and soon hatched plans to conquer the other islands using Russian ships. Scheffer by this time had become intoxicated by his status on Kaua'i and lost sight of the fact that he could not deliver on any of the promises he was making to Kaua'i's King Kaumuali'i. He even renamed Hanalei Valley, calling it Schefferthal with the King's blessing. When Scheffer needed a ship, he bought it and sent the bill and the captain to Alaska (still owned by Russia) for payment.

As Scheffer began building the Russian Fort in honor of Elizabeth, the consort of Emperor Alexander, his sponsors back in Russia were beginning to get a hint of Scheffer's tactics. They sent a ship to Hawai'i to tell Scheffer that he was to pack and leave the island. Scheffer ignored the message and continued building the Fort. By this time Kaua'i's king was becoming suspicious and a group of American businessmen saw an opportunity to rid the island of Scheffer and Russia. They started the rumor that Russia and America were at war. Kaua'i's king abandoned Scheffer who fled the island in a leaky old ship and set sail for O'ahu. The trip took five days and the pumps had to be manned the whole way lest the ship should sink. Once on O'ahu, he was told he would be taken prisoner. He fled to Brazil where he changed his name to Count von Frankenthal and tried to lure colonists to his estate of the same name.

WAIMEA

Back on the main highway you come to the town of Waimea. Off to your right you will see the Captain Cook Monument. It was in Waimea that the great explorer first set foot in Hawai'i in January 1778.

A bit more than a mile up Menehune Road on the mauka side of the highway is the Menehune Ditch. This is one of the few projects constructed by Hawaiians where they cut and dressed the stones. The result is a smooth lined irrigation ditch designed to bring water from the Waimea River to taro fields. Only fifty or sixty feet are now visible. It's impressive to think that the rocks used for its construction came from a quarry over six miles away. Across from the ditch are the remains of the Waimea swinging bridge. It was removed by the Hurricane.

The Waimea (meaning red water) River is full of sediment which dyes the water red. All the beaches in the vicinity of the river are murky due to river runoff and the swimming is correspondingly poor. According to legend, there was a beautiful chief's daughter named Komali'u who was sought after by many men in the village. One day a man named Mano asked her to marry him.

When she refused, he killed her at a nearby waterfall where her blood ran into the river. The chief named the village, canyon, and river Waimea in memory of his daughter.

KEKAHA

From Waimea, most people go up the road to the Waimea Canyon, but we will get to that later. Assuming you are continuing along the coast, you arrive in Kekaha. This is the last town on this side of the island. Many maps list a town farther north called Mana. It was once a thriving little community until the middle of this century. This area was formerly marshy and famous for its mirages. Now the town of Mana is nothing more than two mango trees and a mule. Its former residents recently gathered for a reunion to *talk story* about the old days.

While in Kekaha, Ritchie's Ono Saimin and Bento in the Waimea Canyon Plaza serves excellent shave ice. Try it; you'll need it by the time you get to Polihale.

From here on the beach is pure sand. You will pass the Pacific Missile Range Facility where they do "Star Wars" missile tests on occasion. Offshore, submarine hunting exercises take place almost continuously. This is a repository for some of the most sophisticated sensing equipment in the world and they are capable of detecting a bottle bobbing up and down in the choppy water. Lining part of the base is the Barking Sands Beach. The sand grains at this beach have tiny pockets in them and are supposed to make a barking sound while walking on them if conditions are right (see **Beaches**). You can go through the base to access the beach here if you want, or continue on down the road.

With Ni'ihau and Lehua in the background, a lone boat cruises Polihale from a trip down Na Pali.

POLIHALE

Looking at the map you will notice that the highway ends after the first 32 mile mark. Follow the map and a dirt road will take you to Polihale. From the extreme northern end of the beach, the magnificent cliffs of Na Pali beckon you with their sheer majesty. If it's summer, you might see kayaks coming (or rolling) in for a surf landing. From here you could walk 17 miles in the sand in one direction. There are facilities here including showers, rest rooms, and drinking water.

The dunes of Polihale are up to 100 feet high. There used to be a heiau nearby but its remnants are so vague that they are indistinguishable. The section on **Beaches** provides more information on Polihale.

WAIMEA CANYON

The Waimea Canyon is a spectacular gorge that defies description. When Mark Twain was here, he called it "the Grand Canyon of the Pacific." Indeed, the layers evident on the sides of the canyon are reminiscent of the grander canyon in Arizona. Each layer represents a different eruption and subsequent lava flow. The canyon is 10 miles long, 1 mile wide and over 3,600 feet deep.

To get to the canyon, most opt to take Waimea Canyon Road from Waimea.

The sometimes misty forests of Koke'e demonstrate the contrasts found on the Garden Island

Splendid Waimea Canyon is yet another facet of Kaua'i's personality.

This road has its own mile markers and we will use them as reference points. On your return from the canyon, take Kekaha Road (between the 6 and 7 mile mark) for a different view of the coast.

Before you go up the road, check your gas gauge. There are no stations up there and you've got a forty mile round trip ahead of you with a 4,000 foot elevation rise. The temperature is 10-15 degrees cooler up there and a sweater might be wise depending on conditions. There are more good hiking trails in this area than anywhere in Hawai'i. For more hiking information and a detailed map of the trails in the Waimea/Koke'e area, see **Hiking** under **Activities**.

Going to the canyon, turn mauka onto Waimea Canyon Road just past the 23 mile mark near a church. The road twists and turns its way up the canyon's side. On the way, keep an eye out for Ni'ihau. There are some great views of that private island from up here. Past the 10 mile mark is the Waimea Canyon Lookout. This is one of several vantage points and definitely worth a stop. From here on you will probably see lots of wild chickens about. They thrive in this environment.

The canyon lookout is an awesome vista. At one time three rivers, fed from the island's center by the Alaka'i Swamp on Wai'ale'ale, all ran down the gently sloping shield volcano emptying into the ocean at separate points like the spokes of a wheel. When a fault caused the collapse of part of the volcano's flank, the three rivers were

The Kalalau Valley is best seen from the Pu'u o Kila Lookout.

forced to combine and ran down into the fault. This new opportunistic river carved a place for itself in the splintered and fractured lava flows. The results are extraordinary.

As you drive upward, there are numerous areas along the road from which to view the canyon. From the Pu'u Ka Pele Lookout, the Waipo'o Falls are visible after a heavy rain. The Pu'u Hinahina Lookout, located past the 13 mile mark, has a Ni'ihau Viewpoint in addition to its canyon lookout. If it is clear, the view of Ni'ihau is great.

Shortly after this lookout there is a paved road on your left leading to the Makaha Ridge Tracking Station run by the military in conjunction with the Pacific Missile Range Facility. The road drops 2,000 feet over a relatively short distance and can be a real brake burner.

Shortly before the gate at the station you will see several dirt roads leading into a pleasant forested area with picnic tables.

There are dirt hunter roads all along this part of the coast. The view from the edge of the cliffs is outstanding but they are only open at certain times of the year and used by hunters.

Past the 15 mile mark is the Koke'e Museum. This is a good place to stretch your legs. The museum itself has several interesting displays and their three-dimensional map of the Canyon really gives you a sense of what you are seeing. The Koke'e Lodge next door is a good place to get lunch. (Actually, it's the *only* place to get lunch.)

As you ascend the road note how different the vegetation is up here. Remember how it was down at the bottom near Waimea? Here it is always cool and there is more rainfall than on the plain below.

At the 18 mile mark is the Kalalau Lookout. We suggest that you drive right past it and go to the far superior, but less used, Pu'u o Kila Lookout. You are not about to see another canyon lookout. You are about to be treated to one of the greatest views in the Pacific. The Kalalau Valley is the largest valley on Na Pali. It was inhabited until 1919 and its beach is only reachable by an eleven-mile hike or by kayak (see **Adventures**). For now, just revel in the view. Clouds are always moving in and out of the valley, so if it is cloudy, wait awhile before you give up. It's well worth it. The earlier you go, the less clouds there will be. You can usually see clouds coming from the interior of the island. When they encounter the valley, they sink. Sinking air warms, and warmer air can hold more moisture. So if conditions are right, the clouds disappear into humidity in less than a minute right before your eyes.

A Real Gem

This is the end of the road. As the crow flies, Ha'ena on the north shore is less than 7 miles away, but you ain't no crow. They tried to build a road from here to Ha'ena in the early part of this century. Anybody who has ever hiked the Alaka'i Swamp Trail before they installed a boardwalk on part of it could tell you that a road in these parts is next to impossible. The results of this boondoggle are monuments in the form of heavy earthmoving equipment still stuck in the swamp where the prison work crews left them. A stroll from here down part of the Pihea Trail can be a pleasant diversion. This is where the road to Ha'ena was supposed to start.

From here you could theoretically walk to the north shore. In 1870, Queen Emma made her famous trek to the Alaka'i Swamp and over to the north shore valley cliffs of Wainiha. (As an aside, Alaka'i means "to lead," because it is impossible to get around in there without a guide.) She had a hundred people accompany her and the trip became legendary throughout the islands.

By not having a road completely encircling the island, Kaua'i has been able to escape the fate that has befallen O'ahu. As long as the dots aren't connected, there will always be parts of Kaua'i that are remote.

WEST SHORE SHOPPING

Obviously you won't find as much on this side of the island as other areas, but there are still a few places, in our opinion, worth stopping for. Some have already been mentioned in the tour so we won't list them again.

Hanapepe has numerous galleries worth a look. There you will also find

Kaua'i Kookie, a tiny store with good prices on Kaua'i produced cookies. Hanapepe Bookstore and Espresso Bar has some unique items worth stopping for.

In Waimea, try Collectibles and Fine Junque. Excellent variety of vintage clothing, Hawaiiana, jewelry, and dishes. Captain's Cargo Co. shares a store with Na Pali Boat Tours. Very nice selection of clothing, jewelry, and beach supplies.

In Kekaha, Waimea Canyon Plaza has International and Kaua'i Souvenirs, a nice selection of T-shirts, women's clothing, and Ni'ihau Shell Leis.

WEST SHORE BEST BETS

Best Sunset View—Anywhere along the shore, or a couple miles up Waimea Canyon Road

Best Treat—Shave Ice at Ritchie's or ice cream at Lappert's Hanapepe

Best Hearty Food—Chili and cornbread at the Koke'e Lodge

Best Place for Quiet Contemplation—To the right of the viewing platform at Pu'u o Kila Lookout

Best Swimming—Salt Pond Beach Park

Best Place to View Ni'ihau—Along Waimea Canyon Road or from Pu'u Hinahina Lookout

Best Place to Have Good Brakes—Makaha Ridge Road

Sunset on the west side.

SeaLodge Beach is a secluded little pocket of sand tucked away under a Princeville cliff.

Because Kaua'i is older than the other major Hawaiian Islands, it is blessed with having more sand beaches per mile of shoreline than any other. No part of the island is without sand beaches. Many are accessible by merely driving up and falling into the sand. Others are deliciously secluded requiring walks of various lengths. Some are local secrets, others are unknown even to most locals. In this section we will describe most of Kaua'i's beaches starting from the north shore and working our way around the island clockwise. All of these beaches are located on the maps of the various areas.

One thing you should be aware of is that in Hawai'i, all beaches are public beaches. This means that you can park yourself on any stretch of sand you like. The trick, sometimes, can be access. You might have to cross private land to get to a public beach. The County and State have procured easements to many of the beaches. On our various maps, we have marked these public access routes in yellow. This, along with descriptions and directions, will assist you in finding the beach of your choice.

One of the things you might notice about County park beaches is that some of the pavilions are less than pristine. It seems that these are a low priority for the County and are not expected to be completely repaired until 1995.

BEACH SAFETY

The beaches of Kaua'i, and Hawai'i in general, are beautiful, warm and unfortunately can be dangerous. The waves, currents, and abundant beach use has caused Hawai'i to become the drowning capital of the U.S. If you're going to swim in the ocean, you need to bear several things in mind. We are not trying to be killjoys. There are several reasons why Hawai'i's beaches in particular can be inherently dangerous. The waves are stronger here in the open ocean than most other places. Rip currents can form, cease, and form again with no warning. Large "rogue waves" can come ashore with no warning. These usually occur when two or more waves fuse at sea, becoming a larger wave. Even calm seas are no guarantee of safety. Many people have been caught unaware by large waves during ostensibly "calm seas." Most of the beaches we describe in this book were swam and snorkeled by us on at least two occasions (usually more than two). But beaches change. The underwater topography changes throughout the year. Storms can take a very safe beach and rearrange the sand, turning it

The Hawaiian Monk Seal

The endangered Hawaiian monk seal, such as this one snoozing in front of the Hyatt in Po'ipu, occasionally come ashore after a heavy meal, or to avoid a predator. Many people assume they are sick or injured and attempt to coax them back into the water. If you are lucky enough to encounter one, please leave it be. Beaching is perfectly normal. The fines for disturbing one can range as high as $20,000. The seals dive as deep as 400 feet to feed and are considered the most primitive seals in the world with ancient social behavior. Unlike other seals, they don't come ashore in large numbers.

into a dangerous beach. Hurricane 'Iniki changed the characteristics of many beaches by adding more sand which will erode over time, changing the under-water topography. Just because we describe a beach as being in a certain condition does not mean it will be in that same condition when you visit it. Consequently, you should take the beach descriptions as a snapshot in calm times. If seas aren't calm, you probably shouldn't go in the water. If you observe a rip current, you probably shouldn't go in the water. If you aren't a comfortable swimmer, you should probably never go in the water, except at those beaches that have lifeguards and protected pools, such as Lydgate or Salt Pond. But during abnormally high seas, even these are potentially haz-ardous. Kaua'i averages nine drownings per year—58% of these are visitors. We don't want you to become one of these statistics. There is no way we can tell you that a certain beach will be swim-mable on a certain day, and we claim no such prescience. There is no substi-tution for your own observations and judgment.

In general, the north and east shore beaches are calmest during the summer months (meaning April—September). The south shore is calmest during the winter months (meaning October—May). North shore high surf is stronger than south shore high surf since our location in the northern hemisphere makes us closer to northern winter storms than southern hemisphere win-ter storms.

A few of the standard safety tips apply. Never turn your back on the ocean. Never swim alone. Never swim in the mouth of a river. Never swim in murky water. Never swim when the seas are not calm. Don't walk too close

to the shorebreak, a large wave can come and knock you over and pull you in. Observe ocean conditions carefully. Don't let small children play in the water unsupervised. (In fact, it's best to keep them at the protected ponds such as Lydgate.) Fins give you far more power and speed and are a good safety device (in addition to being more fun). If you are comfortable in a mask and snorkel, they provide considerable peace of mind in addition to opening up the underwater world. Lastly, don't let Kaua'i's idyllic environment cloud your judgment. Recognize the ocean for what it is; a powerful force that needs to be respected.

The beaches with year-round life-guards (most of the time) are Ke'e, Hanalei Pavilion, Lydgate, Po'ipu Beach, and Salt Pond. Occasionally there are lifeguards at other beaches during summer months.

When we mention that a beach has facilities, it usually includes rest rooms, showers, picnic tables, and drinking water.

NORTH SHORE BEACHES

❖ **Ke'e Beach**—This is as far as you can go *by car* on the north shore. The beach here is called Ke'e (also called Ha'ena State Park) and is a swimming, snorkeling, and sunbathing favorite. During summer months the lagoon is usually calm and offers great snorkeling, especially around the reef opening on the left side of the beach. The salient qualifier here is *only when it's calm.* Dur-ing winter months waves wash over the reef creating an excess of lagoon water. This water has

A Real Gem

only one place to go to equalize the volume—out the reef opening on the left side. That's why it's important to observe ocean conditions carefully and check with the lifeguard. The park is equipped with facilities. The stream you crossed .3 miles back makes an ideal place to rinse off the saltwater—be careful, the rocks can be slippery.

The road's end is also where the Kalalau Trail begins. It leads to **Hanakapi'ai Beach** and **Kalalau Beach** which are described in the section called **Adventures**.

If the parking area seems full of cars, take the dirt road to the right for a couple hundred feet and stay to the left. There you will find a perfect place to park, probably all to yourself. One turnout even has a picnic table. We almost never see another car parked here, even when drivers were patrolling the regular parking area like vultures.

❖ **Ha'ena Beach Park**—This very pretty beach has complete facilities as well as a concession truck (usually). It is located across from the Dry Cave. Plenty of parking near the beach. Sand is very coarse (and therefore comes off very easily). Although you might see people swimming here, the shore is totally exposed lacking any reef protection. The smallest of waves have a surprising amount of force. A popular surf spot off to the left of the beach is called Cannons. Since the beach is very steep, a small wave could knock you over and the backwash could pull you in, therefore swimming is hazardous except during very calm seas. Camping with county permit.

Ha'ena Beach Park often displays the most unusual blue colors you'll ever see in the ocean.

Tunnels Beach sports a fabulous reef, perfect for scorkeling, swimming, and SCUBA.

❖ **Tunnels (Makua) Beach**—One of Kaua'i's snorkeling nirvanas. This superb beach has a wide-fringing reef that is so large that it can be seen from space. (Don't believe me? Locate it on the map then look at the cover of this book. The reef is very prominent in this shot taken from the Space Shuttle *Discovery*.) There is often a lateral rip current but it's normally quite weak making Tunnels a good snorkeling spot most of the time. The beach is quite popular and you will

A Real Gem

likely see SCUBA divers here as well as zodiacs dropping off visitors. Surfers and windsurfers also frequent the area. All this makes it sound crowded, but crowds are a relative thing. You will find less people here than on O'ahu's least crowded beach. The kaleidoscope of underwater life is profuse and definitely worth your time to explore. See section on **Snorkeling** on page 138 for some useful tips. See also the **SCUBA** section; both are in the chapter called **Activities**. Public access is by either of two short dirt roads past the 8 mile mark on 560. The first one is .35 miles past the 8 mile mark. The second one is .5 miles past the 8 mile mark. If you don't have a lot of stuff to carry, please use the second one. Windsurfers use the first one to avoid carrying their gear so far.

❖ **Kepuhi Beach**—The snorkeling is good here but not nearly as good as Tunnels. You'll rarely find anyone on this beach, so if you're in the area and want easy access but no crowds, this is the beach for you. This long strip of sand is fronted by an even longer coral reef. The makeup of this reef causes a slightly stronger current. Check out conditions before you snorkel. Because most of it is not located directly off the main highway, it tends to be forgotten, even by locals. It is, however, still used on occasion by throw-net fishermen. Access is at the eastern end of Alamo'o Road. See map on page 48.

❖ **Wainiha Beach Park**—Hazardous surf and its location at the mouth of the Wainiha River make it murky and unsuitable for anything other than shoreline fishing and beachcombing.

❖ **Lumahaʻi Beach**—This is the long, wide, golden, glorious beach you see just after you've passed Hanalei Bay. Pictured on countless postcards and posters, this beach was made famous as a location for the movie *South Pacific*. This is where Mitzi Gaynor spent considerable time washing a man right out of her hair. If you're looking for a huge, picture perfect stretch of sand on the north shore, Lumahaʻi shouldn't be missed. If you're looking for safe swimming, Lumahaʻi shouldn't be touched. This beach, along with Hanakapiʻai on the Na Pali Coast, are the two most dangerous beaches on Kauaʻi. Exposed to open ocean, the waves here, even small ones, are frighteningly powerful. We've come to this beach after seeing it absolutely flat at Haʻena Beach Park a few miles away only to be utterly assaulted by Lumahaʻi's waves. Put simply, Lumahaʻi is almost never safe to swim. The waves, currents, and backwash are not to be underestimated. Lumahaʻi Stream on the left side is sometimes crossable during calm seas and low stream flow. It serves as an estuary for ʻoʻopu during the summer when the shifting sands tend to cut the river off from the ocean. During this time, the closed river mouth is sometimes safe to swim. But absent these conditions, swimming in Lumahaʻi Stream has caused numerous individuals to be swept out to sea. Surfers and boogie boarders often use the left side of the beach near the rocks, but unless you're an expert on Hawaiian surf, this should not be attempted. Separated by lava rock to the right of Lumahaʻi is Kahalahala Beach (technically part of Lumahaʻi, but who's quibbling). Swimming and snorkeling are possible here on very calm summer days. The beach is delightful and the water is quite clear, but the same warnings generally apply here. In short, a fantastic place to visit and sun yourself, but usually not to swim.

Access to these beaches can be obtained either via a trail from the top of the lookout at the eastern edge of the beach (this gets you to the eastern part which is the best part), or from the parking area just before you get to Lumahaʻi Stream. See Map on page 49.

❖ **Hanalei Bay**—The four beaches described below are all part of Hanalei Bay. With its single long crescent of sand, the bay is beautiful to look at, but not great to swim in. Pounding shorebreak, backwash, and rip currents, especially during the winter months makes Hanalei Bay less than ideal as a swimming beach. But that doesn't make it any less pretty. Large surfing waves make Hanalei Bay very popular with surfers, who come from other islands to experience its waves.

❖ **Waikoko Beach**—Easy access and good reef protection at this one portion of Hanalei Bay make this a popular beach during high surf periods, but the water is shallow which makes for marginal swimming conditions. The snorkeling is better than the swimming if stream flow isn't high. Located between the 4 and 5 mile marks as the road begins to ascend. There is a 20 foot long path near the 15 mph sign. See map on page 49.

❖ **Waiʻoli Beach Park**—Located at the end of either Heʻe or ʻAmaʻama

Roads in Hanalei, the underwater topography focuses more of the ocean's force here making the swimming hazardous except during very calm seas. Access is from Weke Road in Hanalei.

❖ **Hanalei Pavilion Beach Park**— Also located on Weke Road in Hanalei it includes facilities. Popular with boogie boarders and surfers, the shorebreak and backwash make for less than ideal swimming conditions.

❖ **Black Pot**—Located near the mouth of the Hanalei River, swimming conditions are marginal. During calm summer surf, boogie boarding is possible near the pier area. Black Pot refers to a large black cooking pot residents used to keep at the beach. This is the area where kayakers put in to paddle up the Hanalei River. Facilities at beach. Camping with County permit.

❖ **Pu'u Poa Beach**—Located in front of the Princeville Hotel in Princeville, the beach has a fringing reef and offers good snorkeling possibilities during summer seas. During the winter, the waters off the outer edge of the reef offer some of the best and most challenging surfing in the state (for experts only). Access is through a cement path starting just at the left of the gate house at the Princeville Hotel. Getting to the beach necessitates negotiating 191 steps. (Yes, we counted them.) From here you can walk all the way to the mouth of the Hanalei River. The other access is to come from Black Pot Beach and wade the usually shallow water at the mouth of the Hanalei River.

❖ **Pali Ke Kua (Hideaways)**—Fifty feet before the Princeville Hotel gate house is a corridor off to the right (next to the Pu'u Poa tennis courts). This path leads *down* to Pali Ke Kua Beach, also called Hideaways. The first half of the descent consists of stairs and a railing. The remainder is trail. All told, it takes 5–10 minutes to get there. There are actually two beaches here, with the second one is off to the right separated by a rocky point. Both offer excellent snorkeling during calm seas. The salient underwater features are good relief and a diverse fish community punctuated by the occasional turtle. With marvelous coarse sand, large false kamani trees for shade, and good summer snorkeling, this beach is a wonderful place to spend the day. You will rarely find more than a handful of people here since it is not widely known and is poorly marked.

A Real Gem

While the beach can be a nice place to bring the kids, some may have trouble negotiating their way down the path. (In fact, you might have trouble too if it has been raining and the path below the steps is muddy.)

When seas aren't calm, rip currents can form. Check ocean conditions carefully. Unusually high surf has been known to generate waves which can sweep across the entire beach. The other part of Pali Ke Kua beach can be reached either from Hideaways or by a paved trail leading down from the Pali Ke Kua condominiums, but this is a private trail available only to guests at Pali Ke Kua.

❖ **Queen's Bath**— One of those little known gems on the north shore. It is actually a large natural pool the size of sever-

A Real Gem

al swimming pools carved into a lava shelf with an inlet from the ocean for fresh seawater to flow. If the surf and tide are high, you would never recognize this place as anything special. But at other times, Queen's Bath is a marvelous pool to swim in. Fish get in through the inlet making it all the more charming. During the summer, if the ocean is *too* calm, the water is not refreshed as much as it should be. During high surf, it would be dangerous as the water flows out the pond. But the rest of the time, Queen's Bath is one of those places you will return to each time you visit Kaua'i. To get there follow the trail from the end of Kapiolani Road in Princeville. Note the shape of the end of the trail on the map on page 49. The trail encounters the ocean where a small waterfall drops directly into the ocean. Go to the left for 300–400 yards. If you can't find it, the ocean probably isn't cooperating. During certain times of the year, low tide is best. Call 335–3611 for tide information.

❖ **SeaLodge Beach**—This wonderful pocket of sand is set in an indentation in the cliff. With plenty of shade courtesy of false kamani trees, and heavenly coarse sand (the kind that won't stick to you with the tenacity of a barnacle), SeaLodge Beach is a real find. This beach is usually empty of people because most don't know it's there. During the summer in particular, it's the ideal secluded beach. Access is via a trail at the end of the long cement driveway located to the right at the end of Keoniana Road. The trail follows a stream part of the way then turns to the left just before you get to the top of a

A Real Gem

waterfall (that sounds complicated, but it's not that bad). Another trail from *Building A* at the SeaLodge resort intersects the trail after a few hundred yards. See map on page 49. Where the trail encounters the ocean, it veers to the left. Look for turtles in the water here. The snorkeling can be outstanding during very calm seas, but entry and currents need to be respected. Depending on the weather, the trail can be slippery and a bit tricky in areas. During periods of unusually high surf, waves have been known to travel all the way to the base of the cliff. Don't come here if this is the case. The entire picturesque hike should take between 10 and 15 minutes and is well worth it.

❖ **'Anini Beach Park**—Protected by a *long* fringing reef, 'Anini Beach has become a popular place for the rich and famous (such as Sylvester Stallone) to build homes. The water can be very shallow, and the snorkeling is usually very good in many areas. The swimming is among the safest you will find on the north shore. The channel at the western end of the beach is where the water flows out so stay away from this part. (See the left side of the map on page 46.) There are numerous areas along this stretch of sand to swim, snorkel, or just frolic. There is a polo field across from the beach, check it out if you are there during the summer. 'Anini Beach is a good place to learn windsurfing. Camping with County permit, facilities at pavilion. The name used to be Wanini Beach but the "W" broke off the sign long ago. It was simpler to change the name of the beach than make a new sign. Take the northern Kalihiwai Road (the one between the 25 and 26 mile marks) and stay to the left on 'Anini Road.

❖ Kalihiwai Beach—Located at the mouth of Kalihiwai Stream, you drive down from either Kalihiwai Road. (It used to be a loop but the bridge was knocked out by a tsunami in 1957 and they declined to rebuild it.) At the bottom of the road you encounter a picturesque bay with a wide sand beach lined with ironwood trees to park under. There are houses on the other side of the road. The beach is popular with boogie boarders in the summer and is a good place to see local keikis learning to ride waves. It's also a good place to just enjoy the water during the summer. During the winter, surfers ride the large waves under the cliff area. The eastern (1st) Kalihiwai Road is the best road to take to the beach.

❖ Secret Beach—Also called Kauapea Beach and known to most locals by the more enticing name of Secret Beach, is a strikingly beautiful beach only acces-

A Real Gem

sible via a 10 minute hike. This fact along with its former anonymity has caused it to become Kauaʻi's premier nude beach. For the record, public nudity is illegal in Hawaiʻi. This long golden sand beach is not swimmable during the winter, but on calm summer days it can be a delight for swimming and offers good snorkeling. It's worth the trip year-round just to see it. There is a small waterfall to rinse off your gear. The island off to your right is Mokuʻaeʻae Island, a bird sanctuary. To get to Secret Beach, turn right off the first (eastern) Kalihiwai road, then right on the first dirt road you encounter. (See map on page 46.) Take the trail to the bottom.

❖ Kahili Quarry Beach—Where Kilauea Stream encounters the ocean is a beach sometimes called Rock Quarry Beach. There is good swimming on the left (western) side and good snorkeling on the right side during calm seas. Since this is a river mouth, the water can get murky at times. (Sharks, which like murky water, have been sighted here

Kahili Quarry Beach is one of a number of good beaches on the north shore.

during periods of heavy stream flow.) This is a popular boogie boarding and surfing site. The river mouth can cause rip currents. Easiest access is from a dirt road off N. Wailapa Road.

❖ **Waiakalua Beach**—A marvelous and undiscovered north shore beach. Although it requires a steep, 5–10 minute walk down from your car, Waiakalua is an undisturbed, serene place to spend the afternoon. Medium coarse sand, a long fringing reef, numerous pockets of shade and a fresh water spring at the far end add to the charm. Observe the reef from up on the bluff. Calm summer snorkeling can be interesting but shallow; watch out for the rip currents. During other times, swimming can be hazardous. At the far end of the beach is a rocky point separating the two halves of the beach. The snorkeling around this point is exciting, featuring clear water teaming with big life. However the rips, surges and surf make this area tricky— only advanced snorkelers need apply. Otherwise, just enjoy the beach. The cool spring at the far end offers sweet fresh water. Bring an empty container and some water treatment pills—all fresh water obtained anywhere in nature should be treated to prevent bacterial disease. To get there, turn onto North Waiakalua Road and take the dirt road on the left side just before the end of the road. Park when you can't drive any more and take the trail off to the left. The beach on your left at the bottom is Waiakalua Beach. The beach boulders off to your right lead to **Pila'a Beach**. It can take 10–30 minutes to reach **Pila'a Beach**, depending on how fast you traverse beach boulders. Otherwise, just stay at Waiakalua Beach. You'll probably have either one all to yourself. See map on page 47.

❖ **Larsen's Beach**—Crystal clear water, lots of beachcombing and seclusion. This beach, named after a former manager at Kilauea Plantation named L. David Larsen, is splendidly isolated but can be accessed by a 5–10 minute walk down a gently sloping trail. Off to the right are a bunch of lava rocks that make for good snorkeling if conditions are right. To the left is a long crescent of sand broken by occasional outcroppings of rock and reef. Underwater topography creates good conditions for beachcombing. Pakala Point is on the left side where the beach ends and lava rock protrudes out into the ocean. Just before these rocks is Pakala Channel. Most of the water you see breaking over the reef, drains through this channel, therefore, *don't swim in or near the channel.* The water leading up to the channel, at times moves so swiftly that it seems more like rapids than rip current. If the ocean is calm, and you stay away from the channel, and if the tide is right, and you have some experience snorkeling, this place can be a snorkeler's paradise. Large amounts of coral and fish in shallow, crystal-clear water greet the eye. You will probably be the only one on the beach if you go during the week. This beach is *not* a swimming beach, just snorkeling due to the sharp reefs and shallow water. During periods of high surf, waves tower above the reef breaking on the edge, which can be quite a spectacle. On the opposite side of Pakala Point are two pockets of sand that are even more secluded. Larsen's is about 20 minutes north of Kapa'a, take the *north* end of Ko'olau Road (second

A Real Gem

Koʻolau if you're coming from Kapaʻa) just before the 20 mile mark. 1.2 miles from the north end of Koʻolau Road, take the left Beach Access road all the way until it ends. (See map on page 47.) Go through the cattle guard and follow the trail to the bottom. The beach is a 5 minute walk down. If you pass through a herd of cows on the trail, try to discourage them from following you down to the beach. Cattle and beaches don't mix.

EAST SHORE BEACHES

❖ **Moloaʻa Beach**—Good snorkeling and SCUBA on calm summer days but entry and exit can be difficult due to the reef. Very pretty beach, but not a great swimming beach most of the year. Off the main highway but easy automobile access makes it a good place for a beach stroll. Take the first Koʻolau Road (before the 17 mile mark) to Moloaʻa Road, follow to the end. Fork to the right or left at the end, it's your choice. See map on page 47.

❖ **Papaʻa Bay**—Very picturesque but trail is difficult to follow and swimming is marginal. In addition, it is one of the few beaches on Kauaʻi where you may detect a fishy smell. Located on Papaʻa road, see map on page 47.

❖ **ʻAliomanu Beach**—The long fringing reef offshore is used heavily by locals for throw-net fishing, octopus hunting, pole fishing, torch fishing, and limu kohu harvesting. This beach, along with Pilaʻa and Larsen's, attracts families who have been practicing limu kohu (an edible seaweed) harvesting on the outer parts of the reef for generations. They pick the top part of the plant, leaving the roots to regenerate.

❖ **Anahola Beach Park**—The area around Anahola is designated Hawaiian Homelands. This is a complicated subject, but suffice it to say that individuals of Hawaiian descent are the primary occupants of the land in this area. In recent years, controversy has broken out concerning the way these lands have been administered and used. As a consequence, emotions can run high. Although the majority of Anahola residents are among the friendliest you will encounter, a few have jealously guarded Anahola Beach Park in recent years. It's probably best to avoid Anahola Beach Park for the time being until the controversy is settled, since there is a chance that a few people might make you feel less than welcome there.

❖ **Donkey Beach**—So named by drifters in the '60s who observed burros and mules being used by Lihuʻe Plantation Company to haul seed cane to the fields nearby. Donkey Beach is a popular nudist beach on Kauaʻi due to its location. This long stretch of sand is also popular with surfers. When you see cars parked on the side of the road past the 11 mile mark north of Kapaʻa, this is where they went (although they didn't *drive* nude). Bear in mind that the road is still on LPCO land and that this access is not legal. The foreshore at the beach is steep, creating a pounding shorebreak and strong backwash. Swimming is usually hazardous.

❖ **Kealia Beach**—Drive north of Kapaʻa and you will often see lots of boogie boarders and surfers in the water here. The powerful waves are fantastic but can be treacherous. The currents and backwash are sometimes ferocious. You can often see water spitting into the air from the collision of an incoming and outgoing wave (called clapotis for the trivia minded). The northern end of the beach is more protected by a breakwater and can be good for wading and occasionally snorkeling on a calm day. If you have never ridden waves, be very careful or you might get drilled into the ground. If the surf is high, definitely leave it for the big boys.

❖ **Kapaʻa Beach Park**—Located in the heart of Kapaʻa, this is used heavily by locals. The area south of the Waikaʻea Canal (used to launch boats) is also called Fuji Beach. Like any beach located close to a population center, Kapaʻa Beach Park is not as pristine as other beaches you will find. That said, the northern section (the part just before the lookout as you leave Kapaʻa going north) offers interesting but shallow snorkeling. Check for currents. The rest of the park, located on Niu Street, is not as memorable. It is, however, a good place for a beach stroll or to watch the sunrise. There are a few large sand pockets along the beach which are swimmable when the surf isn't high. Regular facilities plus a swimming pool.

❖ **Waipouli Beach**—Pretty but not a good swimming beach. There are a few small pockets along the southern portion of the beach which are relatively safe for swimming during calm periods, but be cautious. The area seaward of the beachrock fronting the beach is subject to strong currents year-round. This is normally considered a dangerous beach. There is a paved shoreline trail along much of this beach which is perfect for jogging or a leisurely stroll.

❖ **Wailua Beach**—Across from the Coco Palms Resort, from the mouth of the Wailua River to a rocky point to the north, this is an easily accessible beach. Just drive right up. It is popular with surfers and boogie boarders who appreciate the unprotected waves. Winter swells sometimes keep even these users out of the water. Swimmers should be aware of rip currents in several areas along the beach. The river itself, which is crossable only during periods of *low flow*, can cause tricky water conditions so caution is advised. The ocean and the river are constantly battling for supremacy and the struggle can be dramatic. The ocean builds up a sand bar and the river attempts to erode it. Sometimes the river is stopped up completely. When it finally breaks through the sand bar, it can be fascinating. The sand bar can erode in a matter of an hour or two taking large amounts of sand with it. For a short time thereafter, ancient Hawaiian petroglyphs are exposed on rocks in the mouth of the river.

❖ **Lydgate State Park**—Located just south of the Wailua River, Lydgate (now

run by the County but still called a State park) is composed of a picnic area, a large patch of grass, rest rooms, showers, and two marvelous boulder-enclosed ponds. These ponds are nearly always safe to swim, with the smaller one meant for the keikis (kids). These ponds were created to allow fresh sea water and fish into the pond, while protecting you from the ocean's force. And they work quite well. Lydgate is the most popular fish feeding place on the island. Mornings are the best times. Some chips, bread or rabbit food sparingly squeezed

A Real Gem

through a hole in a zip–lock baggie will usually win you lots of new underwater friends. If you are having trouble attracting a crowd, keep swimming slowly while staying reasonably close to the rocks. Fish like the rocks, as they offer protection from predators. Once a few start eating, continue to swim slowly in order to attract the maximum crowd. For more tips on feeding the fish, see page 139. Please be careful to take the plastic baggie out with you. There are plenty of turtles in the area which can choke on your plastic baggie. Access is just off Leho Road in Wailua. (See map on page 59.)

❖ **Nukoli'i Beach Park**—From Lydgate to the far end of the Outrigger Hotel is a long sand beach called Nukoli'i Beach. This beach includes the area fronting the Wailua Golf Course. This entire stretch of sand, more than 2 miles in length, is never crowded, often deserted. This is surprising given its proximity to Kapa'a, but good for you. There is a road fronting the golf course but it is eroding. In several spots it can be very narrow. If you just want to claim a large spot of beach for yourself, this is as good a place as any. The swimming conditions vary along the beach but are usually marginal. Currents and surf are the usual villains. The area in front of the golf course is the only part worth considering for swimming purposes. The snorkeling can be good when it's calm, and it's fun to hunt for golf balls in the water. You might even find a club hurled by someone having an off day. Access? Just drive right up from the dirt road between the golf course and the Outrigger entrance (not far from the 4 mile mark). Or take the Outrigger entrance to access the southern portion of the beach. Facilities near the Outrigger.

❖ **Hanama'ulu Beach Park**—Water is usually murky due to Hanama'ulu Stream. Sharks are often seen in the area. The waters around Ahukini Pier can offer interesting snorkeling when it's very calm. In general, only good for beachcombing.

❖ **Ninini Beach/Running Waters**—Located below the Westin, good snorkeling off to the left in front of the rocks on a calm day. However, even then it can be surgy and a bit tricky. Access via a walk through the 13th green and a steep trail to the bottom; see map on page 67. Take a drive over to the Ninini Lighthouse. If someone is working there at the time, ask if you can go to the top. The view from up there is outstanding.

❖ **Kalapaki Beach**—With a gently sloping sand bottom and partial protection from the open ocean, Kalapaki Beach is popular with visitors and locals alike. Swimming, bodysurfing, windsurfing, and boogie boarding conditions are usually good except during periods of high surf. Adjacent Nawiliwili Park behind the Anchor Cove Shopping Center is a popular picnic spot. Canoes and twin hulled sailing catamarans often come ashore here. Facilities near Anchor Cove Shopping Center. Access is by a road behind the shopping center, or through the Westin. See map on page 67. This is a good place to be when a cruise ship goes by. When it's calm (which is most of the time) it's a good place to teach your little one how to ride a boogie board.

❖ **Niumalu Beach Park**—Popular place to launch kayaks for trips up the Hule'ia Stream (where the opening scenes from *Raiders of the Lost Ark* were filmed). Camping by County permit. Other water activities are marginal due to its location so far up the river.

SOUTH SHORE BEACHES

❖ **Maha'ulepu Beaches**—This marvelous beach is one of the nicest on the entire south shore and actually consists of three separate areas known as **Gillin's Beach, Kawailoa Bay**, and **Ha'ula Beach**.

A Real Gem

To get to **Gillin's Beach**, park on the right where the road starts to curve left. (See map on page 73.) This beach is named after Elbert Gillin who was the construction superintendent for the Ha'upu Range Tunnel. (This is the half-mile long, single-lane, dirt-lined cane tunnel just north of the Waita Reservoir which has spooked many lost, unwary tourists.) Gillin's House—now Gillin's Chimney thanks to 'Iniki—was built on the beach just off to your right. If you walk past it you'll see a stream which may or may not reach the ocean. Take the trail which fronts the stream on its far (southern) side. After about 2 minutes you'll will see a small triangle-shaped opening off to your left. Inside you will find an ancient circular shaped amphitheater dominated by banyan trees. One was knocked over by the Hurricane (which is difficult to understand since it was completely protected by a wall of rock—take a look and see if you can figure it out). This area is identified as a cave on the map rather than as an amphitheater because we didn't want the casual map reader to think that rock concerts were held there.

To get to **Kawailoa Bay**, continue on the dirt road until it is directly next to the beach. Windsurfing is popular from here to **Gillin's Beach**. They ride the waves faster than the wind and it is a real treat to watch.

Reaching **Ha'ula Beach** requires a walk along an ancient lava field. Although over one million years old, the condition of some parts of the field make it seem like the eruption occurred last week. This is a great place to observe the power of the ocean as it smashes into the cliff. Local fishermen drop their line into the water from here since they can see their prey before they cast. When you reach **Ha'ula Beach** (about a 10–15 minute walk) you will almost certainly have it all to yourself. The beach is backed by high sand dunes. Behind one you will find an old picnic table and BBQ. The beach is rarely visited except by occasional horseback tours from CJM Stables. The swimming isn't very good; in fact it can be quite hazardous depending on conditions. But the beach is a beautiful place to enjoy your solitude.

The area between **Ha'ula Beach** and **Kawailoa Bay** contains lithified sand dunes. Fishing from the top is incredible, but be careful; the dunes can be brittle so don't fall in. The area just north of these lithified dunes often provides lots of goodies for the beachcomber.

Maha'ulepu was the scene of a terrific slaughter in the Spring of 1796. When King Kamehameha launched the first of two invasion attempts, he and his fleet of 1,200 canoes carrying 10,000 soldiers left O'ahu at midnight hoping to reach Wailua on Kaua'i by daybreak. They were in the middle of the treacherous Kaua'i Channel when the wind and seas picked up. Many of his canoes were swamped. Reluctantly, he ordered a retreat but too late to stop some of his advance troops. When they landed at Maha'ulepu, they were exhausted. They awoke to the sound of enemy troops who proceeded to kill all but a few escapees.

The whole of Maha'ulepu makes for fantastic exploring and beach walking. The swimming is often hazardous and seas here are not usually very calm. Entry is difficult in most places. There is a guard shack on the road to the beaches and you must sign a release to drive on sugar plantation land. Please take everything out that you bring in. The plantation company can close this access down any time they wish, so locals are bending over backwards not to give them a reason.

❖ **Shipwreck Beach**—This beach was named for an old unidentified wooden shipwreck now long gone.

Also called Keoneloa Beach, it fronts the Hyatt. Public access road is between the Hyatt and the Po'ipu Bay Resort Golf Course. The beach is used mostly by surfers, boogie boarders, body surfers, and windsurfers who stay toward the eastern end. High surf can create very unfavorable conditions. Even during calm seas, swimming can be difficult. The Hyatt erects flags to signal ocean conditions. Although not always accurate (we've seen red flags there when the ocean was absolutely flat), they are a good indication. The cliff off to your left is called Makawehi Point and is a popular place for pole fishermen. You will often see foolhardy young men jumping off the cliff into the waters below. The Hyatt has some outdoor showers near the beach area to rinse off, but they are technically for guests only.

The water is nice, but entry can be a bit awkward from this spot. Shipwreck Beach can be a good place to sit and watch frustrated fishermen cast off (literally).

❖ **Brennecke Beach**—This was one of the most popular and well-known boogie boarding and bodysurfing sites on the island until Hurricane 'Iwa rearranged the sand in 1982. The beach is now little more than a few feet of sand. Since it is so small, surfboards are not allowed near the shore. The waves are usually great, but they break too close to the rocks and high surf can generate unsafe conditions. You can rent boogie boards across the street at Brennecke's Beach Center under the restaurant. 'Iniki washed away much of what little sand was left at this beach making boogie boarding conditions a lot less favorable than they used to be. As the beach works its way back, it will change in character. Observe conditions carefully before you go in. Not for the inexperienced wave rider.

❖ **Po'ipu Beach Park**—This is the major center of beach activity on the

A Real Gem

south shore. The swimming is nearly always safe just to the left of the tombolo. "What's a tombolo?" Glad you asked. It's a narrow strip of sand joining two pieces of land. If you stand in the middle of one when the tide is right the ocean waves will strike you from both sides of the strip; this is what builds up the sand bar. There are only three such examples in the state, all on Kaua'i (the other two are inaccessible except by kayak; they are Makapili Rock near Kilauea, and Kipu Kai). Many people like to park their beach chairs at the end of the tombolo (also known as Nukumoi Point). Of course, their return trip isn't always dry if the tide is high. The snorkeling around the right side of the point can be fantastic.

Park facilities are present. This is a nice place to enjoy the ocean. Adjacent **Wai'ohai Beach** is not quite as protected but features excellent snorkeling opportunities if the surf isn't high. The swimming here is usually good as well.

❖ **Po'ipu Beach/Sheraton Beach/ Kiahuna Beach**—Take your pick with

A Real Gem

regards to the name. This beach fronts the Sheraton Hotel and Kiahuna Plantation Resort. It is postcard pretty and almost always safe to swim thanks to an offshore reef. Surfers ride waves outside the reef, but you should stay inside unless you really know your stuff. Boogie boarding and snorkeling help make this one of the most user-friendly beaches around. One caveat: As of this writing, the Sheraton Kaua'i Beach Hotel has not begun their rebuilding (after almost a year and a half) due to a dispute with the land owners. Consequently, construction noise, once rebuilding begins, might be heard into 1995. In the meantime, you will never find this beach less crowded than now since the Wai'ohai and Sheraton Hotels are closed.

❖ **Koloa Landing**—An old boat launch used as a SCUBA spot. See **SCUBA** in the chapter on **Activities**.

❖ **Beach House/Lawa'i Beach**— This tiny pocket of sand next to the Beach House restaurant nearly disappears at high-tide. The snorkeling in front of the restaurant is great, but the water is subject to currents during periods of high surf and needs to be respected. At other times it can be calm and a good place for the less experienced snorkeler. Just stay near the shore around the restaurant.

❖ **Palama Beach**—Named after the Palama family of Kaua'i which owns the Nomilu Fishpond nearby, the only way to get to this beach is to take the McBryde Sugar Company's wide haul cane road from the stoplight on Po'ipu Road. From there take one of the feeder roads to the beach. (We didn't put it on the map because these roads are always changing.) All this requires permission from McBryde. If you are still with me, the beach is quiet and nearly always deserted. A half mile offshore is Palama Buoy which marks Lanipu'ao Rock, a popular SCUBA destination.

WEST SHORE BEACHES

There aren't a lot of listings under West Shore Beaches. That's because it's almost *all beach*.

❖ **Salt Pond Beach Park**—This area is distinguished in that it is the only natural salt pond in Hawai'i still used to make salt. Seawater is pumped into containers and allowed to evaporate. More water is added and then it is transferred to shallower pans. The process is repeated until the water is loaded with salt. This is allowed to evaporate completely, leaving crystallized salt behind. During the summer you will likely see people practicing this process. The nearby park and its facilities are a popular place for locals to bring their families. The beach is separated by two rocky points. A natural ridge of rock runs between the two points creating an area of relative calm inside. Swimming is usually safe and children play in the semi-protected ocean water. The exception is during

periods of high surf which can make it unsafe.

❖ **Pakala Beach**—Those cars you might see parked on the side of the road shortly after the 21 mile mark belong to surfers carrying their boards to a very famous surfing site known also as Infinities, so named because the ride seems to last forever. The water is murky and only used for expert surfing.

❖ **Lucy Wright Beach Park**—Lucy Wright was a prominent member of the Waimea community when she died in 1931. It is a testament to how the townsfolk felt about her that the beach was named in her honor, especially in light of the more historic event which happened here. For it was at this spot that Captain James Cook first stepped foot in the Hawaiian Islands in January 1778. The beach itself is not a particularly good beach. The Waimea River mouth is nearby and the silty water colors the beach dark brown. Some guidebooks label this a black sand beach. Don't you believe it. It should more accurately be called a dirty sand beach. Camping by County permit. Across the river are the remains of the Russian Fort called Fort Elizabeth State Historic Park. For more information on the Fort, see page 83.

❖ **Polihale**—This area consists of more than 15 miles of uninterrupted sand beach. There are three regions, called **Polihale State Park**, **Pacific Missile Range Facility**, and **Kekaha Beach Park**. Except for a few small areas, the entire stretch is unprotected which means it is exposed to the ocean's force. During periods of high surf, waves can travel up the beach and pull you in, so be wary. When the seas are calm, you might enjoy the water. The sand can get pretty hot on this side; hot enough to fry your feet, so watch it. Take water with you. It is available only at Kekaha Beach Park, and at the other end at Polihale State Park.

Kekaha Beach Park is the first region you encounter. High surf generates a particularly powerful rip current and the waves can be unbelievably strong, so stay out unless the water is real calm.

Pacific Missile Range Facility is operated by the U.S. Navy. It is here that they train for ASW, or Anti Submarine Warfare. They also conduct "Star Wars" missile tests here. The beach is usually open to the public. Just go through the main gate to the guard house. The beach on the northern part (adjacent to Polihale State Park) is the famous **Barking Sands Beach**. If conditions are right the sand is supposed to make a barking sound with your every step. Don't feel bad if it doesn't happen. We've jumped up and down on that sand until we're blue in the face and we haven't even gotten it to whimper. The sand needs to be real dry. Local legend has it that the barking sound comes from nine dogs buried in the sand. They belonged to their master, a fisherman, in the days when dogs didn't bark. One day, they started acting antsy as the master tied them up before he went fishing. While he was out, a storm broke and forced him off course. A god gave the dogs the power to bark so they could guide their master home. Unfortunately, the dogs were so fearful waiting for their master that they ran around the stakes they were tied to. Around and around and around they ran until they buried themselves in the sand. The fisherman was depressed when he returned and couldn't find his dogs. He would go down to the shore everyday looking for his dogs, but he never found them. The dogs remain there to this day, barking for their master, hoping he will find them.

Polihale State Park is the end of the line. You can't go any farther north on this part of the island without a boat. This is where the Na Pali Coast starts. Rain is rare in these parts. The sand can get real hot in the summer. There are facilities here including a shower, picnic tables, and drinking water (which you will need). The dunes of Polihale are famous throughout the islands. The beach averages 300 feet in width and the dunes can get up to 100 feet high. Walking down a dune like that can be fun, walking up is a monster. Better to walk around unless you are training for the *Ironman Triathlon*. Locals drive their 4WD vehicles right onto the beach after first letting much of the air out of their tires. If you try it, be aware that there is no AAA on the island. A tow from this far out will probably cost you more than your entire vacation. Better to buy a new vehicle.

One area of Polihale that does usually offer safe swimming is Queen's Pond. It is protected by a fringing reef and the swimming is good except during periods of high surf. You can get there by taking the road marked on the map on page 82. That access road is at an intersection marked by a large monkeypod tree. Drive until it ends. Watch out for drifting sand on the access road—it has been known to get deep enough to strand a car.

There are several other beaches located farther up the Na Pali Coast. See **Na Pali Kayak Trip** under **Adventures** on page 143 for more information on these.

If you want more from your Kaua'i vacation than a suntan, Kaua'i offers a multitude of activities that will keep you happy and busy as long as you're here. Whether you're into golf, SCUBA, helicopter sightseeing, fishing, or whatever, Kaua'i offers nearly every activity you can think of. Two exceptions are parasailing and jet skiing which are not allowed by County law. We've listed many other activities here in alphabetical order.

You will see many activity booths scattered around the island. While these can be quite helpful, you should be aware that they are not uninterested parties. They are often nothing more than forums for selling timeshares. In addition, they will "recommend" companies that they have agreements with. So if you are steered to XYZ helicopter company and assured that they are the best, consider the source. We walk up to these booths frequently. What we

hear is usually wrong, and sometimes comical. We have no stake in any company we recommend. We just want to steer you in the best direction we can.

Beachcombing

Beachcombing. The word brings to mind someone strolling along the beach and finding a bottle with a note in it (saying you are behind in your payments on your student loan). Recommending particular beaches for beachcombing can be hazardous. A beach might contain some real prizes one day and nothing the next. The following beaches are *relatively* consistent in accruing beach litter (which is what beachcombing is all about, right?). Directions to them can be found in the section on **Beaches: Wainiha Beach, Larsen's Beach, Hanama'ulu Bay,**

Wainiha Beach is one of the better beachcombing beaches on the north shore.

Maha'ulepu Beach between Ha'ula Beach and Kawailoa Bay.

There is another place that needs some explaining. In Lihu'e there is a beach that is perfect for beachcombing. About 70 feet wide, the size, shape, and location make it a natural repository for beach litter. The "beach" actually has virtually no sand; it is piled *several feet high* with coral and shells. Unfortunately, beach litter is not the only kind of litter you will find here. Consequently, we hesitated telling you about its existence out of sheer shame. While easy to get to, you will find the short path to it strewn with abandoned cars and trash left by inconsiderate jerks who don't appreciate the paradise that they live in. If you aren't dissuaded by this (and don't say we didn't warn you), you will find it on the right side of Ahukini Road just north of the airport off a 50 foot dirt road located between two sets of old train tracks just before you see the entrance of an auto wrecking yard (whew!). It's labeled as an X on map #3 because we didn't want anyone to go there without reading our disclaimer.

Bicyclists will be disappointed to learn that there are almost no bicycle paths on Kaua'i. Most roads have two lanes with narrow shoulders.

There are many places to rent and ride mountain bikes. Po'ipu is a popular place to ride mountain bikes and the only place on Kaua'i where bikes are common on the roads. The cane roads in this area, especially near Maha'ulepu, can be fun.

If you are interested in renting a mountain bike, call any of these companies. **Outfitters Kaua'i** in Po'ipu at 742–9667. **Bicycle John** in Lihu'e at 245–7579 and in Kapa'a at 822–3495. **Bicycle Kaua'i** in Kapa'a at 822–3315. **Pedal 'n Paddle** in Kapa'a at 822–2005 and in Hanalei at 826–9069. Expect to pay $20–$35 per day.

For organized bicycle tours, there are three companies offering very different tours: **Kayak Kaua'i Outfitters** at 826–9844 in Hanalei or 822–9179 in Kapa'a offers bike and swim tours from Hanalei or Kapa'a everyday. Price is $45 per person. **Outfitters Kaua'i** in Po'ipu at 742–9667 has a Koke'e Mountain Bike Ecotour along the back roads above Waimea Canyon for $78 per person. **Kaua'i Downhill** at 245–1774 offers an *early* morning 12 mile downhill bicycle cruise from Waimea Canyon for $60 per person.

BOAT TOURS; See either Ocean Tours or River Trips.

Boogie boarding is where you ride a wave laying on top of what is essentially a sawed-off surfboard. It can be a real blast. Short fins are worn to assist in catching the wave. If you've never done it before, start on small waves.

Underestimating larger wave strength is a big mistake. They can drill you into the ground if you are not careful. The section on **Beaches** describes the more popular sites. Observe ocean conditions and don't go if the waves look too big for you. **Tip:** Men should wear T-shirts lest you rub raw certain tissue not accustomed to trauma. Women, you are already covered.

Your hotel activity desk is the first place to check for renting boards. It should cost you $5–$8 per day and $20–$25 per week. Hard shell boards are best. Other places include:

NORTH SHORE—**Hanalei Surf Co.** at 826–9000, **Kayak Kaua'i Outfitters** at 826–9844, **Pedal 'n Paddle** at 826–9069.
EAST SHORE—**Kayak Kaua'i Outfitters** at 822–9179, **Pedal 'n Paddle** at 822–2005, and **Ray's Rentals** at 822–5700.
SOUTH SHORE—**Progressive Expressions** in Koloa at 742–6041 or **Kaua'i Seasports** in Po'ipu at 742–9303.

CAMPING

The ultimate in low price lodging is offered by Mother Nature herself. Kaua'i is a great place to camp with 13 different areas—6 State campsites and 7 County campsites. See map below. To camp at a State controlled site, you need to contact the **Division of State Parks** in Lihu'e at 3060 Eiwa Street, Room 306, Lihu'e, Hi. 96766-1875 (808) 241-3444. You are *strongly* advised to get your permit before you arrive as the sites can fill up, especially during peak season (May—December). The State requires that you send them a copy of the driver's license or passport of every adult who will be camping as well as the names of any minors, along with your dates of travel. The permits are free and should be acquired as far in advance as you can. They recommend 6 months in advance during the busy months.

County sites require a County permit. Write to: **Division of Parks and Recreation**, 4193A Hardy Street, Bldg #5, Lihu'e, Hi. 96766 (808) 241–6670. They will send you an application. The cost is $3 per person per night.

If you need to rent camping or hiking gear, your best sources will be **Pedal 'n Paddle** in Hanalei at 826–9069 and Kapa'a at 822–2005, **Kayak Kaua'i Outfitters** in Hanalei at 826–9844 and Kapa'a at 822–9179, and **Outfitters Kaua'i** in Po'ipu at 742–9667.

Good places to buy gear include the variety stores around the island: **Village Variety** (826–6077) in Hanalei, **Waipouli Variety** (822–1014) in Kapa'a, and **Discount Variety** (742–9393) in Koloa. Others are **Stan's** in Hanapepe and the **PayLess** stores in Kapa'a and Lihu'e.

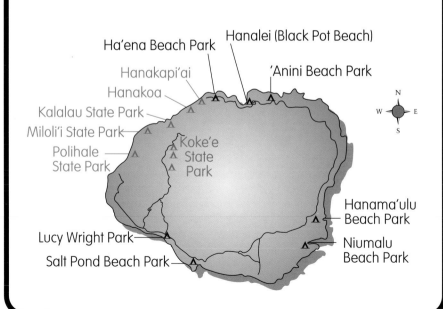

Campsites Requiring Permits

State Parks Written in Red; County Parks written in Black

Ha'ena Beach Park

Hanalei (Black Pot Beach)

Hanakapi'ai

'Anini Beach Park

Hanakoa

Kalalau State Park

Miloli'i State Park

Koke'e State Park

Polihale State Park

N
W · E
S

Hanama'ulu Beach Park

Niumalu Beach Park

Lucy Wright Park

Salt Pond Beach Park

Kaua'i's waters contain abundant fish. Of course it's one thing to have 'em, and another thing to catch 'em. Whether you want to go deep sea fishing, sit by a lake, or cast off a cliff, you will be pleased to know that all are available on Kaua'i.

Deep Sea Fishing

If deep sea fishing's your game, there are several charter companies around. They all provide the necessary gear. Tuna, wahoo (ono) and marlin among others are all caught in these waters. The seas around the islands can be rough if you're not used to it, and it's fairly common for someone on board (maybe you) to spend the trip feeding the fish. We advise that you take Dramamine *before you leave*. Scopolamine works better but requires a prescription and can make you sleepier than Dramamine. See your doctor (I've always wanted to say that).

Before deciding *who* to go with, decide *where* you want to go. It might be calm on one side of the island and rough on another. Current ocean conditions can be obtained by calling 245–3564 for Hawaiian waters, 245–6001 for the weather forecast.

Reputable charter companies are:

'Anini Fishing Charters at 828–1285 fishes off the north shore and has the cheapest rates on the island. Light and medium tackle are their specialty but they'll go heavy if you like. $75 for a half day, Bob will stay out longer if things are really jumping. 30 foot craft will take 6 persons, minimum of 3.

Gent-Lee at 245–7504 fishes on the east side and uses 36 foot Radons to carry 6–8 customers per trip. 4 hour trips cost $90, 6 hour trips are $120. They won't go out with less than 4 persons, but rarely have trouble filling a boat.

Robert McReynolds Sports Fishing at 828–1379 fishes off the north shore and specializes in medium tackle to maximize the chance that everyone will catch a fish (they will go for the big stuff if you like). In business for twenty years, they are one of the few that will go out even if you are the only one. Their 30 foot craft will accommodate up to 6. $85 for half day, $130 for all day. They provide a cooler, you fill it.

True Blue Charters and Ocean Sports at 246–6333 fishes off the east shore and specializes in the big stuff. Their 4 hour trip is $90, 6 hour trips are $120. They will go out with 2 people, to a maximum of 6 on their 30 foot craft.

Wayne's World Charter Service at 338–1312 fishes on the west side and uses a 27 foot Cris Craft for nonstop trolling. $85 for 4 hours, $110 for 6 hours. Snacks and beverages included; lunch for the 6 hour trip. They won't go out with less than 3 persons.

Liko Kaua'i Cruises provides cruises up and down the Na Pali Coast (northwest side). Trolling takes place on the return for about 25 miles. The rest of the 4–5 hour trip is for sightseeing and snorkeling. $75 per person.

Freshwater Fishing

There are dozens of lakes (actually man–made reservoirs) strewn throughout the island. Many of them are on private property and require permission.

You'd never know this if you went to one on the weekend—locals pretty much fish where they want and are rarely hassled. Waita Reservoir in Po'ipu, the Wailua Reservoir, and the Wailua River are all very popular. Large-mouth bass are plentiful. You will also find smallmouth bass, and the tough-fighting South American import called tucunare or peacock bass (bright orange or red sinking crankbait are said to work best for this aggressive fish). Avoid fishing when the water is real muddy after a heavy rain, the fish won't bite.

The Pu'u Lua Reservoir in Koke'e (on the west side, see map on page 82) as well as several feeding streams are stocked yearly with rainbow trout finger-lings. Lake waters here are too warm for trout to spawn. Trout season there is the first 18 days of August, then weekends and holidays until the end of September. (They are considering extending this, call 241–3400 to get more information).

The Division of Aquatic Resources, Department of Land and Natural Resources at 241–3400 can fill in any additional blanks you may have. Three places you can obtain licenses are:

Lihu'e Fishing Supply at 245–4930 in Lihu'e. **Stan's Fishing and Liquor Supplies** at 335–5213 in Hanapepe. **Waipouli Variety** at 822–1014 in Kapa'a. Squid and shrimp can be obtained at almost any supermarket.

Shore/Surf Fishing

The island is replete with areas to fish from. Drive along the shore for ten minutes and you will see plenty of places to fish. We will tell you about our absolute favorite.

Maha'ulepu in Po'ipu (see map on page 73) is outstanding. Even if you don't fish, it will make you want to learn. From the top of an inward leaning lithified sand dune, you can look into the crystal clear waters, spot the fish, and drop your line. Located between Ha'ula Beach and Kawailoa Bay. The lava cliffs near the Ha'ula Beach section of **Maha'ulepu** are also outstanding. You will find pole holders driven into the lava here. If the surf is too high, don't go.

FLYING

If you're a pilot and want to rent an airplane on Kaua'i, **Lihu'e Aviation Center** at (808) 246–8776 rents a Piper Cherokee 140 for $78 an hour wet. You pay for the time the craft is in operation. The 4 seat tricycle cruises at 120 mph and can be a perfect way to see the island at your own pace. Check rides are required as well as the necessary pilot's proof.

The Wailua Reservoir can be one of the more relaxing places to fish.

With its bountiful nightly rainfall and warm, sunny days, Kaua'i is a perfect environment for golf. Its eight golf courses are diverse, ranging from a wealthy sugar magnate's private course donated to the island, to a world class resort course rated number one in the all the islands by *Golf Digest*. If golf is your game, Kaua'i is sure to please. The prices described under Fees in the box below reflect the highest category of fees. Check the specific course descriptions below for more information and possible discounts.

Princeville Resort Kaua'i; The Makai Course (808) 826-3580

Designed by Robert Trent Jones, Jr. and first opened in 1972, the **Makai Course** consists of 3 sets of 9 holes called the **Ocean**, the **Lakes**, and the **Woods**. For 18 holes you get your choice of two with **Ocean/Lakes** being the most popular. The Hurricane partially denuded the trees on the **Woods** course. Since most of these trees are slow-growing Norfolk Island pines, it could take some time before the **Woods** loses its recently acquired windy reputation. The **Lakes** offers an impressive 9, with holes 3-7 commanding outstanding views. Hole 9 requires a buttery touch as it shoots over the water onto a small green located just behind it. The **Ocean** is the most challenging and interesting of the three, as well as the longest. The 6th and 7th holes offer dramatic views of the north shore coastline from the edge of a steep cliff. In fact, hole 7 shoots across a menacing gorge. Located off Highway 56 inside Princeville, see map on page 49. Fees are $100 for standard, $75 if you're staying at a Princeville resort, and $60 if you're staying at the Princeville Hotel. Kama'aina rate is $45. Carts are included in price and are mandatory.

Note: the proper golf attire rule is more rigidly enforced at Princeville courses.

Princeville Resort Kaua'i; The Prince Course (808) 826–5004.

Now you've reached golfing nirvana. This course is usually rated #1 in all the islands, and for good reason. With 390 gorgeous acres to work with, Robert Trent Jones, Jr. took full advantage of the cliffs, gorges, and natural rolling scenery. When it opened in 1990, the Prince Course was hailed by *Golf Digest* as the best new resort course in the Country. Since

A Real Gem

then, it has quickly become known throughout Hawai'i as one of the most challenging and rewarding courses one can play. The design stresses unobstructed expansiveness, with the rolling topography and deep gorges serving as the main hazards and obstacles. There are nine miles of cart paths, and the layout allows for considerable room between holes. Hole 6 offers a delightful march toward the ocean cliffs. At hole 7, you must shoot over a gorge onto a narrow finger of land containing the green and little else. The 14th green is accompanied by a charming waterfall coming out of a hole in the mountain. You won't find a lot of flat areas on this

Course	Par	Yards	Rating	Fees
Princeville Resort Kaua'i;				
Makai Course *	72	6306	69.7	$100*
Prince Course	72	6521	71.0	$110*
Wailua Municipal Golf Course	72	6585	71.9	$18–20
Kaua'i Lagoons Golf and Racket Club;				
Lagoons Course	72	6108	68.0	$100*
Kiele Course	72	6164	69.1	$145*
Po'ipu Bay Resort	72	6021	69.0	$120*
Kiahuna Golf Club	70	5631	66.5	$78*
Kukuiolono Golf Course	72	6154	70.0	$5

* Indicates power cart included in fee

course, but you will find tough, challenging world class golfing. In fact if you're *really* into self-flagellation, the black tees measure a whopping 7309 yards with a rating of 74.6. The Clubhouse is spectacular and not to be missed. If you've never played golf before, this probably isn't the course on which to learn. But if you have a little experience and don't mind being humbled a bit, this course can't be beat.

Located just before Princeville off Highway 56, see map on page 49. Fees are $110 for standard, $85 if you are staying in Princeville, $60 if you're staying at the Princeville Hotel, and $55 for kama'ainas. Standard fees go up $20 in July 1994. Carts are included in price and are mandatory.

Wailua Municipal Golf Course (808) 245–2163

This course is consistently rated as the best *municipal* course in Hawai'i, and one of the best in the U.S. As it parallels the beach on Kaua'i's Coconut Coast, Wailua constantly reminds you that you are near the ocean. The smell of sea air, the constant crosswind, and the roar of the surf are all comforting companions, making this course extremely popular with locals. (The $6 kama'aina rate might also be a factor). Weekends are very busy. While the course is long, there are relatively few hazards making it a leisurely course. Wind is always a consideration here. Hole 17 requires restraint, lest you drive it into the sand (the **real** sand, and its accompanying surf). Expect the grounds to be less than scrupulously maintained (it is supported by the County). The Clubhouse was devastated by the Hurricane and the County is slow to rebuild (golf courses are considered a low priority). The expectation is that they will reopen the Clubhouse and pro shop in late 1994, and all the accompanying services such as club rental will resume then. In the meantime, they are open for business *sans* these services. **Paradise River Rentals** at 245–9580 rents clubs if you can't find them elsewhere.

Kaua'i Lagoons Golf and Racket Club; Lagoons Course (808) 241–6000, or (800) 634–6400

This is one of the two courses operated by Kaua'i Lagoons and is not part of the Westin Kaua'i. Designed by Jack Nicklaus and opened in 1989, the **Lagoons** has become popular with locals due to its lower fees. Not as challenging as the **Kiele** course, the **Lagoons** also seems to receive less maintenance and has been relegated to the status of the less deserving cousin course. While the **Lagoons** offers a pleasant golfing experience, it is not spectacular and might disappoint those who have been told to "make sure you golf at the Westin." The adjacent airport and its accompanying jets can be a bit annoying. If your golfing days are few and precious here, consider playing the **Kiele** or driving to the north shore. But if you have golfing days to burn, the **Lagoon**s is a pleasant, if somewhat unremarkable course.

Located at Kaua'i Lagoons, take the Rice Street entrance and proceed past the guard gate. Fees are $100.

Kama'aina rates available. Carts are included in the price. Push carts are available upon request.

Kaua'i Lagoons Golf and Racket Club; Kiele Course (808) 241–6000, or (800) 634–6400

This is considered one of the tougher courses around and is replete thick, lush, woodsy areas along the cart paths and luscious ocean views. Also designed by Jack Nicklaus, and opened in 1988, the **Kiele** was the finest course on the island until the **Prince** opened up on the north shore. It is still an outstanding course. The greens at hole 16 command a fabulous view of the ocean chiseling its way inland. Many of the holes are difficult and rewarding. You might recognize it from the *1991 PGA Grand Slam*, and it's usually rated in the top 100 courses by various magazines. You start at the *Happy Buddha* (all the holes are named and have corresponding statues standing guard at the tees).

Located at Kaua'i Lagoons, take the Rice Street entrance and proceed past the guard gate. Fees are $145. Kama'aina rates available. Carts are included in price and are mandatory.

Kiahuna Golf Club (808) 742–9595

At one time Kiahuna Golf Club's owners boasted that their Robert Trent Jones Jr. designed course was the best on Kaua'i. Those days, if they ever existed, are long gone. Now it is somewhat rundown and its current owners seem to have lost interest. There is a slightly cramped feel to it. The course's main boast is not its play, but the *heiaus* and other ancient structures on the course. The greens are usually extremely slow. With a par of 70, and fairly easy holes, **Kiahuna** is good for the ego but lacks pizzazz. In general, we recommend against **Kiahuna**—not because it is a bad course, but because it gives you no reason to want to return. In short, it is unremarkable. Located on Kiahuna Plantation Drive off Poʻipu Road (520), see map on page 73. Fees are $78 for standard 18 holes, $35 for 9. Kamaʻaina rate for 18 holes is $45. Carts are included in the price and are mandatory.

Poʻipu Bay Resort (Hyatt) (808) 742–8711

There was much anticipation preceding the opening of this (here he is again) Robert Trent Jones Jr. designed course. With its location on the "sunny south shore," **Poʻipu Bay Resort** is a sprawling 210 acres of wide open golfing. In fact if it has a flaw, it's that it is too wide open. Even course personnel privately mumble about a dearth of hazards. But this nitpicking aside, **Poʻipu Bay Resort** offers spectacular scenery, impeccable grooming and attention to detail (they like to brag that they imported their bunker sand from Australia and Idaho). Its ocean links style is nicely done with particularly smashing views from holes 15–17. Look for turtles in the water when you're near the *heiau* (an ancient Hawaiian structure) on hole 16. During winter months you might even see whales off the coast. The course is not exceedingly challenging, and those less comfortable in the game will enjoy it as much as the more advanced.

Located off Poʻipu Road (520), see map on page 73. Fees are $120 for the general public, $85 for Hyatt guests and a kamaʻaina rate of $60. Carts are included in price and are mandatory.

Kukuiolono Park and Golf Course (808) 332–9151

In 1919, sugar magnate Walter D. McBryde donated his personal 9 hole golf course and some surrounding land to the people of Kauaʻi. This land, complete with a trust, has been cherished by Kauaʻi residents ever since. To get into the park you pass through a magnificent metal gate with lava stone pillars. Once inside, the personal nature of the course is apparent. One can't help but feel like you're golfing among friends. The links are not as lavish as others on the island; its location in Kalaheo does not afford it much rainfall and the maintenance budget is not in the same league as the big boys. And it wasn't designed by Robert Trent Jones Jr.; in fact they don't know *who* designed it. But this course might leave you with a smile. Course personnel even sell bird seed to feed the ubiquitous tamed chickens. The price can't be touched. $5 per *day* with power carts costing $6 and pull carts $1, both per nine holes. If you're playing 18 holes, play from the blue tees for the back nine, which will provide 6154 yards of pleasant, easy-going golf. Especially good for those who have never played before. If you want to personally thank Mr. McBryde, you'll find him buried near the 8th tee, in the middle of his lovely and cherished Japanese garden. This charming garden is definitely worth a look; in fact local weddings occur in it almost every weekend.

Open to everyone, this course is located .8 miles from Highway 50 on Papalina Road (the only stoplight in Kalaheo). Look for the gate on your right.

If ever there was a place made for helicopter exploration, it's Kaua'i. Much of the island can be seen only by air, and helicopters, with their giant windows and their ability to hover, are by far the best method. Going to Kaua'i without taking a helicopter flight is like going to see the Sistine Chapel and not looking up. You will see the ruggedly beautiful Na Pali Coast and marvel at the sheerness of some of its cliffs. This is an area where razor-thin, almost two-dimensional mountains rise parallel to each other leaving impossibly tall and narrow valleys between them. You will see vertical spires and shake your head in disbelief at the sight of a goat perched on top. The awe–inspiring Waimea Canyon— dubbed "The Grand Canyon of the Pacific" by Mark Twain—unfolds beneath you. A good pilot will come up over a ridge suddenly exposing the glorious Canyon, often timed to coincide with a crescendo in the music you hear in your headphones. You will see the incredible Olokele Valley with its jagged twists and turns and stair-step waterfalls. It is impossible to keep track of all the waterfalls you will see on your flight. You will get a different view of Kaua'i's fabulous north shore beaches and reefs. You might see turtles, dolphins, or whales depending on the time of year. And best of all, you will be treated to the almost spiritual splendor of Wai'ale'ale Crater. You have never seen anything like the Crater—a three sided wall of waterfalls, greens of every imaginable shade, and a lushness that is beyond comprehension. Many people find themselves weeping when they enter the crater. Others find that they stop breathing—it happened to one of us the first time. If it has been dry lately, it's simply great; if it's been "pumping," it is spectacular.

When you are finished with the flight, you will either be speechless or babble like a fool—it happens to everyone.

One concern you may have is safety, and that's a valid point. As far as the industry safety record is concerned, there have been crashes and "incidents," when a craft has had to make an unscheduled landing. You can ask the companies directly about safety but

Company	Phone #	Status	Helicopter Type	Departure
Inter–Island	335–5009	Recommended	Hughes 500D	Hanapepe
Island	245–8588	Qualified	A-Star	Lihu'e
Jack Harter	245–3774	Recommended	Bell Jet Ranger	Lihu'e
Ni'ihau	335–3500	Specialized	Agusta	Hanapepe
Ohana	245–3996	Recommended	A-Star and Bell Jet Ranger	Lihu'e
Papillon	245–9644	Qualified	A-Star	L H and P
Safari	246–0136	Recommended	A-Star	Lihu'e
South Sea	245–7781	Qualified	Bell Jet Ranger	Lihu'e
Will Squyres	245–8881	Qualified	Bell Jet Ranger	Lihu'e

you should be aware that when we tried it, we were often misled or directly lied to. Not every time, but many times.

When we checked with the FAA we discovered that, like many things, safety evaluation isn't that simple. A company might be cited for maintenance violations—*that* sounds ominous. Then you find out that the maintenance was carried out properly, but a log was dated wrong, or the company didn't fill out a particular form. Should we steer you away from them for this reason?

In the end it comes down to a matter of judgment. Below is a list of companies that we feel are qualified. Not all have spotless safety records. Things happen—a warning light comes on and you have to land immediately. Even if it was a false alarm it is still considered an "incident." These companies struck us as honest and forthright in their concerns about safety. All are 135 certified, meaning they adhere to stricter safety standards than those certified 91. There are others around but we **specifically** don't recommend them for one reason or another. Helicopter safety should not be trifled with.

As far as seating is concerned, the front seat is the best—in consoling you some companies might tell you otherwise when they direct you to a back seat. From the front, the island rushes at you with incredible drama. The problem is that seating arrangements are made on the basis of weight. Lighter people are generally seated up

If you ever saw Jurassic Park, *you'll remember this waterfall. Real name Manawaiopuna Falls, the only other way to see it is by helicopter (unless your last name happens to be Robinson).*

front. If you are seated in the back, the right seat is the best since much of the action will be on the right side (by common agreement all the companies fly clockwise around the island making the Na Pali and other areas best from the right side). A-Stars have two passengers up front and four in the back, leaving two people in the middle. Helicopter companies like these crafts since they can fly six passengers at a time. There are usually no windows which open so glare will be a factor with your pictures. Bell Jet Rangers have one passenger up front, three in back. They also have a small window to open to get better pictures. The back middle seat on this craft is the worst helicopter seat you will find. Hughes 500Ds have two in the front and two in the back, by far the best arrangement. The Hughes is also the only craft to have the pilot sit on the left side, out of the way. They have large removable windows. While the back is a little cramped and doesn't allow the forward view that other back seats allow, their side views are better. Unfortunately, only one recommended company uses these, **Inter–Island**. This is because the Hughes cost more to operate than the Bell Jet Rangers and they don't carry 6 people like the A-Star.

Another consideration is the takeoff point. Port Allen Airport in Hanapepe is the best location from which to take off since there is no "dead time," or travel over non-scenic areas. However, you don't get to see Kipu Kai or Wailua Falls from there as you do if you leave from Lihu'e. But from Lihu'e, the flight seems *slightly* rushed. The qualified companies which have flights from Port Allen Airport are **Inter–Island** and **Papillon**.

The difference between helicopter companies is the difference between a very pleasant flight, and really experiencing the island. It's the difference between coming off the craft with a pleasant smile, and coming off with a stupid grin on your face that won't leave all day. Between having a tale to tell, and experiencing something so moving that it will stay with you for a lifetime. All this said and done, our personal favorite is **Inter–Island**. Their helicopter, location, and pilot all come together to provide an outstanding flight. They are small, and lack the slickness that some others have, but their tours are executed flawlessly and in our opinion they are far and away the best on the island. Also, if you request it, they will remove the back window on your side which allows you to get unbelievable photographs since you can lean out the window with your camera (keep your seat belt fastened and bring a light sweat jacket if you do this). They will even remove the whole door if you like. Their Hughes 500D is well suited for this purpose and is the only helicopter where we don't object to being in the back seat. They also have a "Full Moon Flight." Kaua'i by moonlight is only available 3 nights per month.

From Lihu'e, **Jack Harter** and **Safari** are recommended. Their tours are well done. **Jack Harter** was the first and used to be considered by many to be the best. Although this is no longer the case, he is still quite good. **Safari** prides itself on its videos of your trip. Although we generally prefer videos that were professionally prepared showing each of the locations at their best, if you want a well made video of *your* trip, **Safari** is the place to go.

They provide a more gentle flight from a slightly higher elevation which will please those who have an innate fear of helicopters, or frighten easily. Owner/operator Preston Myers has helicopter experience all over the world. **Papillon** is the largest company around, with flights throughout the islands. Although their trips are reasonably pleasant and they use talented pilots, some might feel like they are on a tour bus rather than with a pilot passionate about the island. We also found the music unimaginative. Their support staff is very professional, and we hope that they will be able to shake those big company blues.

When it comes to prices, expect to pay between $120 and $150 per person for a flight of between 50 and 75 minutes. **Jack Harter** provides a comprehensive 90 minute flight for $160.

These prices often include a video. Charter rates are between $600 and $1,000 per hour. Four passenger Hughes 500Ds and Bell Jet Rangers are cheaper than the big A-Star. **Inter–Island, Jack Harter,** and **Safari** have two–way communications, a plus for charters.

Other helicopter tips...
• Never take a flight less than 50 minutes, you will only get your appetite whetted.
• Still photographs work better than video and some companies don't permit video cameras.
• Zoom lenses work best since the size of the field changes rapidly.
• Use automatic shutter speed if you have it, you'll never be able to keep up manually.

Na Pali by air is utterly unforgettable.

- Use fast film—ASA/ISO 400 or better.
- With a camera capable of it, set the aperture to a low f-stop to create a large lens opening. This will help the camera to see through the window and any foreign matter that may be on it.
- Beware of the glare from the inside of the windows.
- If you're in a craft that has two-way communication, don't be afraid to ask the pilot to turn so you can take a shot of something.
- If there are four or more of you, consider chartering a helicopter. It might actually be cheaper and will allow you to call many of the shots during the flight. "Pilot, please hover here for a few minutes, and turn a little more to the right." If only your group is on the flight, you are effectively chartering the flight whether you realize it or not so take advantage of it.
- Morning is often the best time for flights.
- When you see people getting off a helicopter after their tour, try not to be downwind from them; they are often frothing at the mouth from their experience and might drool on you.

For a unique helicopter experience, **Ni'ihau Helicopters**, owned by the powerful Robinson family, flies groups to the privately owned island of Ni'ihau. The Robinsons bought this Ferrari of a helicopter to take care of emergency medical problems on their island and use it for tours to help subsidize its cost. For $235 you get a 90 minute flight, circumnavigating Ni'ihau and landing for a few minutes on one of its beaches. If you are staying at the Hyatt and want to part with $250, they will give you a similar tour and also provide you with a lunch, snorkel gear and allow 5 hours on one of Ni'ihau's beaches to frolic. The problem you will encounter with **Ni'ihau Helicopters** is that they require at least 4 people on a flight and don't have enough customers to ensure a flight for you. If you are determined to take the flight, contact them as much in advance as possible to maximize the chance that they can organize a flight, but don't be surprised if it doesn't work out.

If you don't like helicopters and still want to see Kaua'i by air, **Fly Kaua'i** at 246–9123 provides tours by airplane. They also have a Ni'ihau fly–by. While nowhere *near* as thrilling as a helicopter tour, it's cheaper and is better than no air tour at all.

HIKING

Of all the Hawaiian Islands, none offer more trails or better hiking than does Kaua'i. You could spend an entire month in Kaua'i, hiking every day and not see half the trails that the island has to offer. And that's just the official *maintained* trails. If you have hiked here in the past and think you have seen it before, we have a surprise for you. In one way, Hurricane 'Iniki turned out to be a big blessing for hikers. After the Hurricane, large amounts of Federal money poured into the park system. The result? Many of the trails at Koke'e that had been closed for *years* were reopened thanks to extra work crews.

In addition, the **Alaka'i Swamp Trail**, which used to be a fascinating but incredibly muddy experience, has a wooden boardwalk between the trailhead and the **Pihea Trail** intersection. They are continuing the boardwalk which should eventually go past the **Pihea Trail** for several miles.

There are entire books dedicated to the subject of hiking Kaua'i. As of this writing, none have been written after the Hurricane. This is important since many trails changed after the storm. The best one on the market today is *Kaua'i Trails* by Kathy Morey. Though dated, it is a good hiking companion.

The Koke'e area in particular is rich with hiking areas and its altitude makes for cool, pleasant hiking conditions. The Koke'e map that follows will be of assistance. Several hikes that are reasonably easy but rewarding are **Kukui Trail** (as far as you want to go), **Waipo'o Falls** (Halemanu Valley Road to the Canyon Trail), **Pihea Trail** and the **Alaka'i Swamp Trail**. It's always best to check in at the Koke'e Lodge before you hike to get up to date information. If you plan to do a lot of hiking, contact the agencies below for information packets on their trails.

Division of State Parks
3060 Eiwa Street, Room 306
Lihu'e, Hi. 96766-1875
(808) 241-3444

Division of Parks and Recreation,
4193A Hardy Street, Bld#5
Lihu'e, Hi. 96766
(808) 241–6670

If you need to rent camping or hiking gear, your best sources will be **Pedal 'n Paddle** in Hanalei at 826–9069 and Kapa'a at 822–2005, **Kayak Kaua'i Outfitters** in Hanalei at 826–9844 and Kapa'a at 822–9179, and **Outfitters Kaua'i** in Po'ipu at 742–9667

Good places to buy gear include the variety stores around the island: **Village Variety** (826–6077) in Hanalei, **Waipouli Variety** (822–1014) in Kapa'a, and **Discount Variety** (742–9393) in Koloa. Others are **Stan's** in Hanapepe and the **PayLess** stores in Kapa'a and Lihu'e.

Outside of Koke'e, the Wailua area has several trails that are outstanding for a short day hike.

Nounou Mountain Trail

See map on page 59. Also called the Sleeping Giant Trail. This is a moderately difficult trail. The vertical elevation

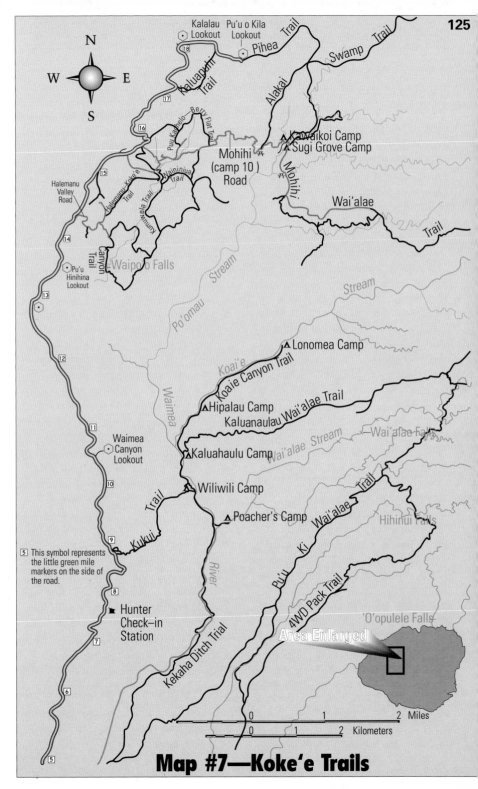

Map #7—Koke'e Trails

you will gain on this hike is 1,000 feet. A thousand feet sounds like a big rise (OK, it *is* a big rise), but this is a hike worth experiencing. Nearly the entire hike is through forests with stunning views. This is a real trail, not an abandoned road like some other hiking trails. Shortly after the .5 mile stake, the trail seems to split into 2 paths. *Do not take the left fork which is on the side of the mountain!* This is probably a pig trail and not part of the main trail. You won't like it. When you get to the main fork in the trail, (diligently guarded by Hala trees) take the fork to the left for 3 or 4 minutes to the picnic tables. From here you can see the entire Wailua Valley from Anahola to Lihu'e. The view is not to be missed and well worth the climbing effort expended. Anyone who becomes dizzy from heights should be aware that there are areas along this hike where the view off to one side is quite steep.

Up at the picnic tables, there is a short trail leading south to the Giant's forehead. Or is it his nose? Hard to say. The view from up there is literally, once in a lifetime. The vista is without rival. Think *real hard* before you take this part. It is steep, and the spine is almost vertical on both sides. A wrong step, or a slip anywhere near the nose would almost certainly cost you your life. This part of the trail is what they call a real okole squeezer. Stop at the picnic table unless you are very brave, very foolish and very well insured.

Either retrace your steps or, for a one way hike, continue on the **Nounou West Trail**. It's all downhill and fairly steep in spots. After you pass through a magnificent strand of Norfolk Island pines (a very tall and straight pine tree

highly prized in the Age of Discovery for its value as a ship's mast), you come to the junction of **Nounou West** and **Kuamo'o-Nounou Trail**. To the left is **Kuamo'o-Nounou Trail**.

Kuilau Ridge Trail

1.75 miles past the University of Hawai'i at Manoa, Kaua'i Research Station. The trailhead marker is on the left side, park at the Keahua Arboretum.

This is one of the nicer hikes on the island. The first half hour is a gentle, but constant incline which takes you past a myriad of birds. Watch and listen for them. At the end of the incline, you will come to a small picnic area overlooking a lovely valley. If it's clear, you will get a stunning view of Mount Wai'ale'ale. This is a nice place to have lunch or just enjoy a long sip of water. *Make sure you go past the picnic tables.* The payoff is 5 minutes later. You will be rewarded with a breathtaking razor back, winding, rolling, trek into paradise. There are lush hillsides filled with ferns of every size and shape. Off in the distance you can see the ocean at Kapa'a and all the way to Lihu'e at another point. The views are unmatched. Turn around when you reach a fork about .25 mile past a quaint wooden bridge. The entire hike should take you 2.5 to 3 hours if you hike at a semi-steady pace. Bring water. Hiking boots recommended but tennis shoes OK.

Jungle Hike

If you want a *taste* of the steamy jungle and forest (but without the need for a machete and a gallon of insect repellent), this one might just be the ticket. It leads to a government stream gauging station and passes through some breathtaking scenery. Your reward at the end is a picturesque, stair-step little stream adjacent to a LPCO diversion ditch (the word ditch has ugly connotations but oftentimes these small dams can make a nice place for a picnic). To get there, take Kuamoʻo Road (580) all the way until it becomes dirt. When it ends, go right and look at your odometer. At .5 miles is a Y. Take the left fork. At 1.3 miles is a left branch. Don't take it, go straight. Then at almost 1.4 miles is another Y, take the left fork. At 1.7 miles is the gate. Park here and walk down the dirt road (the gate is on State land and was erected to prevent vehicles from going any farther, but it's perfectly legal to go through the gate and continue on foot). The views into Waiʻaleʻale Crater from this dirt road can be exceptional. At about 10-15 minutes into the walk as you come upon an

A Real Gem

ascent, there will be an old turnout on the left side, keep a sharp eye open for it, it's easy to miss. The trail off to the left from this turnout immediately parallels for a short time a LPCO ditch and passes through extremely lush territory. The ferns, birds, and trees are abundant along this easy-to-follow but sometimes slippery trail. A pleasant 10-15 minute trek will bring you to a nice, fresh water pool, formed by the small dam. The area around the dam is covered with plant life and can be slippery. A wonderful, secluded spot for a picnic.

This jungle hike is fairly easy and rewards you with a nice place for a picnic.

The Kalalau Trail

The ultimate hike is also the most famous hike in all Hawai'i. Eleven miles of switchbacks, hills, and beautiful scenery. This hike can be a real adventure. Because of this, we discuss it in detail under **Adventures**. If you want to get a taste of it, two miles into the trail is Hanakapi'ai Beach. This is a beautiful but treacherous beach to swim. From here there is a two mile side trip to Hanakapi'ai Falls, one of the more spectacular falls and pool on the north shore. Many people like to reward themselves by swimming in the pool under the falls. Watch out for falling rocks. This is as far as you can go without a permit. The authorities assume anyone going past Hanakapi'ai will be camping.

Guided Hikes

If you want to hike with the comfort and security of a guide, **Kayak Kaua'i Outfitters** at 826–9844 has several types of hiking tours; from half day to 6 day, depending on what you are up for. They go to a waterfall off the Wailua River, the Kalalau Trail, and Koke'e.

Horseback Riding

If you want to let someone else do the walking while you tour the island, horseback riding is available from several outlets.

Po'oku Stables at 826-6777 has a marvelous four hour ride to *beautiful* Kalihiwai Falls (the falls seen from the bridge right after mile marker 25 on the north shore). Tours leave at 9:00 a.m. and 11:00 a.m. each day except Sunday. $90 per person; includes 1 hour for swimming and a snack. 220 pound weight limit. Bring your camera and something to swim in.

CJM Country Stables at 742–6096 has several rides available. An 8:30 a.m. Breakfast Ride—2 hours of riding, 1 hour for a continental breakfast. The ride is over mountains and along the coast to a "secret" (Ha'ula) beach. $65 per person. Then there's a 10:00 a.m. Hidden Beach Ride—2 hours of riding on mountains and along the coast. Beverages included. $48 per person. Finally there's a 1:30 p.m. Ride—1.5 hours of riding on mountains and along the coast. $40 per person. Reservations the day before for the Breakfast Ride; otherwise, reservations the same day. No riding experience necessary. 250 pound weight limit. **CJM Country Stables** is also involved in several types of rodeos. Call them for more information.

Garden Island Ranch at 338–0052 is in the Waimea/Kekaha area. They offer a 1 to 1.5 hour day ride limited to 5 people on the 130 acre ranch and along the ocean. $40 per person. There is a slightly longer sunset ride of about 1.5 hours, also limited to 5 people. $50 per person. 220 pound weight limit. A lower western rim Waimea Canyon ride on private land is offered (2 riders only) for 2–4 hours. Cost is $150–$225 depending on the length of the ride. Soft drinks included.

Can you see all four goats in this picture? They are all out in the open.

Hunting

The State of Hawai'i is generally considered friendly to hunters. Although tightly regulated (hunters should not take this personally, *everything* is tightly regulated here), hunters are welcome and even encouraged in Hawai'i and this is one of the few places where big game is available all year-round.

The problem you will encounter here is the complexity of the regulations. For example, you can only hunt at such-and-such valley with a knife, on the northern bank of the stream, on months with a B in them, if your last name ends with an S, on Tuesdays when the moon is full. Prosecutors will be Violated.

Therefore we recommend that prospective hunters contact the Department of Land and Natural Resources, Division of Forestry and Wildlife (808) 241-3433 for their hunting regulations—ask for the 12 volume set (just kidding). Licenses are required. For

these call (808) 241-3521. In general, the Na Pali wilderness will be your most accessible area to hunt. Goats are plentiful there and pigs are often seen. Both are considered pests in the islands. Goats can be especially destructive to native flora. Also available are black tailed deer and a multitude of game birds. Koke'e State Park and Waimea Canyon State Park are probably the nicest areas to hunt with lots of game and unbeatable scenery. However, getting a permit takes more effort there. The State takes great pains to ensure the health of the parks. Poaching has taken its toll. As a consequence, tighter management of the area is necessary. Field Forestry personnel do an outstanding job and you will find them quite helpful and knowledgeable.

A good island source for information on the subject is Scott Evans at **The Hunting Shop** at (808) 246-2644. He also owns **The Travel Company of Kaua'i** which specializes in organizing hunting trips to all the islands.

If you are *really* looking for the unique hunting experience, the "Forbidden" Island of Ni'ihau is available. The

Robinsons, who have owned the island for more than a century, have a sheep and pig problem. With no natural predators, they have decided to reach out to hunters to clear the island of these pests. For $1,200 their company **Ni'ihau Safaris Limited** at (808) 335–3500 or 338-9869 will fly you over to the island on their private helicopter **(Ni'ihau Helicopters)**, provide you with a guide and two skinners, and allow you to take two animals back to Kaua'i. This day trip is available to two or more hunters at a time. If you are by yourself, they will *consider* it.

JET SKIING

Jet ski rentals are outlawed on Kaua'i, so if this is what you came to the Island to do, you're out of luck.

A kayak can be a marvelous way to see Kaua'i. The quiet, peaceful nature of kayak travel appeals to many. There are three rivers on Kaua'i you can kayak and, of course, there is the open ocean.

Of the three rivers, the Hanalei is the longest but goes mostly through plains (beautiful plains, but plains). The Wailua is very scenic and has the **Fern Grotto** three miles up. It passes through very lush areas. Expect to share the river with riverboats and an occasional water skier. The Hule'ia River in Lihu'e is where they filmed the opening scenes of *Raiders of the Lost Ark*. You paddle past the **Menehune Fish Pond** and through a wildlife refuge.

Ocean kayaking can be an experience of a lifetime. Most opt for guided tours

down the Na Pali Coast (for more information on this trip, see **Adventures** on page 143). There are also guided trips on the south shore. Or you can take a sea kayak to other places independently.

The companies described below provide a variety of services.

Kayak Kaua'i Outfitters in Hanalei at 826–9844 and in Kapa'a at 822–9179. Ocean kayaks rent for $35 per day for 1 person kayak, $60 per day for 2 person. River kayaks are $48 for two person. Roof tie–down included. From May through September they have one day guided Na Pali tours for $115 per person. Lunch included at either **Miloli'i** or **Nu'alolo Kai**. Snorkeling is fabulous at Nu'alolo Kai. Six day Na Pali trip is $900 (See **Adventures**). Arrange in advance. They also have trips to **Kipu Kai** on the south shore (which is only reachable by water) and several other trips. The more involved the trip, the better it is to call them in advance.

Outfitters Kaua'i at 742–9667 has one day guided tours down the Na Pali Coast for $115. They also have river kayak tours and others. Owner Rick Haviland is the guy who guided Paul Theroux down Na Pali in November 1990 in Theroux's book *The Happy Isles of Oceania*. They contend that they screen tourists to determine if you're "up to the job" of a tour.

Although well qualified, we have repeatedly detected a condescending attitude toward tourists. Maybe we are just being sensitive, but we wanted to let you know.

Pedal 'n Paddle in Hanalei at 826–9069 or in Kapa'a at 822–2005. This place specializes in one stop shopping. They rent camping supplies, kayaks, mopeds, and snorkel gear. May through September they have guided one day Na Pali tours for $115. **Pedal n Paddle** and **Kayak Kaua'i Outfitters** strongly compete with each other, so expect roughly equivalent prices.

Paradise River Rentals 245–9580 rents one–man river kayaks for $35, two–man kayaks for $45. Located in Kilohana between Lihu'e and Po'ipu.

Luana of Hawai'i at 826–9195 offers kayak tours from the mouth of the Hanalei River to the Hanalei Bridge for $65. There's not much to see but that's O.K. because you don't go very far. Your $65 can probably be better spent elsewhere. If you really want to river kayak, the Wailua River is more attractive.

Kaua'i Water Ski & Kaua'i Surf Company at 822–3574 has hard shell river kayaks available for $25 for single kayaks, $50 for doubles. Wailua River only. The benefit here is that the kayak is already on the river–just get in and paddle.

Island Adventures aka **Kaua'i by Kayak** at 245–9662. They provide 2.5 hour guided kayak trips up the Hule'ia River for $39. Easy paddling.

With its almost constant trade winds from the northeast, Kaua'i is a rather dependable place to fly a kite. If you want to rent a stunt kite (or just a plain ol' regular kite), the first place you should check is the activities/concierge desk where you are staying. At the present time the only outside company that rents them is **Paradise River Rentals** at 245–9580, near Lihu'e at Kilohana Plantation. The only kite store on the island is **Kaua'i Kite and Hobby Company** at Princeville Center at 826–9144. Stunt kites start at under $20. You can usually buy stunt kites at **Cost-U-Less** in Kapa'a at cheap prices.

Makapili Rock is the best example of a tombolo (see page 106) in all the Hawaiian islands and can only be reached by kayak.

Ocean Tours

When the directors of the 1976 *King Kong* remake wanted to find a beautiful, remote coastline studded with majestic cliffs and glorious valleys, they chose Kaua'i's Na Pali Coast. From the sea, this area of the island takes on a magical quality. Many people dream of seeing the Hawaiian Islands by sea. The Na Pali region is surely the most popular area to cruise, but there are others as well. This can be a fantasy trip. Rough seas are rarely part of the fantasy, but can be part of reality depending on conditions.

If you want to experience Kaua'i by sea, you have several options. From largest to smallest we have big **Cruise Ships** which trek between the islands, briefly stopping at some of the main islands. **Sailing Yachts** cover short distances up and down the coasts. **Big Power Crafts** usually leave from Hanapepe or Hanalei for Na Pali trips and often offer snorkeling. **Power Catamarans** ply up and down Na Pali with similar services. They are a bit rougher and wetter than the bigger power crafts. **Zodiacs** are sturdy inflatable boats which zip up and down Na Pali. Like the power Catamarans, they go in and out of the various sea caves and offer snorkeling, but they are much bumpier and wetter than the power catamarans. The last way to see the island by sea is by **kayak**.

BIG CRUISE SHIPS

American Hawai'i Cruises at (800) 765–7000 has two ships that cruise throughout the islands with brief stopovers. Prices start at $689 for 3 day trips, $839 for 4 day trips and $995 per person for 7 day trips.

SAILING YACHTS

Captain Sundown Catamaran Sailing at 245–6117 has marvelous sailing trips. From October to mid-May they leave from Nawiliwili and sail to Kipu Kai. This is a beautiful long beach not accessible by land (unless your last name is Rice). Here you can swim ashore for snorkeling and strolling. Whale sightings from here are guaranteed or your next trip is free. (That's what they say!) The rest of the year they leave from Hanalei Bay and sail down Na Pali to Honopu Beach, turn around and come back. For the real adventurous, ask about "riding the net." Full lunch included. Prices for their 5 hour trip are $70 per person after May 1994, when they use a new 40 foot catamaran. Only 12 passengers per trip. Sunset trip also available. **Blue Water Sailing** at 822-0525 has a 42-foot Pearson ketch-rigged sailing yacht. From October to mid-May they sail out of Port Allen Harbor in Hanapepe and snorkel at Wahiawa Bay (which is 1 mile from where you start). From mid–May to October they sail out of Hanalei. 4 hour trips are $75 per person; 6 hour trips are $115 per person. 12 person maximum per trip. They also have a $45 sunset cruise. Humpback whales are often encountered between December and March. **Catamaran Kahanu** at 822–0818 puts 20 people on a 36 foot cat for 4 hour Na Pali tours at $85 a pop, February through October. **Captain Andy's Sailing Adventures** at 822–7833 has a four hour trip to either Kipu Kai or Lawa'i Kai for $65 per person, snorkeling

Ocean tours down the Na Pali are wildly popular with visitors. They go in and out of various sea caves and expose passengers to incomparable sights.

when conditions permit (Rx masks available). They put 40 people on their 46 foot catamaran and serve simple foods and beverages. They also have a two hour sunset trip for $40 per person.

BIG POWER CRAFTS

Liko Kaua'i Cruises at 338–0333 offers 4.5 to 5 hour tours of the Na Pali on a 38 foot Radon Craft. Leave from Kikiaola Small Boat Harbor near Kekaha and cruise to Kalalau Beach. On the way back you stop and snorkel at Nu'alolo Kai (which is a fabulous snorkeling spot) if conditions permit. Ask Captain Liko, and they will let you troll for fish on the way back. Liko, a native Hawaiian, fills the trip with narrations, legends, and stories. $75 for adults, $55 for kids, includes snacks and sandwiches.

POWER CATAMARANS

Power catamarans and zodiacs are the two most popular ways to see the Na Pali Coast. Both offer similar trips with zodiacs being rougher but more "thrilling." The choice is yours, but if you have a bad back, go with the catamarans which slice through the waves rather than bouncing over them. We recommend the power catamarans because they are more comfortable. All have similar tours. All of them leave from the north shore. All have a shorter trip up and down the coast that includes about an hour of snorkeling at Nu'alolo Kai, and a longer trip which is similar but *lands* at Nu'alolo Kai. Snorkel and/or hike to an old Hawaiian fishing village. **Hanalei Sea Tours** at 826–7254 has catamaran trips. 4 hour trips for $75 per person, 5.5 hour trips for $100 per person. **Na Pali Adventures** at 826–6804 has 3.5 hour trips for $65 per person, 4.5 hour trips for $85 per person.

ZODIACS

These can provide a rough ride. They were chosen initially because they used to be able to land on beaches all along Na Pali. Now they are being gradually replaced by the power catamarans. If you want to see Na Pali by zodiac, **Captain Zodiac** at 826–7197 has several tours ranging from $75–$105. They also have a winter trip to Kipu Kai for $75. Snorkel or frolic on an "inaccessible" south shore beach for an hour. **Hanalei Sea Tours** at 826–7254 has two zodiac tours identical to the catamaran trips described above.

TIP: If you take the Na Pali trip by power catamaran or zodiac, try to sit on the right side going out and the left side coming back in order to face the coast. Also remember that boats are always a lot smoother in the back than the front.

KAYAK

If you want to see Kaua'i by kayak, see page 130 for more information.

PARASAILING

Parasailing and jet ski rentals are outlawed in the County of Kaua'i. The County wants to avoid becoming too much like O'ahu.

River Trips

There are three ways to take a river trip. You can take a riverboat ride up the Wailua River (often referred to as the only navigable river in all Hawai'i but this is a relative term). **Smith's Motorboat Service** at 822–4111 or **Wai'ale'ale Boat Tours** at 822–4908 go three miles up the river and stop at the Fern Grotto, a large natural

River trips up the Wailua River take you to the Fern Grotto, a fern filled natural amphitheater.

amphitheater with ferns squeezing out every crevice. This is a popular place to get married. It's 30 minutes each way and they spend 30–45 minutes at the site. $10 per person.

You can rent a kayak at any of several places and paddle the Wailua, the Hanalei River, or the Huleʻia Stream. There are also guided river kayak tours. See section on **Kayaks**.

If you want to go up the Wailua on your own but don't like paddling, small power boats are available for rent. **Paradise River Rentals** at 245–9580 rents several types of boats, from small collapsible Porta–botes for $95 per day, to a 6 man Boston Whaler, complete with Jeep for $245 per day. This company also rents all sorts of other items and is a good source for activity related rentals.

Ray's Rentals and Activities at 822–5700 in Kapaʻa rents Porta–botes for $99.

Kauaʻi is justly famous for many things; its incomparable lushness, gorgeous beaches, and balmy nights. But Kauaʻi is not famous for its diving. This is a shame because Kauaʻi has some fabulous dive spots, many of them shore dives. Turtles are common with many of them being downright gregarious. Lava tubes, ledges, and walls are sprinkled around the island. Fish are abundant and varied. Coral growth is not as good as around the Big Island—

at 22° latitude, Kauaʻi is on the fringe of the coral belt. Kauaʻi's many rivers and streams cut visibility in some areas, but you can still see over 100 feet on good days.

Granted, you might find better conditions on the Kona coast of the Big Island. It is dryer there and consequently receives less runoff from its rivers. But this should not dissuade you from enjoying the wondrous underwater sights the Garden Island has to offer.

Kauaʻi's ocean pattern is small summer surf on the north shore, larger summer surf on the south shore and the reciprocal during winter months, so you should plan your diving activities accordingly. Most of the dive operators, however, operate their tours on the south shore year-round since the local government doesn't allow the boats to moor on the north shore. Many also have dives on the west side at Mana Crack and at Lehua Rock, off the coast of Niʻihau. These dives are generally considered advanced dives due to the depths involved. The Niʻihau dive in particular involves at least an hour travel time each way, so those who get seasick should take Dramamine *before* they depart.

Off Niʻihau, however, you will be treated to ridiculously clear water, lots of big life (sharks, rays, turtles, and your best chance at a Hawaiian monk seal) and a close view of the "Forbidden Island." (The Robinsons, who own Niʻihau, *hate* it when you call it that.) See **Adventures** for more on this dive.

Shorties are usually sufficient for most people. Surface water temperatures range from a low of 73.4° in February to a high of 80° in October. Nitrox is available on Kauaʻi at **Nitrox**

Dive Operator	Services	Price of Boat Dive	Rent Gear for a Day	Camera Rental	Dive Computer	Ni'ihau 3–Tank Dive	Dive Certification	Rx Masks
Aquatic Adventures 822–1434	Dive Shop & Boat Dives	$70 – $90	$50 – $65	$50 – $75	$30 Extra	$200	$395	No
Dive Kaua'i 822–0452	Dive Shop & Boat Dives	$75 – $90	$35 – $41	$35	Included	$200 – $215	$395	Yes
Fathom Five 742–6991	Dive Shop & Boat Dives	$75 – $90	$30 – $35	$20	None	$200	$350	Yes
Bubbles Below 822–3483	Boat Dives	$75 – $90	None	None	Included	$200	$350	Yes
Kaua'i Seasports 742–9303	Dive Shop & Boat Dives	$75 – $90	$40	None	None	$200	$295	Yes
Ocean Odyssey 245–8681	Boat Dives	$70 – $85	$39 – $49	$35	Included	$175	$295	Yes
Sunrise Diving 822–7333	Shore Dives	None	None	None	None	None	None	None
Bay Island Water Sprts 826–7509	Shore Dives	None	$45	None	None	None	$425	Yes

Tropical Divers at 822–7333, the same people who run **Sunrise Diving**. Nitrox is a mixture containing more oxygen and less nitrogen and is reported to double your bottom time by creating less residual nitrogen in your blood. Supposedly you can get a 40 minute bottom time at 100 feet (assuming you can stretch your tank that far). We stress that we have not received adequate technical literature on the subject and recommend you consult PADI or NAUI for more information before you breathe the stuff. For advanced divers only.

If you're not sure if SCUBA is for you, **Sunrise** offers free swimming pool opportunities at many hotels around the island. They specialize in offering shore dives to those who have never dived before. For $98, you get a patient and gentle shore dive. Many companies offer dives for those who have never dived before.

As with most places, underwater scooters are not available here.

For the heavy breathers among you, **Bubbles Below** and **Dive Kaua'i** have 100s available.

Dive computers are not available when you rent gear for your own independent dives. *Disposable* underwater cameras in a watertight box for SCUBA are available at most dive shops. The cameras we describe in the chart above are either compact 35MM cameras or SLRs. Price spreads in rental or boat dives are due to different equipment needs. The outfits we recommend are **Bubbles Below** and **Dive Kaua'i.** They are well qualified, professional and knowledgeable. **Bubbles Below** in particular excels at finding great dive spots. Perky Linda and laid back Ken have been doing it here since 1984 and their love of the sport still shows through. You won't go wrong with them. We've had mixed encounters at **Fathom Five** and **Kaua'i Seasports.** Kaua'i's hyperbaric (recompression) chamber is at Kaua'i Veteran's Memorial Hospital in Waimea.

Po'ipu Kapili in Po'ipu is establishing itself as a diver–friendly resort. They are installing facilities to take care of gear and are directly ashore from Sheraton Caves, a popular boat dive spot (or shore dive if you've got the gumption to swim it.) **Hotel Coral Reef** is run by a diver and is gearing up to tailor itself to divers. **Po'ipu Kapili** is the finer of the two.

Kaua'i has many boat dive spots. Since the more resourceful operators such as **Bubbles Below** are always finding new spots, and since you basically go where the boat operators go, we'll forgo a detailed description of all boat dive destinations. Suffice it to say that Sheraton Caves, General Store, Brennecke's Ledge, Turtle Bluffs, and Fishbowl are all popular and all good.

Below is a list of the best **shore dives** on the island:

♦ **Ke'e Beach**; North shore—If the seas are flat on a calm summer day, this area offers interesting shallow relief. The area near the reef dropoff is good, again on calm days.

♦ **Tunnels**; North shore—Arguably the best shore dive on the island with easy access, lots of turtles, reef sharks, lava tubes, caves, and nice underwater relief.

♦ **Cannons**; North shore—Similar to and almost as good as Tunnels. Easy access a decided plus.

♦ **The Hole**; North shore—Located just off the Princeville Hotel. Like the name says, a hole in the reef. Acceptable underwater relief, easy access (especially if you rent your gear from the dive facility just a few feet away, **Bay Island Water Sports**). They will give you precise directions if you call them.

♦ **Kahala Point**; East shore—Entry and exit is a bugger on the lava rocks with crashing surf. Underwater relief is good and there are lots of fish.

♦ **Koloa Landing**; South shore—Easy entry, usually calm conditions year-round and decent coral near the shore. After slightly murky water on entry, the sea is usually quite clear.

♦ **Nohili Point**; West shore—If you're willing to walk with your gear for about 20 minutes on the sand (have I lost you yet?) you'll find good diving just past the big machine gun bunker. Lots of lobster and fairly pristine conditions are the highlight of this dive. Locals drive on the beach with their 4WD vehicles (after letting much of the air out of the tires) but you better be real sure of yourself before you try it in a rental Jeep. The fee for a tow this far out is just short of your first born male child. Only dive during calm conditions, be careful of the sharp rock ledge during entry and exit.

Snorkel

If you have ever looked into a saltwater aquarium and marveled at the diversity of the fish life, snorkeling is an experience you might want to try. Anyone who has ever hovered over hundreds of colorful fish can attest to the thrill you feel from being in their environment.

Where to snorkel depends on how good you are and what kind of experience you want. The best place for beginners is **Lydgate State Park** in Wailua. There you will find an area protected by a ring of boulders which shield you from the strong ocean. Mornings are best. The intermediate snorkeler will find **Ke'e** or **Tunnels** on the north

shore to be fabulous when calm. **Hideaways** is also great during calm seas. **Po'ipu Beach Park** on the south shore usually offers good snorkeling and calm seas on either side of the tombolo. The section on **Beaches** has a description of all the beaches and the different characteristics they possess.

As far as gear goes, there are several places to rent gear on the island. Many people prefer to rent gear when they get here and leave it in the trunk so they may snorkel when the opportunity arises. Your hotel or condo may have gear available. If they don't, try any of the following:

Snorkel Bob's has two small shops; one next to the video store on Ahukini Road in Lihu'e, and the other located just past Po'ipu Shopping Village in Po'ipu. Prices range from $15/week

Ke'e Lagoon offers great snorkeling when it's calm.

for the cheapest to $40/week for the better equipment. Expect to pay more rather than less. Although the equipment is good and we have experienced friendly service on occasion, we are usually treated to unimaginable rudeness at the Lihu'e location. Take your chances here. Rx Masks available. You can also rent in Kaua'i and return equipment to any other island.

Kaua'i Snorkel Rental at 823–8300 rents silicone mask, snorkel, fins, and bag for $4 per day, $10 per week. Although it's more "used" than say, Snorkel Bob's, the price can't be beat. Located in the Coconut Marketplace in Kapa'a.

Brennecke Beach Center rents beach equipment including snorkels and the like. The gear is cheap, but so are the prices. $5 per day for mask, snorkel and fins.

Hanalei Surf Company at 826–9000 has pretty good equipment for only $5 per day, $20 per week.

Pedal 'n Paddle at 826–9069 in Hanalei or 822–2005 in Kapa'a rents gear for $7 per day, $20 per week.

Fathom Five in Po'ipu has gear for $5 per day.

If you've never snorkeled before and desire lessons and assistance, **Sea Fun Kaua'i** at 245–6400 offers guided snorkel tours for $48 per person (children under 12 cost $36). For this price, they'll pick you up at your hotel, take you to a place like Tunnels or Po'ipu Beach, and provide you with gear, snacks, and assistance. Prescription masks are available.

Bay Island Water Sports at 862–7509 has snorkel tours off the Princeville Hotel for $35.

If you're going to be snorkeling, here are a few tips:

• Tropical gloves make snorkeling much more enjoyable. You can grab rocks to maneuver in shallow or surgy areas (please don't grab coral, however).

• Reef shoes with fins designed to fit over footwear are strongly recommended. Although you should never walk on a reef, the rocks and other sharp objects in the ocean make reef shoes a wise investment. Any SCUBA shop can supply them, but alas, nobody rents them. (We rarely go into the ocean without reef shoes).

• Use *Sea Drops* or another brand of anti–fog goop. Spread it *thinly* on the inside of a dry mask, then do a quick rinse. The old fashioned method of spitting in the mask is not very effective and will surely identify you as a former Seahunt fan. (Now you know why Mike Nelson never chewed tobacco. Yuck!)

• Don't use your arms much or you will spook the fish. Gentle fin motion. Any rapid motion can cause the little critters to scatter.

• If you want to feed the fish (and we are not talking about getting seasick) at Lydgate or a similar location, use rabbit food. You can find it at Foodland in Kapa'a. Fill a ziplock bag and at the proper time, make a small slit in a corner to let the water fill the bag. You can dispense the food by squeezing the bag and using a slight wiggle motion to attract the fish. Be careful that the zip part doesn't unzip—a common occurrence. If you can get a few fish interested and they start darting around, others will come. Dispense the food *sparingly*, too much and they will grab a bite and run. If they have to compete, they will increase in numbers. Too much food also makes the water murky—fish don't like murky water and will depart. If you don't want to use rabbit food, a tightly compressed ball of bread works well. Again, dispense *sparingly*. Don't use frozen peas. Although many think that this food is benign, in fact it can be harmful due to the fish's inability to digest it properly. We cannot stress enough the importance of not losing your plastic bag in the water. If a turtle encounters it, he will surely think it to be a jellyfish and choke to death. If you encounter a bag discarded by a thoughtless jerk, please pick it up and wedge it in your suit until you get out of the water.

- Fish are hungriest and most appreciative in the morning (before their coffee).

- If you have a mustache and have trouble with a leaking mask, try a little Vaseline. Don't get any on the glass—it can get *really* ugly.

- Several manufacturers, including Kodak and Fuji, sell disposable waterproof cameras. They are cheap and can provide you with wonderful souvenirs.

If you've always wanted to see what it's like to SCUBA dive but are a bit worried or don't want to go through any hassle, try SNUBA. That's where you take an air tank and place it on a raft which floats above you. From the raft is a 20 foot hose which attaches to a regulator. There you are, underwater up to 20 feet; no tank on your back, no hassle. You have some instructions before you go under and the dive master stays with you the whole time. It can be an exciting way to see the underwater world for the first time. On Kaua'i, try **SNUBA Tours of Kaua'i** at 823–8912. They do their thing off Beach House Beach on the south shore. $49 per person, it should take about an hour.

There are two spas on the island that are worth recommending. **Anara Health and Fitness Spa at The Hyatt** at 742–1234 in Po'ipu has a fabulous full service spa—guaranteed to turn you to jelly. **The Prince Health Club and Spa** at 826–5030 in

Name	Phone #	Fees	# of Courts	Pro Shop	Racquet Rental	Locker Rooms
North Shore						
Princeville Resort Tennis Complex	826–3620	$9–$12 pp per hour	6	Yes	Yes	No
East Shore						
Kaua'i Lagoons Racquet Club	241–6000	$5 pp per hour	8	No	Yes	No
South Shore						
Hyatt Regency Resort and Spa	742–6251	$20 per hour	4	Yes	Yes	No
Po'ipu Kai Tennis Complex	742–1144	$5 pp per hour	8	Yes	Yes	Yes

* Price at the Hyatt includes racquet rental and ball machine.

Princeville is also highly recommended. Both offer the works, and will relax you enough to breeze through the toughest IRS audit.

If you're a real surfer dude or babe, or want to become one, there are several sites around the island which will do quite nicely. Hanalei Bay is justly famous island-wide as one of the best and *most challenging* in Hawai'i. The section on **Beaches** can assist you in picking beaches with surfing possibilities. If you want lessons, the best source on the island is **Margo Oberg's Surfing School** at 742–1750. She is a seven-time world champion. For $40 per hour she will take you to the beach in front of the Kiahuna Plantation

Resort and teach you the basics. If you just want to rent a board, contact your hotel activity desk, Margo, or any of the following: **Progressive Expressions** in Po'ipu at 742–6041. **Hanalei Surf Company** in Hanalei at 826–9000. **Kaua'i Waterski and Surf Company** in Kapa'a at 822–3574.

If you are into tennis, Kaua'i has no shortage of courts. Many hotels offer free courts for their guests. If your hotel doesn't have one, you may contact the courts above to arrange court time. None have lighted courts. Kaua'i County has nine separate municipal courts

scattered around the island. Some were in marginal condition before the Hurricane and the County is taking the opportunity to "repair them right." Consequently, none were open as we went to press and (this is gonna make someone mad) probably won't be open when you get here—they are considered a low priority. But that's OK, the private courts available provide more than enough court space.

At **Kaua'i Water Ski & Kaua'i Surf Company** (822–3574), you can waterski the Wailua River. They rent a ski boat for $85 per hour, $45 for half hour. This includes the boat, driver, ski equipment, and lessons if you wish. Since you pay for the boat and not for skiing, non–skiers can come along for free.

Although whale watching season is December through March, you'll rarely see more than a few scouts before the end of February. March through May are the best months for seeing whales *en masse*. The humpbacks don't come to Hawai'i for the food, but rather to bear their calves. These gentle giants are very social and have been known to come right up to the boats to check out the sightseers. Regulations prohibit the boat companies from initiating this kind of intimacy, but they get close enough to enjoy the whales. If you want to go on a whale watching boat tour, see **Ocean Tours** for a list of the tour boat operators.

winDsurfing

If want to do some windsurfing (formerly known as sailboarding), you'll find that your options are limited on Kaua'i. **Hanalei Surf Company** used to rent boards and give lessons on the north shore, but they decided to get out of the business when the Hurricane hit. Since then, two of their ex–employees, Celeste and Foster have decided to make a go of it. Celeste at **Windsurf Kaua'i** at 828–6838 specializes in lessons for beginners on the north shore. Rates are $75 per person for 3 hours of lessons and practice. Foster is at **'Anini Beach Windsurfing** at 826–9463 and specializes in more advanced lessons and board rentals. He charges $25 per hour for lessons and $15 per hour for practice, or you can rent a board for $50 per day. Since County laws prohibit renting boards at the beach, you will probably have to pick up a board at another location if you don't want any lessons. In any event, Felicia at **Hanalei Surf Company** at 826–9000 will be your best source for windsurfing information should you fail to get results at the above described companies. Other than that there are no other companies in the windsurf rental or lesson business on Kaua'i.

ZODIACS; See Ocean Tours

Beaches don't get any finer than Honopu Beach on Kaua'i's Na Pali Coast.

The activities described below are for the serious adventurer. They can be experiences of a lifetime. We are assuming that if you consider any of them, that you are a person of sound judgment, capable of assessing risks. All adventures carry risks of one kind or another. Our descriptions below do not attempt to convey all risks associated with an activity. These activities are not for everyone. Good preparation is essential. In the end, it comes down to your own good judgment.

NA PALI KAYAK TRIP

If you really want adventure, consider a kayak trip down the Na Pali Coast. June through August are normally considered the only months where ocean conditions permit kayak transit. Kayakers often put in at Ke'e Beach on the north shore, exiting at Polihale Beach on the west shore, a total of 16 miles. Along the way you will encounter incomparable beauty, innumerable waterfalls and sea caves, pristine aquamarine seas, turtles, flying fish, and possibly dolphins. At night you can camp on beautiful beaches, sleeping to the sound of the surf. The experience will stay with you for a lifetime.

There are two ways to do this trip— either on a guided tour, or on your own. Guided tours usually do the entire trip in one day (but not always; see below), offering a more structured, though less leisurely way to see the coast. These trips, usually led by experienced guides, offer the *relative* safety of an expert. The drawbacks to this method are a lack of independent movement, a more brisk paddling pace, and usually a lack of an opportunity to camp. Doing it on your own allows *you* to set the pace and the schedule. You go when you like, how you like, where you like, and at the speed you like. You can rent a two person kayak if you like. The drawback to going it alone is the lack of accompanying expertise. Consideration of this method necessitates a dispassionate evaluation of your skills, abilities, strengths, and weaknesses. Although you don't need to be an expert kayaker, it doesn't hurt. When we did it on our own, our only kayak experience had been a three hour trip up the Wailua River. After experiencing some trouble negotiating the kayak, we came ashore and were fortunate enough to encounter someone who was able to instruct us in the proper paddling and loading techniques. On the trip we experienced ideal conditions, which don't always occur, even during the summer. Please bear in mind that this trip is not for everyone. The Na Pali Coast is wild and unpredictable and you are exposing yourself to the ocean's caprice. The usually calm June through August seas can become difficult with surprising suddenness. Most of the zodiac companies can tell you stories about kayakers who have had to be rescued when they got in over their heads (so to speak).

If you decide to do it on your own, here are a few things to keep in mind. (1) Learn as much as you can about kayaking (*Paddling Hawai'i* by Audrey Sutherland was our main reference when we made the trip), proper paddling and loading techniques are essential. (2) Contact the kayak rental companies for additional information (see page 130 for list of kayak companies). (3) Apply for camping permits well in advance (as much as 6 months in advance might be needed for some Na Pali campsites). (4) Tell someone locally about your itinerary, leaving instructions on what to do if you don't arrive on time. (5) Think through your food requirements (don't assume you'll be living off the land). (6) Any water source you utilize along the way will require water treatment pills to avoid possible contraction of Leptospirosis. Water filters are not considered reliable due to the corkscrew shape of the Leptospirosis bacterium. Fresh water is present at the following beaches along

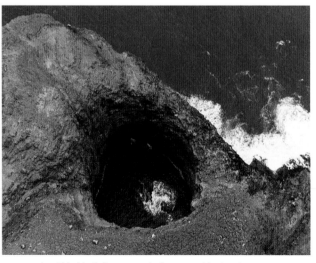

This Na Pali sea cave is frequented by kayakers.

the route: Keʻe, Hanakapiʻai, Kalalau, Honopu, Miloliʻi, and Polihale. (7) Normal June through August conditions mean that the wind and sea are both pushing you in the direction you want to go; but *normal* doesn't mean *always*. Monitor ocean conditions by calling 245-6001 for National Weather Service weather, 245-3564 for National Weather Service; Hawaiian Waters, and 335–3611 for the KUAI Surf Report. (8) In addition to other essentials, make sure you bring waterproof sunblock, a hat, sunglasses, Chapstick and possibly Dramamine. (9) Paddling in the early morning usually offers the calmest seas (sometimes like glass if you are lucky) and easier launchings.

Here's some of what you can expect...

From Keʻe, Hanakapiʻai Beach is slightly over a mile. With campgrounds and a fresh water stream, Hanakapiʻai is a favorite place for hikers to camp (but a little too soon for you). Past Hanakapiʻai, you will start to see caves and waterfalls to your heart's content. Some of the caves are horseshoe–shaped, with separate entrances and exits, and are visited by the zodiacs.

Keep an eye out for dolphins and turtles which become more plentiful as you get farther down the coast. At Kalalau, you have paddled 6 miles. This is a good place to camp with half a mile of sand, fresh water, and portable toilets. Kalalau is as far as hikers can go, so from here on you are in exclusive company.

A mere half mile past Kalalau is Honopu Beach. Check with the State Parks office (808) 241-3444 for their current policy on landing kayaks at Honopu. At the time of this writing, landing crafts of all types including *surfboards* are prohibited. (Although that didn't seem to be stopping anyone during our trip, the penalties, if pursued, are severe.) Technically, the only legal way to visit Honopu Beach is to swim there from Kalalau Beach (which can be hazardous), or to anchor your craft offshore and swim in (which can also be hazardous).

In all the Hawaiian Islands and perhaps in all the world you'll never find a more glorious, moving, and mystical beach than Honopu. Unspoiled Honopu is only accessible by sea. It is actually 2 beaches, separated by a gigantic arch carved into the Na Pali by Mother Nature's furious waves. During the summertime when the pounding Na Pali surf weakens, Honopu is reclaimed from the sea. As you approach by kayak, you're left speechless by the sheer majesty of what unfolds before you. *Vertical* walls 1,200 feet in height are the first characteristics you see from the sea. If you're lucky enough to land, the giant arch draws you towards it like a magnet. As you approach it, you can just make out the cascading waterfall around the bend. This is no mere trickle. This immense cataract can knock you down from its force. The stream continues through the arch and out to sea providing a superb way to rinse off the saltwater. The southern beach of Honopu actually makes a better kayak landing than its northern counterpart but the northern beach is the most dramatic and its unfolding vista will surely stay with you forever.

Past Honopu, listen for goats. Although considered pests by island officials, it's a delight to hear them from your position on the water. At 9 miles you come to a pair of reefs fringing a beach called Nualolo Kai. The waters inside the reef offer world class snorkeling during calm seas (and you wouldn't be here if the seas weren't calm, right?) The buoy markers that are supposed to be here marking the channel opening weren't here, but the opening was easy to see from the water.

Miloli'i is 11 miles into your journey. Camping and fresh water make Miloli'i an inviting respite. There is a reef all along the beach. There are supposed to be buoy markers here also, indicating where there is a channel in the reef, but alas, there were none during our visit (which was in early July, the middle of the kayak season). If they are not there for you, look for the reef opening yourself or keep going to Polihale.

After Miloli'i, you will see a radio transmitter on top of a mountain belonging to Pacific Missile Range Facility. From the transmitter, it's only 3 miles to Polihale. After your surf landing there, you can look forward to dragging your kayak through 1,000 feet of sand in searing heat (unless you sprung for a pickup service from one of the kayak companies, a wise investment if we ever saw one).

Congratulations, you have now joined an elite club of adventurers who have braved the Na Pali. A not–so–quick shower at Polihale Beach and you are ready to dance all night. Or maybe not.

If you don't want to do it on your own (which is a perfectly reasonable decision) consider **Kayak Kaua'i Outfitters'** six day trip. Three days are spent camping at Kalalau Beach. It costs $900, but for that you get the security of an expert.

KALIHIWAI FALLS HIKE

If you dream of finding a beautiful and secluded waterfall to enjoy a picnic or just to ponder, Kalihiwai Falls is probably what you envision. These falls are among the most beautiful on the island (the upper pool especially). To get there you can take the trail across from the turnout near the 25 mile mark on the north shore. Starting at the "Falling Rocks" sign, it goes down through jungle onto a grassy plain. From there you go left following the permanent tire marks until it trails off to the right and encounters Kalihiwai Stream. Pay attention to where it encounters the stream so you can find it on your way back. From here you must walk in the stream for a couple hundred yards until you see a trail on the *other* side of the stream to the falls. Stay near the bank, the rocks are smaller there. You will be able to hear and maybe see the lower falls from this trailhead. From the lower falls, there is a very short but steep trail to the upper pool where you will encounter a magnificent waterfall and pool. The hike to the falls should take 25–30 minutes from the bridge. The trail is heavily used by locals who fish in the stream using a mask and a spear, but it can be difficult to follow where it encounters the stream and is not a professionally maintained trail, so be forewarned. Expect some slippery mud if it has been raining. Hiking boots are recommended. One caveat; the only people you might encounter are riders from Po'oku Stables who park their horses above the falls and hike *down* to the upper pool. They have been known to ask people to leave even though they don't own or even lease the land from the Japanese beverage

The upper pool of Kalihiwai Falls is a fantastic reward for the 25–30 minute hike.

Map # 8—Kalalau Trail

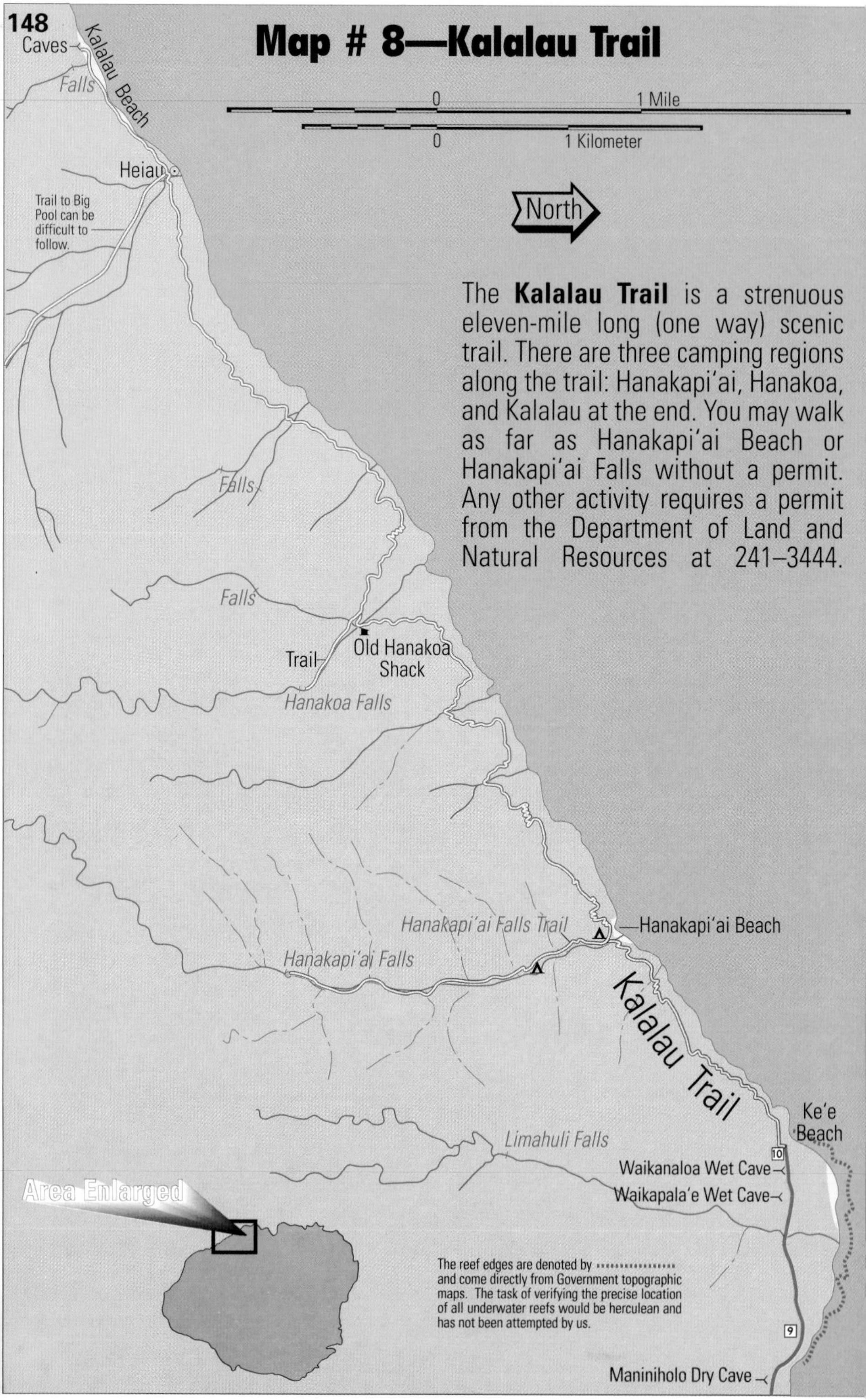

Caves

Falls

Kalalau Beach

Heiau

Trail to Big
Pool can be
difficult to
follow.

0   1 Mile

0   1 Kilometer

North

The **Kalalau Trail** is a strenuous eleven-mile long (one way) scenic trail. There are three camping regions along the trail: Hanakapi'ai, Hanakoa, and Kalalau at the end. You may walk as far as Hanakapi'ai Beach or Hanakapi'ai Falls without a permit. Any other activity requires a permit from the Department of Land and Natural Resources at 241–3444.

Falls

Falls

Trail — Old Hanakoa Shack

Hanakoa Falls

Hanakapi'ai Falls Trail — Hanakapi'ai Beach

Hanakapi'ai Falls

Kalalau Trail

Ke'e Beach

Limahuli Falls

Waikanaloa Wet Cave

Waikapala'e Wet Cave

10

Area Enlarged

The reef edges are denoted by ••••••••••••
and come directly from Government topographic
maps. The task of verifying the precise location
of all underwater reefs would be herculean and
has not been attempted by us.

9

Maniniholo Dry Cave

company which owns it. Use your best judgment. Only for the pioneer. If the trail changes between when we write this and when you hike it, you're on your own.

THE KALALAU TRAIL

The ultimate hike is also the most famous hike in all Hawai'i. Eleven miles of switchbacks, hills, and beautiful scenery. See map on facing page. Much of the trail is narrow and not without hazards. The trail calls for several stream crossings. Don't cross if the water is too high. Don't go if overnight hikes are a problem. To get the proper permits contact:

Division of State Parks
3060 Eiwa Street, Room 306
Lihu'e, Hi. 96766-1875
(808) 241-3444

Two miles into the trail is Hanakapi'ai Beach. This is a beautiful but treacherous beach to swim. From here there is a two mile side trip to Hanakapi'ai Falls, one of the more spectacular falls and pool on the north shore. Many people like to reward themselves by swimming in the pool under the falls. Watch out for falling rocks.

This is as far as you can go without a permit. The authorities assume anyone going past Hanakapi'ai will be camping. If this is your plan, and you have your State camping permit, keep on going. Only nine miles to go from here. At Hanakoa, you have the choice of either camping, continuing to Kalalau, or taking the side trip to Hanakoa Falls which is even lovelier than Hanakapi'ai. Less broken rock around here means less falling rock, so you stand a better chance of not being beaned by a falling rock if you decide to linger under the falls. If you've come as far as Hanakoa, go see the falls, it's not very far and worth the walk.

Back on the trail, you will eventually find yourself at Kalalau Beach. Wow! This is the glorious valley you see from the top of Waimea Canyon Drive at the Kalalau Lookout. The beach, the valley, and the isolation all make Kalalau a magic place. There is a two mile trail inland which takes you to "Big Pool," a large natural pool in the stream.

Have you ever read *Koolau the Leper,* by Jack London? It's the true story of Koolau who fled to Kalalau in the 1880s after authorities refused to let his wife accompany him to the Kalaupapa Leper Colony on Moloka'i. On July 2, 1893 a ship carrying twelve police, fourteen soldiers, the sheriff, many rifles, and a howitzer came ashore to capture Koolau and the other lepers who had joined him. After Koolau shot two of the soldiers dead and a third accidentally shot himself in the head, the authorities decided to leave Koolau alone. He died in Kalalau in 1896 from his affliction.

As you stand on the beach at Kalalau, it's amazing to think that the entire valley had once been populated. It was only in 1919 that this isolated valley was finally abandoned as people sought the life available to them in Lihu'e and other towns. This is as far as you can go. A half mile farther down the coast is the most beautiful beach in all the islands, maybe in all the Pacific. Honopu Beach. There is none finer. Period. The only legal way to visit the beach is to swim there. If you do this, beware that the current is against you coming back. Only during calm seas, only with fins, and

ADVENTURES

Sunset from Hanakapi'ai Beach is only available to hikers and kayakers.

only for strong swimmers. Occasionally Kalalau Beach snakes its way a bit closer and people walk on the rocks most of the way to Honopu. Beware of unexpectedly large waves if you do this. For more information on Honopu, see the **Na Pali Kayak Trip** above.

Kalalau has portable toilets. The waterfall provides freshwater which should be treated before drinking. In fact, all freshwater in nature should be treated to avoid possible bacteriological contamination from animals or people polluting the stream.

If you only want to hike the Kalalau Trail one way, the zodiac tour companies offer drop off and/or pickup service. This can make it delightful since you only have to carry half the supplies you would need for a round trip. See **Ocean Tours** in the **Activities** chapter.

If you want to hike with the comfort

and security of a guide, **Kayak Kaua'i Outfitters** at 826–9844 has a six day guided hike into Kalalau for $900.

NI'IHAU DIVE

For SCUBA divers looking for clean, clear, virgin waters, several dive operators offer three tank dives off the privately owned island of Ni'ihau. (For more information on Ni'ihau, see **Introduction**.) Since this island is in the rain shadow of Kaua'i, there are no permanent streams on the island (and consequently no runoff).

The waters are rich in critters, arches, caves, and pelagics. There's a good chance you will share the water with sharks, so be prepared. The dive requires a forty mile round trip and involves dropoffs, currents and sometimes rough seas. This is not for the inexperienced diver.

No jacket required.

By their very nature, restaurant reviews are the most subjective part of any guidebook. Nothing strains the credibility of a guidebook more. No matter what we say, if you eat at enough restaurants here, you will eventually have a dining experience directly in conflict with what this book leads you to believe. All it takes is one staff person to wreck what is usually a good meal. Many of us have had the experience where a friend referred us to a restaurant using almost reverent terms indicating that they were about to experience dining ecstasy. And, of course, when you go there, the food is awful and the waiter is a jerk. There are many variables involved in getting a good or bad meal. Is the chef new? Was the place sold last month? Was the waitress just released from prison for mauling a customer? We truly hope that our reviews match your experience. If they

don't, please drop us a line and we will reevaluate the restaurant.

We have purposely left out restaurant hours of operation because they change so frequently that the information would be immediately out of date. We *often* leave out whether they serve breakfast, lunch or dinner for the same reason. These decisions are usually made quite capriciously in Hawai'i. If you're going to drive a long way to eat at an establishment, it's best to call first.

Restaurants that stand out from the others are highlighted with a ✓

For each restaurant, we list the price *per person* you can expect to pay. It ranges from the least expensive entrees to the most expensive and includes a beverage and usually appetizers. *The price excludes alcoholic beverages since this component of a meal can be so variable.* Obviously, everyone's ordering pattern is different, but we

Index of Restaurants

thought that it would be easier to compare various restaurants using dollar amounts, than if we used different numbers of dollar signs or drawings of forks or whatever to differentiate prices between various restaurants.

Remember, when we give directions to a restaurant, *mauka side* of highway means "toward the mountain" (or away from the ocean). The shopping centers we mention are on the maps to that area.

Very few restaurants care how you are dressed. A few discourage tank tops and bathing suits and the only ones with dress codes are Dondero's and the Prince Restaurant. Their dress code requires casual resort wear, meaning covered shoes, collared shirts for men, etc.

The difference between local and Hawaiian food can be difficult to classify. Basically, local food combines Hawaiian with American, Japanese, Chinese, Filipino, and several other types and are (not surprisingly) frequented mainly by locals.

Lu'aus, those giant outdoor Hawaiian parties, are described at the end of this section.

If you find yourself with a selection of foods you've never heard of, the descriptions below of various local foods might help. Not all are Hawaiian, but many might be unfamiliar to you.

ISLAND FISH

Ahi–Yellowfin tuna; excellent eaten raw as sashimi.

Ahu–Skipjack tuna, a heavier meat than Ahi.

A'u–A billfish such as marlin or swordfish; steaks are usually broiled or barbecued; meat is firm and white.

Hapu'upu'u–Grouper; white, firm meat.

Kumu–Goatfish; firm, white meat. Steamed kumu is an island specialty.

Mahimahi–Dolphinfish (not the mammal!) White, delicate, moist, firm meat.

Mano–Shark; firm, white meat.

Moi–Threadfin fish; excellent eating fish.

Ono–Wahoo; moderately coarse, white meat that is very moist and 100% delicious.

Snappers–White, firm, yet tender with a mild flavor. 'Opakapaka, Kalekale, and Onaga are the best.

Ehu–Red snapper.

Kalekale–Pink snapper.

Onaga–Red snapper.

'Opakapaka–Pink snapper; especially good to eat.

Uku–Gray snapper.

Ulua and Papio–Jack fish with white, firm, flaky meat.

LU'AU FOODS

Chicken lu'au–Chicken cooked in coconut milk and taro leaves.

Haupia–Coconut pudding.

Kalua pig–Pig cooked in an underground oven called an imu, shredded and mixed with Hawaiian rock salt (outstanding!).

Laulau–Pork, beef, or fish wrapped in taro and ti leaves and steamed.

Lomi salmon–Chilled salad consisting of raw, salted salmon, tomatoes, and 2 kinds of onions.

Namasu–A Japanese salad of raw vegetables marinated in rice vinegar.

Pipi kaula–Hawaiian beef jerky.

Poi–Steamed taro root pounded into a paste. It's a starch that will take on the taste of other foods mixed with it. Some prefer it 1 to 2 days old as the sour taste is more appealing. Visitors are encouraged to try it so they can badmouth it with authority.

OTHER ISLAND FOODS

Apple bananas–A smaller, denser, smoother texture than regular (Wilson) bananas.

Azuki beans–Japanese sugar sweetened red beans; served at the bottom of shave ice.

Barbecue sticks–Teriyaki marinated pork, chicken, or beef pieces barbecued and served on bamboo sticks.

Bento–Japanese box lunch.

Breadfruit–Melon-sized starchy fruit; served baked, deep fried, steamed, or boiled.

Crackseed–Spicy preserved fruits and seeds.

Guava–About the size of an apricot or plum. The inside is full of seeds so it is rarely eaten raw. Used primarily for juice, jelly, or jam.

Huli huli chicken–Hawaiian BBQ chicken.

Kim chee–A Korean relish consisting of pickled cabbage, onions, radishes, garlic, and chilies.

Kona coffee–Grown on the Kona Coast of the Big Island. Smooth, mild flavor; available everywhere.

Kulolo–Steamed taro pudding.

Liliko'i–Passion fruit.

Loco moco–Rice, hamburger patty, egg, and gravy eaten for breakfast.

Lychee–A reddish, woody peel that is discarded for the sweet, white fruit inside. Be careful of the pit. Good large seed lychees are so good, they should be illegal.

Macadamia Nut–A large, round nut grown primarily on the Big Island.

Malasada–Portuguese doughnut dipped in sugar.

Mango–Bright orange fruit with yellow pink skin.

Methley plums–A wild fruit harvested with a permit at Koke'e State Park during the summer months.

'Opihi–Limpets found on ocean rocks. Eaten raw mixed with salt. Texture is similar to clams or mussels.

Pao dulce–Portuguese sweet bread.

Papaya–Melon-like, pear shaped fruit with yellow skin best eaten chilled.

Plate lunch–An island favorite as an inexpensive, filling lunch. Consists of "two scoop rice", a scoop of macaroni salad, and some type of meat, either beef, chicken, or fish. Also called a Box Lunch. Great for picnics.

Portuguese sausage–Pork sausage, very highly seasoned with red pepper.

Pupu–Appetizer, finger foods, or snacks.

Saimin–Noodles cooked in either chicken, pork, or fish broth.

Shave Ice–A block of ice is "shaved" into a ball with flavored syrup poured over the top. Can be served over ice cream or sweet Japanese azuki beans. Very delicious.

Smoothie–Usually papaya, mango, frozen passion fruit, and frozen banana but almost any fruit can be used to make this milk shake-like drink. Add milk for creaminess.

Taro chips–Sliced and deep fried taro, resembles potato chips.

North Shore Restaurants—American

BEAMREACH

Renowned for their outstanding steak and seafood, the Beamreach is widely considered one of the finest restaurants on the north shore. Nearly all entrees are delicious. They use pure Kansas beef. The ono fish is highly recommended when it's available. Their strawberry daiquiris are legendary.

There were only four restaurants still closed as we went to press which were scheduled to reopen, and this is one of them. **Beamreach, Charo's,** and **Bali Hai** will probably be open by the time you read this, but we wanted to be thorough. The **Beach House** in Po'ipu was scheduled to reopen in July 1994. All the remaining restaurants listed are open. Prices for the Beamreach are $15–$40. Reservations required. Located in Princeville next to Pali Ke Kua condominiums.

BUBBA'S BURGERS 826–7839

Funky place to get decent (but a bit small) burgers and very popular with locals for their down home feel. Their motto is, "We cheat tourists, drunks, and attorneys." So if you are a drunk attorney visiting the island, you're on your own, counselor. $5–$10. Located in Hanalei and Kapa'a, can't miss em.

CHARO'S 826–6422

Steak and seafood with a bit of Mexican thrown in. Owned by Charo (aka chuci chuci) they have garnered a reputation as being a good place to have a drink, not a great place to eat. Their reopening brings several changes. The food will be more Sizzler style; order at the counter and they will bring it out to you. The manager tells us that tips are not expected. (Oh, the staff will love us for that.) The oceanfront view is now enhanced with large spotlights illuminating the waves. Regarding the food, we'll have to wait and see. They were in the final stages of rebuilding as we went to press and should be open by the time you read this. $10–$25. Credit cards, no reservations. Lounge and gift shop on premises.

CHUCK'S STEAK AND SEAFOOD 826–6211

Located in Princeville Shopping Center. As the name implies, steak and seafood. Western atmosphere (complete with hanging saddles). $5–$10 for lunch, $15–$25 for dinner. Average wine list. Reservations recommended. Credit cards.

HANALEI DOLPHIN RESTAURANT 826–6113

A north shore tradition with very good seafood in a pleasant, open air atmosphere. They are often busy and don't take reservations–so if waiting bothers you, arrive early or you're out of luck. The seafood chowder is usually great. So is most everything else. $15–$30. Dinner only. Located in Hanalei, can't miss it.

HANALEI GOURMET 826-2524

The owner, "Big Tim" Kerlin is a friendly fellow and his staff will make you feel comfortable. Dinner menu is mostly deli but be sure to ask about the specials. This place can be pretty busy in the evening, and it's a good place to stop and have a drink after a hard day's exploring. Free entertainment most nights, full bar. Breakfast, lunch, and dinner. Take-out sandwiches from the adjacent deli. Small capacity. Fun place. Dinner is $7–$15. In Hanalei Center in Hanalei. Credit cards.

PRINCE RESTAURANT AND BAR 826–5030

Located at **The Prince** golf course, they offer steak and seafood. Lunches are $10–$15, with dinners $15–$25. Reservations recommended. Banquet facilities available. Located just before Princeville in the Prince Golf Course. Credit cards.

ZELO'S CAFE AND ESPRESSO BAR 826-9700

Burgers and salads are the order of the day at this small cafe. Large coffee and espresso selection. Brunch on Sundays. Although classified as a cafe, they have a full bar and use it to its maximum. Live music some nights with no cover charge. Food will cost you $5–$12. Located in Princeville Center. Credit cards.

North Shore Restaurants—Pacific Rim

CAFE HANALEI 826-2760

This is a hard restaurant to classify. They have a vast menu with entrees from all over the world. Not just Pacific Rim but Mediterranean as well. In general, it falls in the Pacific Rim category with lots of American, Japanese, and a few local entrees. For breakfast you can have oatmeal for $3.25, a Choshoku breakfast for $25.00 and many things in between. Menus are long and change often. Lunch generally will run you $10–$15 featuring hamburgers, steak, seafood, and numerous Japanese entrees. Dinner includes lamb, sauteed shrimp with steamed taro, Hawaiian snapper and a host of others. Expect to pay $15–$35 for dinner. Located in the Princeville Hotel in Princeville. Credit cards. Nice view of Hanalei Bay, outdoor seating available.

North Shore Restaurants—Italian

CASA DI AMICI 828-1388

Pastas, fresh fish, and other Italian dishes in a small setting. Their pastas and sauces are listed separately so you can mix and match as you like. Many entrees are offered as light or full portions, a nice option. Most nights they have piano entertainment. Decent wine list. $15–$35. Reservations recommended. Credit cards.

HANALEI BISTRO 826-9436

Northern Italian food well prepared and presented. In addition to pasta, they have steaks, fish, homemade sausages, and several other intriguing entrees. Pizzas come with ingredients such as shrimp, papaya, and asiago. Dinner will run $15–$25. No view. They accept mainland checks. Located in Ching Young Village in Hanalei. Credit cards.

KILAUEA BAKERY & PAU HANA PIZZA 828-2020

This very small (seats 10 indoors and out) combination bakery and pizza parlor offers fresh-baked pastries and bread in the morning starting at 7:00 a.m. The pizza is slightly above average with distinctive toppings you've probably never tried such as Feta cheese, Swiss chard, smoked mahimahi, and Kalamata olives. Located in the Kong Lung Center in Kilauea. Price for pizza, $5–$15. Pizza by the slice available.

LA CASCATA 826-2761

Upscale Italian food. Try the sauteed Hawaiian snapper with wild mushroom custard, spinach leaves and a pommery mustard sauce. Or the cannelloni of roasted duck with wilted greens, chives veal jus. Or settle for the linguine with chicken breast, sun-dried tomatoes and shiitake mushrooms. Hard to go wrong here, unless, of course, you're on a budget. Dinner only. Reservations recommended. $15–$45. Located in the Princeville Hotel in Princeville. Credit cards.

PIZZA HANALEI 826-9494

Located in Ching Young Village, the pizza is decidedly average. If you don't mind driving 10 minutes, Pau Hana Pizza in Kilauea is better. $5–$15.

North Shore Restaurants—Hawaiian

BLACK POT LUAU HUT 826-9871

Hawaiian cuisine, local favorite. Family owned business for 10 years. Vegetables are grown in a home garden. Fish from local fishermen or personally caught. Very small, like you're eating in a friend's kitchen. They make kalua pig the old-fashioned way—they bury it! Come here if you want good local food in a friendly environment, but not if you want your dinner served on Baccarat crystal. $6–$10. No reservations. Located on Aku Road in Hanalei.

North Shore Restaurants—Local

HANALEI WAKE-UP CAFE 826–5551

Good place to grab a quick breakfast in the morning. Cheap, and reasonably good food, good coffee, and efficient service. The theme here is surfing. The omelettes are acceptable but the french toast is great. Try a muffin to go. $5–$8 per person. At night, they *occasionally* serve Mexican food for $8–$12.

TAHITI NUI 826–7320

Ask someone who lives on Kaua'i about the best place to have dinner on the north shore, and many will tell you Tahiti Nui. Hours used to be notoriously flexible, you just had to go with the flow, and that was half the fun. With their reopening, they claim a new dedication to reliability. They also now serve breakfast in addition to lunch and din-

ner. Lunch consists of burgers and the like. Dinner prices have gone up a bit with their new attention to food quality. The result is a restaurant that is easy to recommend. The bar at night is the center of the action with local talent brought in to keep things jumping. The local color is delightful. You never know what will happen at Tahiti Nui. The dinner menu consists of local dishes, steak, and seafood. They have a lu'au, usually on Wednesdays and Fridays. Although occasionally disappointing, Tahiti Nui is a great north shore spot to enjoy the local flavor. $6–$12 for lunch, $15–$30 for dinner. About $35 (drinks not included) for the lu'au. Credit cards. Reservations required for the lu'au.

VILLAGE SNACK AND BAKERY SHOP 826-6841

Their baked goods are *excellent* and reasonably priced. Ambiance is. . .well, they don't have any. But if you want a place that sells lunch, cake, and jewelry, then this is the place for you. Decent, cheap food. $7–$10. Plate lunches $6. Located in Ching Young Village.

North Shore Restaurants—Mexican

TROPICAL TACO

The green van you see on your right as you pull into Hanalei is a familiar island fixture. Tropical Taco has been serving good, hearty, and cheap Mexican food since 1978. Owner Roger Kennedy will serve it any way you like it. Don't confuse this with a "Roach Coach." Roger's food is excellent. With no beverages other than lemonade, and no place to eat, Tropical Taco is still an island favorite and a great place to grab a bite to eat when you're on the run on the north shore. The Fat Jacks are tasty and plate lunches are a bargain. No phone, no credit cards, no checks, no tables—No kidding!

East Shore Restaurants—American

AL AND DON'S 822-4221
There is only one reason to eat here, and frankly it's a pretty compelling reason. From the window booths, you can hear, see, and smell the ocean. With regards to the food, the quality is adequate and the price is quite reasonable. If you're looking for an obsequious wait staff, go elsewhere. Indifference will no doubt be the special of the day. Breakfast generally will run about $5. Dinners are $8–$15. Go for the breakfast. Located in the Kaua'i Sands Hotel in Kapa'a. No reservations. Credit cards.

AUNTIE SOPHIE'S GRILL 823-0833
Slightly above average burgers and hot dogs. $4–$10. Decent bargain. Located in the Coconut Marketplace in Kapa'a.

BARBECUE HOUSE 822-7872
Cheap oriental BBQ if you don't mind being ignored. $5–$8. Located in Kapa'a Shopping Center (the one with a Big Save in it).

BUBBA'S BURGERS 823-0069
See Bubba's review under North Shore.

BULL SHED 822-3791
Quite popular with locals and tourists alike and known for good hearty fish and seafood. All entrees come with a choice of salad or. . . salad. Sorry, no soup. The window seats are particularly close to the water (we've been there when the waves actually splashed against the glass), but

arrive 10–15 minutes before they open to get one. Although the service is slow, the food is good and the portions are on the large side. $18–$25. Heck of a bargain for the price if you have a window seat. Located in Kapa'a on the ocean side of the highway across from Kaua'i Village. Credit cards. Reservations only for six or more.

BUZZ'S STEAK AND LOBSTER 822-0041
Located in the Coconut Marketplace, they have above average food in a pleasant atmosphere with good service. The salad bar is gone, but otherwise it's still the same old Buzz's. $7–$15 for lunch, $15–$25 for dinner. Credit cards. No reservations.

CHARLIE'S PLACE 822-3955
Sandwiches with a few other specialties. No reservations. $6–$10 for lunch, $6–$17 for dinner. Located on mauka side of highway in northern Kapa'a. Credit cards.

DUANE'S ONO-CHAR BURGER 822-9181
Duane's Ono-Char Burger is an institution on Kaua'i. Now into their second decade, Duane's still serves the best burgers on the island (*sans* Duane). Although a bit too pricey, their specialty burgers such as the teriyaki burger and the mushroom burger are the tastiest you'll find anywhere. One order of fries is enough for two people, and their marionberry shakes are outstanding. The cement outdoor tables come complete with shade from the large monkeypod tree, and scrawny cats who subsist almost solely on french fries. $7–$14. Located on the highway in Anahola, can't miss it.

Fish Hut 822-1712

Fish and chips with a few fish steaks and sandwiches. $6–$10. Located in the Coconut Marketplace, Kapaʻa.

Flying Lobster 822-3455

Located in the Kauaʻi Coconut Beach Resort, this restaurant is called **THE VOYAGE ROOM** during breakfast and lunch. This open-air restaurant has views of the ocean and reasonably good food. Their buffets, although lacking a desert and bread, are well-prepared, nicely presented, and a good value at around $13. The menu has changed several times over the years. Service is cheerful and attentive. Be sure to take a walk along the beach after dinner. If sand is not your thing, there is a paved path going south, interrupted for a bit. Breakfast buffets are usually good. $15–$25 for dinner. Most entrees come with a choice of lobster in addition to the main entree. Reservations recommended. Credit cards.

Garden Isle Bake Shoppe 245-9593

Sandwiches and pastries. Nothing special. In the Pacific Ocean Plaza in Nawiliwili.

Gaylord's Restaurant 245-9593

Excellent continental food in a beautiful, open air lanai setting. Evenings here are romantic for honeymooners. $10–$15 for lunch, $20–30 for dinner. Reservations recommended. Located in Kilohana just south of Lihuʻe. Credit cards.

Ginger's Grille 822-5557

Steak and seafood. Not much service, not as clean as we would like. $8–$20. You can do better. Located in Kauaʻi Village in Kapaʻa. Credit cards.

Jacaranda Terrace 245-1955

Steak and seafood with occasional dinner buffets. Good food at slightly elevated prices. Their breakfast buffets are very well prepared and cost a little over $10. Friendly service in a calm, relaxed atmosphere with pleasant views overlooking the pool. $20–$35. Located in the Outrigger Hotel between Kapaʻa and Lihuʻe. Credit cards.

JJ's Broiler 246-4422

Steak and seafood. JJ's has been a fixture on Kauaʻi since 1968 and opened this new building in 1989. Try the Slavonic steak (cooked filets quickly dipped in wine, garlic, and butter). With a grand view of Kalapaki Bay, large glass windows, and sailboats hanging from the ceiling upstairs, JJ's rarely disappoints. The lounge downstairs has beachfront outdoor tables but is known for their weak drinks. $15–$35. Located in Anchor Cove Shopping Center in Nawiliwili. Reservations recommended. Credit cards.

Jolly Roger 822-3451

Part of a chain, this is a good place to get cheap, dependable meals. Popular with locals for their bargain breakfasts. In the same genre as Sizzler with some outdoor tables. No reservations. $5–$15. Located behind Coconut Marketplace in Kapaʻa. Credit cards.

Kalapaki Beach Burgers 246-6330

Gourmet burgers such as buffalo, mahi-mahi, *even beef*. The buffalo is leaner and more loosely packed making for delicious eating. $5–$10. This is the guy who sold Duane's to Duane. Located next to Anchor Cove Shopping Center in Nawiliwili.

KAPA'A FISH AND CHOWDER HOUSE 822-7488

With a name like Kapa'a Fish and Chowder House, you expect great clam chowder and although *slightly* lacking in clam and potatoes, the chowder is outstanding. The entrees are very good (the coconut shrimp is a dream) but the portions are on the small side. They have a new policy (I feel a rant coming on). After your first serving of bread, they charge you almost $2 per extra helping. Any place that charges close to $20 per entree and delivers small portions should be *stuffing* you with free bread (OK, end of rant). Ambiance is calm and restful; tables placed to allow for privacy. Service attentive but not intrusive. $15–$30. Reservations recommended. Located on mauka side of highway in northern Kapa'a. Credit cards.

KAUA'I SMOKEHOUSE 822-7427

BBQ specialists who serve hearty food such as BBQ ribs and chicken, rice, beans, and macaroni salad prepared for take out. $5–$10. Located under the clock tower in Kaua'i Village in Kapa'a.

(LIHU'E) BARBECUE INN 245-2921

Steak and seafood with an some oriental dishes, (Lihu'e) Barbecue Inn is very popular with locals who appreciate the good food and the large portions. The pies are a heck of a bargain. A good value all around. Located on Kress Street in Lihu'e—don't let the outside condition fool you. $10–$25.

ONO FAMILY RESTAURANT 822-1710

This is the place to fill that long standing need to eat buffalo (tasty but stronger than beef). The food is good,

the service is pleasant but not always efficient. $5–$7 for breakfast, $5–$15 for dinner. No reservations. Located on ocean side of the highway in downtown Kapa'a. Credit cards.

PACIFIC ROOM AT THE KAUA'I RESORT 245-3931

Steak and seafood. Located in the Kaua'i Resort in Kapa'a, they like to brag about their buffets which are not available every night. The breakfast buffet selection is not very good with a better dinner buffet. The food is generally good with uneven service. They usually have earlybird specials for around $10. These are a great deal. Otherwise, expect $10–$25. Credit cards.

PAPAYA'S NATURAL FOODS 823-0190

A health food store that also serves a few plate specials such as vegetarian lasagna, mixed vegetables, etc. $5–$10. Located in Kaua'i Village in Kapa'a. Credit cards.

PARADISE CHICKEN N RIBS 822-2505

Chicken and ribs are the specialty (*boy, that's a surprise*) in this little stand in the Coconut Marketplace in Kapa'a. $6–$10.

PLANTER'S RESTAURANT 245-1606

Located on the highway in Hanama'ulu in an old plantation building. This steak and seafood restaurant specializes in prime rib which they do fairly well. The interior is decorated with old sugar plantation machinery and fixtures. Service is difficult to predict. $15–$30. Tables are a bit cramped but booths are fine. Reservations recommended—ask for a booth next to the small waterfall. Credit cards.

ROB'S GOOD TIMES GRILL 246-0311

Sort of a sports/Karaoke bar with burgers and similar type entrees. $5–$10. Located in the Rice Shopping Center off Rice Street in Lihu'e.

SIDEOUT BAR & GRILL 822-7330

More of a bar than a grill. Have a hot dog or burger with your beer. $4–$8. Located on ocean side of highway in downtown Kapa'a.

SIZZLER 822-7404

Just like the Sizzlers on the mainland but a bit nicer. $5–$15. Located on mauka side of highway in southern Kapa'a across from the Shell Station. Credit cards.

THE TERRACE RESTAURANT 241-6080

Located in the Lagoons near the Westin Kaua'i, they are only open for lunch. Good place to stop after a morning round of golf—which is why it is the only restaurant open in the Lagoons. Around $15.

TIP TOP CAFE AND BAKERY 245-2333

Their motto is "serving the people of Kaua'i for 75 years." This place is recognized by locals as an outstanding bargain for breakfast and lunch. They also have a bakery and counter service. The menu includes some non-traditional breakfast items such as Beef Stew and Oxtail Soup served first thing in the morning. Banana and macadamia nut pancakes come large, fluffy, light, but hardy and very filling. Good coffee. $5–$7, no entrees are more than $6. Pleasant service. They were a bargain even when they were kind of run down. But their recent remodeling makes them a steal. Check out the bakery

before you leave. Their baked goods are always good. Unpretentious hardiness. Located on Akahi Street in Lihu'e.

VOYAGE ROOM—SEE FLYING LOBSTER

WAILUA MARINA RESTAURANT 822-4311

Located in Smith's Tropical Paradise near the Wailua River, they serve good steak and seafood (the fresh fish is particularly good). Weather permitting, the seating on the lanai overlooking the river is best, whereas the interior is nothing special. They tend to get a lot of tour bus business so you may end up dining in a crowd. Reservations recommended, small wine list. Owned by the same family that owns the Green Garden in Hanapepe. $7–$10 for lunch, $10–$30 for dinner. Credit cards.

East Shore Restaurants—Italian

ALOHA KAUA'I PIZZA 822-4511

Pizza stand located in Coconut Marketplace in Kapa'a. Average pizza for a pizza stand. $5–$10.

CAFE PORTOFINO 245-2121

Upscale Italian food with a nice open-air ambiance and lanai with partial view of Kalapaki Bay. Located in the Pacific Ocean Plaza in Nawiliwili. Adequate wine list. Excellent food. Very popular, reservations recommended. They often have a live jazz band in the lounge. Dinner is $15–$25. Credit cards.

East Shore Restaurants—French

WILD PALMS BISTRO 822-1533

Located in Coconut Marketplace in Kapa'a. Formerly South of the Border

Mexican Restaurant and still the same owners. They started out French and are moving toward continental. We'll put them in French until they settle on their category. Good food but ambiance needs to improve to justify price. Pretty good wine list. $15–$30. No view. Credit cards.

East Shore Restaurants—Pacific Rim

A PACIFIC CAFE 822–0013
Hard to classify this one. Sort of the best from many places around the world. Since it opened in 1990, chef Jean-Marie Josselin has won numerous accolades for his world class food and exquisite attention to details. We've never heard a bad word spoken about the food. Everyone has a favorite. Presentation is almost as good as the food itself, and the setting is pleasant (but no view). The only criticism people have is that you can spend a lot of money and still leave hungry. $15–$40 per person. Reservations strongly recommended (usually full). Located in Kaua'i Village in Kapa'a. Credit cards.

East Shore Restaurants—Mexican

NORBERTO'S EL CAFE 822–3362
Consistently good Mexican food at reasonable prices. Service is usually friendly. $7–$15 per person. Located on the main highway in downtown Kapa'a.

SI CISCO'S MEXICAN CANTINA & RESTAURANTE 246–1563
This quasi-upscale Mexican restaurant garners mixed reviews. You'll pay half the price and get better food at either Taqueria Nortenos in Po'ipu, or the Tropical Taco van in Hanalei but you can't (or won't) sit down at either one. Their food is better than Pancho and Lefty's in Koloa, but that's not saying much. $10–$15 for dinner. Sporadic nightly entertainment. Located in Kukui Grove Shopping Center in Lihu'e. Credit cards.

TACO DUDE 822–1919
A taco bar in Coconut Marketplace. They serve good food at cheap prices. Good place to talk to others while you eat. $3–$6.

East Shore Restaurants—Chinese

DRAGON INN 822–3788
Probably the best Chinese food on the east shore. The Dragon Inn is located on the second floor in the Waipouli Plaza (mauka side of Kuhio Highway between 580 and 581). The food is excellent, the service is excellent, and the portions are large. $10–$20 for dinner with lunch specials for $5. Ambiance is clean and unadorned. Credit cards.

HO'S CHINESE KITCHEN 245–5255
Unappetizing Chinese food in unclean surroundings. Eat here at your own peril. $7–$15 per person. Located in Kukui Grove Shopping Center in Lihu'e.

KAUA'I CHOP SUEY 245–8790
Quality Cantonese food in reasonably pleasant surroundings. Although the service is uneven, this is still a good value (although not as good as it used to be). They specialize in sizzling platters (where food is placed on a metal plate hot enough to ignite upholstery from three feet away). Located in Pacific Ocean Plaza in Nawiliwili. $7–$15.

MEMA THAI/CHINESE 823-0899

Good food, friendly and attentive service. They have very imaginative dishes (example; an appetizer consisting of coconut milk, peanut butter, Kaffir leaves and seasoning with cucumber sauce on the side served with fish or shrimp). The food is excellent and not too expensive. Owned by the same family that owns the King and I, another winner. $6–$10 for lunch, $10–$20 for dinner. Located in Sizzler shopping center in southern Kapa'a across from Shell Station. Credit cards.

PANDA GARDEN CHINESE RESTAURANT 822-0092

This is an above average Chinese restaurant with pleasant, light surroundings. The food is good and fresh. The hot and spicy is not much of either. The portions are a bit small so order with this in mind. Located in Kaua'i Village Shopping Center in Kapa'a. $10–$15. Credit cards.

PO'S CHINESE KITCHEN 246-8617

This is *literally* a hole in the wall. With its location inside the Shell gas station in Lihu'e (don't laugh), they dispense the cheapest food on Kaua'i. *Most* items are under $1. Hot box lunches. The ambiance? Get real. No Credit cards, (not even Shell)

WAH KUNG CHOP SUEY 822-0560

Good selection of quality Cantonese food at a very reasonable price. Take out available. Located in the Kinipopo Shopping Center in southern Kapa'a next to the Shell Station. $5–$10.

East Shore Restaurants—Korean

KOREAN BBQ 823-6744

Like the name says, served as plate lunches in a clean environment. A reasonable amount of food for the money. $5–$10. Located in the Kinipopo Shopping Center in southern Kapa'a next to the Shell Station.

KUN JA'S 245-8792

You would never think of going in if someone didn't turn you on to this place. Well, someone just did. *Very* simple surroundings (and an unfortunate exterior), they are renowned for their consistently good food at cheap prices. Customers are all repeats (since few venture into it for the first time). Located on Rice Street in Lihu'e near Hardy Street. $5–$10.

East Shore Restaurants—Japanese

ELSIE'S BENTO AND RAMEN 823-8314

Unpretentious Japanese plate lunches. $5–$8. Located in Kaua'i Village in Kapa'a.

HANAMA'ULU CAFE, TEA HOUSE & SUSHI BAR 245-5211

Both Japanese and Chinese food served in a delightful atmosphere. There are gardens out back, a koi pond, individual tea rooms (if you reserve one) and relaxed but attentive service. Oh, and did we mention that the food is consistently great and well presented? You will almost certainly like this place. Sushi bar. Located on the main highway (56) just outside of Lihu'e in Hanama'ulu. $8–10 for lunch, $10–$25 for dinner. Reservations recommended. Credit cards.

KIIBO RESTAURANT 245-2650

Much more Japanese than other Japanese restaurants with more traditional entrees (the menu consists of photos of each dish). The food is usually good, the service usually acceptable (though a bit slow). Nearly all the customers will be Japanese and they don't take credit cards because, they tell us, "it's not the Japanese way." Oh, OK. Sushi is well prepared. $10–$25.

KINTARO RESTAURANT 822–3341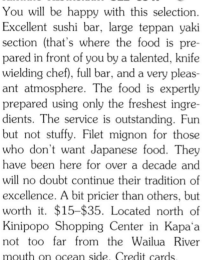

You will be happy with this selection. Excellent sushi bar, large teppan yaki section (that's where the food is prepared in front of you by a talented, knife wielding chef), full bar, and a very pleasant atmosphere. The food is expertly prepared using only the freshest ingredients. The service is outstanding. Fun but not stuffy. Filet mignon for those who don't want Japanese food. They have been here for over a decade and will no doubt continue their tradition of excellence. A bit pricier than others, but worth it. $15–$35. Located north of Kinipopo Shopping Center in Kapa'a not too far from the Wailua River mouth on ocean side. Credit cards.

SUMO RESTAURANT 246–0113

Unfriendly, ungracious, and overpriced given the setting. The sushi scared us. We think you can do *much* better down the street at Tokyo Lobby. $15–$25. Located in Kukui Grove Shopping Center. Credit cards.

TOKYO LOBBY 245–8989

Located in the Pacific Ocean Plaza in Nawiliwili. Clean, pleasant, and comfortable Japanese restaurant with a gracious and attentive staff. Good food, good Sushi Bar, good restaurant. $10–$15 for lunch, $15–$25 for dinner. Reservations recommended. Credit cards.

East Shore Restaurants—Thai

KING AND I THAI CUISINE 822–1642

You won't find anybody who has a bad thing to say about the King and I; and for good reason. Owned by the same family that owns Mema Thai/Chinese Cuisine, the food, service, and value are excellent. We'd like to recommend a particular dish, but they're all good. Located in the Waipouli Plaza, mauka side of highway in Kapa'a. $10–$20. They burn incense as an offering to Buddha when they open everyday, so wait a bit longer if the smell of *strong* incense bothers you. Credit cards.

MEMA THAI/CHINESE CUISINE

See review under Chinese food.

East Shore Restaurants—Filipino

MANILA FAST FOOD RESTAURANT 822–0521

Just like the name says. They also serve local style food in a cheap setting. Prices are $5–$8. Located in the Sizzler shopping center in southern Kapa'a across from the Shell station.

East Shore Restaurants—Hawaiian

ALOHA DINER 822–3851

This small diner is a good place to try simple, hearty Hawaiian food without shelling out the money you pay for a lu'au. The kalua pig is acceptable, but not as good as you will get at a lu'au. They also have lomi salmon, poi, laulau and 'opihi when available. The food is usually good. The staff is friendly and very laid back. $7–$12. Located in the Waipouli Complex, mauka side of highway in Kapa'a.

East Shore Restaurants—Local

DA BOX LUNCH PLACE 245-5151

Da best place to stock up for a picnic lunch. Box lunches normally include things like chicken, hash, shrimp, egg rolls, rice balls, macaroni salad, etc. and are very popular on Kaua'i. Quality food, at a cheap price. Only open from 6:00 a.m. to 1:00 p.m. $4–$9. A real good bargain. Located on ocean side of main highway in Lihu'e.

DANI'S RESTAURANT 245-4991

Adequate local food. At $5–$10 per person, a good value. Located on Rice Street in Lihu'e.

HAMURA SAIMIN STAND 245-3271

There's no good way to put it, so let's be blunt; the place is a dump. You half expect cock fights to be going on in the corner. That said, they have *some of the best saimin on Kaua'i*. It is wildly popular with locals, and people come from other parts of the island to eat here. Their selection is scant, but the food is excellent. Available for take out. As a bonus, they have *wonderful* shave ice which we strongly recommend. (That part of the business is called **HALO HALO SHAVE ICE**.) Make sure to get it with ice cream on the bottom. Located on Kress Street in Lihu'e (off Rice Street).

JONI HANA LOCAL GRINDS 245-5213

Very popular for lunch. If you're interested in trying some local dishes, you can see them and ask about them before you buy since it's served cafeteria style. $4–$7. Located in Kukui Grove Shopping Center in Lihu'e.

KINO'S KITCHEN 246-0106

This was a truly vile place when it was Kino's Kaua'i Kim Chee. They changed the menu and name just as we went to press. We'll have to see if they are any better. Located in Kukui Grove Shopping Center in Lihu'e.

KOUNTRY KITCHEN 822-3511

Dandy place to get breakfast in the morning with quality food at reasonable prices. Lunch and dinner are also a good value. You might have to wait during peak eating times. Simple American/local food in a simple atmosphere. $5–$8 for breakfast, $7–$12 for lunch or dinner. Located on mauka side of highway in northern Kapa'a.

MA'S FAMILY RESTAURANT 245-3142

A little hole in the wall on rarely visited Halenani Street in Lihu'e (Rice to Kress to Halenani). They serve surprisingly good food and have a friendly staff. Breakfast is a bargain; try the papaya pancakes or kalua pig omelettes. Coffee is free with meals—nice touch. Breakfast or lunch will cost you $4–$10. Give them a try if you don't mind the location.

OK BENTO AND SAIMIN 245-6554

The bento is just OK (what did you expect). The atmosphere is decidedly dirty. $4–$8. Located on Rice Street in Lihu'e.

OLYMPIC CAFE 822-5731

The Olympic Cafe has been on Kaua'i since before WWII. The interior is spartan and dull. Although classified as local, they have a lot of American dishes at reasonable rates. Don't expect potted plants and indoor waterfalls—

expect decent service, decent food, and decent prices. That's why they've been here so long. Located on mauka side of highway in Kapa'a. $5–$10.

RS Restaurant 823-6181

Definitely unpretentious but popular with locals. Eclectic menu. $3–$7 for breakfast, $5–$7 for lunch, $10–$15 for dinner. Located in Waipouli Complex on mauka side of highway in Kapa'a.

Sampaguita's 245-5322

Cheap, simple breakfasts and box lunches. $3–$6. Located across from the Shell Station in Hanama'ulu.

Sidewalk Cafe 245-3581

Dirty. If you are at Kukui Grove already and want some local food, walk over to Joni Hana Local Grinds. $5–$10. Located in Kukui Grove Shopping Center in Lihu'e.

Tammy's Okazu-Ya 246-0460

Box lunches to go. $3–$6. Located on Rice Street in Lihu'e.

Violet's Place 822-2456

Located in Kaua'i Village in Kapa'a. Eclectic menu, from chop suey to pigs feet to hamburger to prime rib. OK, it's hard to be good at everything; you take your chances. $5–$15.

Waipouli Restaurant 822-9311

Located in the Waipouli Town Center in Kapa'a. Very popular with local families due to their hearty food and ample portions at cheap prices. Good value for the money. $4–$10. Credit cards.

South Shore Restaurants—American

Beach House Restaurant

A long time south shore landmark. Steak and seafood with unbelievably good ocean views right on the water. There were only four restaurants still closed as we went to press which were scheduled to reopen, and this is one of them. Because they were right on the water, the restaurant was essentially destroyed by the Hurricane. They anticipate reopening in July of 1994. Food and service had been deteriorating before they closed. With an entirely new management, we'll have to wait and see how they do.

Brennecke's Beach Broiler 742-7588

A south shore landmark. Great steak and seafood, good service with wonderful views of the sunset (except during summer months when the Sun's location doesn't cooperate). They've recently added a salad bar. Brennecke's rarely disappoints. Breakfast and lunch is $7–$15 (try the prime rib and eggs). Dinner is $15–$40. Reservations recommended. They also have a deli downstairs that serves plate lunches, salads, sandwiches, and shave ice. Located across from Po'ipu Beach Park. Credit cards.

Cafe Venturi 742-9168

Located in the Po'ipu Shopping Village, this tiny restaurant features fresh fish, steak, and a few specialties. They guarantee dinners or your money back (but they reserve the right to make you feel like a weasel). The price isn't consistent with the atmosphere, but the food is well prepared. $6–$10 for lunch, $10–$20 for dinner. This is the guy who used to own the **Road Kill Grill**. Just thought you'd like to know.

Camp House Grill 332-9755

Good place to get ribs, steak, seafood, chicken, or burgers. Food is good, service is usually good and the value is definitely good. Their pies are also excellent. Popular with tourists and locals alike. Kids will like it too. Easy to recommend this place. Located on mauka side of main highway in Kalaheo, can't miss it. $5–$8 for breakfast, $5–$15 for lunch and dinner. Credit cards.

House of Seafood 742-6433

Located on Po'ipu Road in Po'ipu, they offer high priced seafood served with skill and care. Both the Hawaiian spiny lobster and the abalone are $38 each. All entrees served a la carte. Salads and many deserts are prepared tableside. Huge selection of fresh fish served in a variety of ways. Attentive staff. Large selection of deserts. Good wine list. $25–$60. Dinner only. Credit cards. They are highlighted because their fish selection is so vast.

Ilima Terrace 742-1234

Located in the Hyatt Po'ipu, they offer good food in a comfortable, open air setting near the Hyatt's waterfall. Although breakfast is a bit overpriced at $10–$20 ($16 for the buffet), lunch is fairly reasonable and dinner is a downright bargain. Lunch features pasta, pizza, sandwiches, and some specialties and will run $10–$20. Dinners however are all buffets with different choices every night. Island buffet, BBQ buffet, prime rib buffet; they are all bargains at less than $20 offering a great selection of well-prepared choices. Reservations strongly recommended. Credit cards.

Kalaheo Steak House 332-9780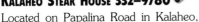

Located on Papalina Road in Kalaheo, they serve outstanding steak and seafood at *very* reasonable prices. This place is a real find for anyone looking for good, hearty food served by an eager staff. You can get a whopping 24 ounces of prime rib for $20, or a 10 ounce frozen ono steak for $12. That is some of the cheapest ono on the island. No view, just good food that won't hurt your wallet. No reservations. Dinner only. Credit cards.

Keoki's Paradise 742-7534

This is a special sort of place that people either love or hate (we love it). The ambiance is the story here with plants everywhere, a large fish lagoon, waterfalls, and thatched roofed booths (try to say *that* three times). It's the South Pacific that never really existed except in movies. There is a taco bar where some wait for their table, and others make a meal of it to save money. The tables are arranged in several levels. Purists will sniff that it's not real—so what! It is still exotic inside. If you are in the right mood, this is the sort of place you will remember for a long time to come. As for the food, it's a steak and seafood restaurant with slightly above average food and service. Quite good, but not great. Several of the entrees, such as the prime rib and the lasagna, are only served as long as they last. They have a 26 ounce prime rib for the ridiculously hungry. The place can get pretty busy which can have an effect on the service. Reservations strongly recommended. $15–$30. Located in the Po'ipu Shopping Village in Po'ipu. Credit cards.

Koloa Broiler 742-9122

This is a fun spot. The food is almost always good. . . after all, you cook it. Just the basics here; hamburgers, steak, fish, shish kabobs, served rare—OK raw. They have a gigantic grill and gigantic spatulas. Off to the side are two big ol' pots of steamed rice and baked beans along with a salad bar. These are all you can eat. The food is inexpensive and the environment is decidedly casual complete with undemanding cats roaming around the veranda area, and rest rooms marked "Pointers" and "Setters." A great place to bring kids if they're old enough to respect the grill. Veranda seats are best. Drinks are good but prices aren't marked. One drink called a Kona Nut Cooler is absolutely delicious. But you have to get the right bartender, otherwise it's just good. Friendly staff. $7–$13. Located in Koloa, can't miss it. Credit cards.

MUSTARD'S LAST STAND/ CAPT'N HELMS 332–7245

Slightly above average fish and hot dogs. Surfboards are strewn all around (including a surfboard table and bench, and a surfboard with fake wave for pictures). With a small miniature golf course for the kids and wandering peacocks and bunnies, this is a great place to bring the kids if they are getting antsy (which is why we highlighted it). $4–$8. A nice souvenir shop adjacent to the stand makes for a good diversion. Located in Lawa'i at the corner of Koloa Road (530) and the main highway (50).

PO'IPU BAY GRILL & BAR 742–8888

Breakfast, lunch, and dinner. Lunch features sandwiches, burgers, and the like for $8–$15. Dinners are steak and seafood with a bit of pasta for $15–$25. Nice views overlooking the golf course with some ocean views from right corner tables. Located next to the Hyatt at the Po'ipu Bay Golf Course. Credit cards.

TIDEPOOLS 742–1234

Located at the Hyatt Po'ipu, their best feature is a very romantic atmosphere. A thatched roof, a stocked freshwater lagoon next to your table, and flickering tiki torches outside provide a calm, quiet dining environment. The entrees include rack of lamb, fresh fish, steak and several Japanese dishes. $20–$55. Service is adequate. Reservations recommended. Dinner only. Credit cards.

South Shore Restaurants—Italian

BRICK OVEN PIZZA 332–8561

Without question the best pizza on Kaua'i. This family-owned pizza parlor has been in Kalaheo since 1977. They pride themselves in making their own sauce, sausage, and other ingredients. In the more traditional Italian vein, the sauce takes on less importance. The crust is very thin with scalloped edges and brushed with garlic butter with tasty results. Simple Italian atmosphere, attentive service and excellent pizza—what more can you ask for? Prices are $5–$15. No reservations. No smoking allowed. Located on mauka side of highway in as you enter Kalaheo, can't miss it.

DONDERO'S 742–1234

Located in the Hyatt Po'ipu, they feature regional Italian food. Entrees include sauteed scallops, shrimp, lobster, and clams in a tomato broth; delicious! Rack of lamb, fresh fish, and several pasta dishes. Outstanding wine list. Elegant dining; their dress code requires casual resort wear, meaning covered shoes, collared shirts for men, etc. $15–$40. Reservations recommended. Credit cards.

Pizza Bella 742-9571

Average sandwiches and pasta, their pizza used to be very good but has slipped a bit in recent years. Their Mexican pizza comes complete with refried beans and jalapeño peppers. Gourmet pizzas are unusual but the quality isn't always high. Located in the back of Po'ipu Shopping Village in Po'ipu. $5–$15. Credit cards.

South Shore Restaurants—Mexican

Pancho & Lefty's 742-7377

Food is sometimes good, service is always bad (bad enough to walk out, a rarity on Kaua'i). Look at your check carefully to see that you are not overcharged. If you're lucky, they might even bring out what you ordered. Prices not justified given the shabby treatment by the staff. You deserve better. $8–$15. Located in Koloa at corner of Koloa Road (530) and Po'ipu Road (520). Credit cards.

Taqueria Nortenos 742-7222

Very good food, embarrassingly large portions, and a small price make this place an excellent choice for Mexican food on the south shore. Their food is fresh and tasty. Located past the 4 mile mark on Po'ipu Road (520) in Po'ipu Plaza. Their dining area isn't much to speak of (we recommend you take out) but there are few places on Kaua'i where two people can eat all the good food they want for about $10.

South Shore Restaurants—Chinese

Hai-Tides Chinese Take Out 742-7149

Acceptable Chinese food for $6–$9. Same owner as Cafe Venturi next door. Located in the Po'ipu Shopping Village.

South Shore Restaurants—Japanese

Taisho 742-1838

Simple Japanese food and sushi bar featuring tempura, mushroom chicken, pork, tofu etc. Very average. $10–$20. Dinner only. Credit cards.

South Shore Restaurants—Local

Green Garden 335-5422

Very diverse menu. From meatloaf to lobster to spaghetti to Chinese dishes to omelettes (for dinner). Our classification of it as a local restaurant is a cop out on our part; it's a little of everything (wait, that *is* the definition of local restaurants). Call it quasi upscale local food. They have been here since 1948 so they must be doing *something* right. That *something* is serving quality food at a reasonable price. Be sure to ask about the specials. The homemade pies are great, especially the liliko'i pie. Ask for a table away from the main road. $10–$25. Credit cards.

Lawa'i Restaurant 332-9550

Located on mauka side of main highway in Lawa'i, they have a large selection of local food and are frequented almost solely by locals. Their food is more than acceptable and some of the selections are a real adventure, but the ambiance is dismal. Expect to stand out if you go, especially at dinner. $5–$10. Credit cards.

West Shore Restaurants—American

Grove Dining Room 338-2300

Steaks with a bit of local thrown in, the Grove Dining Room is the best place to eat in Waimea. To be honest, there aren't a lot of places to eat on this part of the island. That said, the food is good and the service has a real family feel to it. The porterhouse steak is about $25, but for that you get a full pound of beef. The prices for most items are reasonable and their combos can be a real bargain. Located on the ocean side of the highway between the 23 and 24 mile markers in Waimea. $6–$15 for lunch, $10–$30 for dinner. Credit cards.

KOKE'E LODGE 335–6061

Hearty. That's the word that comes to mind. They classify themselves as local soul food. We particularly like the cornbread and chili polished off with some "killer fudge cake." Lunch only for the most part. $5–$10. Located *waaaay* up the road in Koke'e on Waimea Canyon Road past the 15 mile mark. This is the road you take to get to Waimea Canyon and the Kalalau Lookout.

West Shore Restaurants—Italian

HANAPEPE BOOKSTORE & ESPRESSO BAR 335–5011

A neat little place located on Hanapepe's main street, they classify themselves as "gourmet vegetarian Italian," but they do use some dairy products. Breakfast features real homemade oatmeal, multi-grain waffles and pancakes; no eggs. Lunch and dinner offer a small but satisfying selection such as spinach lasagna or pasta prima vera. Oh, and did we mention that they have books and espresso? $10–$20 for lunch or dinner. Dinner reservations recommended. Call to see which days they are open. Credit cards.

West Shore Restaurants—Mexican

SINALOA TAQUERIA & TORTILLA FACTORY 335–0006

High end Mexican food in a medium end atmosphere. Tasty, creative entrees spiced any way you want. Popular with residents and visitors alike and for good reason. Lunch is $5–$15, dinner is $10–$20. Reservations recommended. Located on mauka side of highway in Hanapepe. Credit cards.

West Shore Restaurants—Thai

TOI'S THAI KITCHEN 335–3111

Amazingly good Thai food in a nondescript atmosphere. $5–$10 which is a heck of a deal given the superb quality of the food. Located in 'Ele'ele Shopping Center before Hanapepe, ocean side of the highway near 16 mile mark. Their new location is inside the Port Allen Bar. They might not look like much, but they sure are good.

West Shore Restaurants—Local

LC'S PLACE 335–3991

Little unobtrusive place in Hanapepe. Friendly service, simple hearty food such as saimin, hamburgers, chicken, and kalua pig (baked in an imu instead of being prepared on a stovetop). Breakfast will run you about $5, lunch and dinner $4–$8. Located on Hanapepe's main street. Credit cards.

RITCHIE'S ONO SAIMIN & BENTO SHOP 337–1428

The best thing about this place is the shave ice. The rest is standard local fare. $4–$6.

Lu'aus

If you've ever seen a movie that takes place in Hawaii, odds are there was a lu'au scene. This is where everyone stands around with a mai tai in one hand, and a plate of kalua pig in the other. There's always a show where someone is twirling a torch lit at both ends, and of course the obligatory hula dancers. And the truth is, that's not far from reality. The pig is baked in the ground for up to several days and is absolutely delicious. Shows are usually exciting and fast moving. Although the lu'aus on O'ahu can make you feel like cattle being led to slaughter, Kaua'i's lu'aus are smaller and much more pleasant. At the present time, there are three *consistent* lu'aus held on the island, **SMITH'S TROPICAL PARADISE** at 822–4654 ($43.75 per person), **KAUA'I COCONUT BEACH RESORT** at 822–3455 ($45 per person) and **TAHITI NUI** at 826–6277 ($35 per person). The former two are in Kapa'a with the latter held in Hanalei. Prices include all the food, drinks, and show you can swallow except for **TAHITI NUI** where drinks are extra. Nobody holds lu'aus every night, so call to find out which nights they are having them. Reservations are required.

Fortunately for you, all three of Kaua'i's lu'aus are good and all are distinct from one another. **TAHITI NUI** has a more "authentic" luau. This means it is very informal. The show isn't as flashy, the ambiance is more like a friend's party. This will appeal to many, but some people want an experience more akin to a show. **SMITH'S TROPICAL PARADISE** has fantastic gardens to roam around in, a splashier show full of wonders, and good food. **KAUA'I COCONUT BEACH RESORT** was recently selected as the statewide winner in the *Keep it Hawai'i* program by the Hawai'i Visitors Bureau so expect increased authenticity.

All in all, lu'aus can be a real blast. If your time allows for one, it is highly recommended.

Night Life

Many people who visit Kaua'i for the first time expect the night life to be on par with that of Honolulu. It's not. That said, there is more than enough night life on Kaua'i to satisfy most people's needs. Many of the restaurants feature entertainment at night but the schedules are always changing. You can call the restaurant you choose from the listings above and inquire as to their entertainment. People have different desires when it comes to night life. Here we simply try to describe what's available and let you pick what you want.

Po'ipu

The south shore's best night life is at the Hyatt. **KUHIO'S NIGHT CLUB** at 742–1234 is a small, elegant nightclub that usually features comedy ($12 cover) or dancing ($5 cover). Call them to see what they have going on. They have relaxed their dress code a bit; shorts and covered shoes are now allowed. **STEVENSON'S LIBRARY** also at the Hyatt is designed to appeal to anyone who ever wanted to visit the private library of one of the Rockefellers. Richly decorated, bookcases filled with the classics, pool tables (not billiards), large aquarium, chess tables, and a terrace. The bar is the center attraction and is beautifully crafted out of strips of koa and monkeypod. Some of the staff can be a bit snotty, but otherwise it's a nice place to have a drink. Things can get surprisingly lively.

The **SEAVIEW TERRACE** commands a fabulous view of the resort and can be a relaxing place to have a drink after a long day.

Lihu'e

In Lihu'e and Nawiliwili, it all depends on what you want. **GILLIGAN'S** (245–1955) at the Outrigger Hotel just outside Lihu'e going toward Kapa'a is considered the island's premier meat market. By that we mean mostly young (21–35) people rocking away to the latest music. This has become a popular place for locals in recent years and the place is nearly always packed. No cover except when they have comedy ($12). When Gilligan's closes, everyone heads over to **LEGENDS** (246–0491) in the Pacific Ocean Plaza in Nawiliwili where the dress code is nonexistent and the place is a bit scruffier. No cover. Legends brags that they are the only cabaret on the island and occasionally offer "adult entertainment." The place is always empty until Gilligan's closes.

The **OAR HOUSE** (245–4941) in Nawiliwili is considered the best place in Kaua'i to get a beer bottle smashed over your head. Run down and rickety, the place is full of character. But it might not be the kind of character you are looking for. The place is getting creakier all the time and it's only a matter of time before it falls down.

HAP'S HIDEAWAY on Rice Street is a local sports bar, as is **ROB'S GOOD TIMES GRILL**. The latter also offers karaoke at times. **THE KARAOKE KLUB** on Highway 56 in Lihu'e has just what the name implies. The pupus (appetizers) are free and the drinks are not overpriced.

THE OUTRIGGER HOTEL has a free Polynesian show every Wednesday evening that is worth stopping for. Movie goers can call **KUKUI GROVE CINEMAS** at 245–5055 for a listing of their features.

Kapa'a

Kapa'a is not as lively as Lihu'e, where most go for their nightly entertainment. **COOK'S LANDING** lounge at the Kaua'i Coconut Beach Resort usually has free nightly entertainment. Many like to grab a drink here and stroll along the beach. The **JOLLY ROGER** behind the Coconut Marketplace usually distinguishes itself by having two-dollar mai tais. They're weak, but what do you expect for two bucks. **TRADEWINDS, A SOUTH SEAS BAR** in the Coconut Marketplace is a small but lively little bar.

SMITH'S TROPICAL PARADISE and **THE KAUA'I COCONUT BEACH RESORT** both have good lu'aus (see Lu'aus above). Movie goers should check the **PLANTATION CINEMA** at 822–9391 to see what's showing.

North Shore

Your options are a bit more limited here. **TAHITI NUI** (826–7320) is a great place to explore the local color and their lu'au, when they have it, is always recommended. **THE HAPPY TALK LOUNGE** in the Hanalei Bay Resort, reopening in April 1994, has always been one of the best places in Princeville to have a drink and appreciate the night air. **CHARO'S** (826–6422) in Ha'ena has a lounge with good ocean views (see review). **HANALEI GOURMET** (826–2524) across from Ching Young Village occasionally has music and can be a small but fun place when it's jumping. **ZELO'S CAFE** in Princeville Shopping Center is either alive or dead, it just depends.

The Princeville Hotel (826–9644) has the **LIBRARY LOUNGE**. A bit subdued with great views of Hanalei Bay.

Hotels on Kaua'i

Condominium Resorts on Kaua'i

Your selection of where to stay is one of the more important decisions you'll make in planning your Kaua'i vacation. To some, it's just a place to sleep and rather meaningless. To others, it's the difference between a good vacation and a bad one.

There are four main types of lodgings on the island: hotels, condominium resorts, bed and breakfasts, and single family homes. The vast majority of you will stay in one of the first two types. But B&Bs and single family homes are often overlooked and can be very good values. If your group or family is large, you should strongly consider renting a house for privacy, roominess, and plain ol' value. There is a list of rental agents at the end of this section, each willing and happy to send you a list of homes they represent. As far as B&Bs are concerned, see page 186 for more information.

We have *brilliantly* labeled the four main sections of Kaua'i as North Shore, South Shore, East Shore, and West Shore. We separate hotels and condominiums. Hotels usually offer more services, but smaller spaces and no kitchens. Condos usually have full kitchens but you won't get the kind of attention you would from a hotel, including daily maid service. There are exceptions, of course, and we will point them out when they come up.

In general, you will get a bit more bang for your accommodation buck at north shore resorts. Wailua/Kapa'a/Lihu'e on the east shore is a bit pricier but closer to more facilities. Po'ipu offers more sunshine and reasonable rates. The west offers few, but unique accommodations.

All prices given are RACK rates, meaning without any discounts. Tour packages and travel agents can sometimes get better rates. Most offer discounts for stays of a week or more and some will negotiate price with you. Also, be aware that these prices are subject to a 5% Room Tax and a 4.17% General Excise Tax.

The gold bar indicates that the property is exceptionally well priced for what you get.

Solid Gold Value

The gem indicates that this accommodation offers something *particularly* special, not *necessarily* related to the price.

A Real Gem

HOTELS

As we go to press, almost a year and a half after Hurricane 'Iniki, five big hotel resorts are still closed. The **Westin Kaua'i**, the **Sheraton Kaua'i Hotel**, the **Stouffer Wai'ohai Beach Resort**, **Po'ipu Beach Hotel**, and the **Coco Palms Resort** have all made it clear to us that they will not be reopening until sometime in 1995. It's easy to hear this and misinterpret it to mean that Kaua'i has not recovered yet. This would be a big mistake. None of these resort reopening delays are due to their inability to repair their properties until then.

These resorts have reasons for not reopening that aren't all hurricane related. Some were purchased prior to the Hurricane just before the worldwide recession began, when real estate was at its peak, and their new owners are not hot to pour money into them now. None of them have had their insurance settled yet. Some felt that Kaua'i had too many hotel rooms before the Hurricane and they can't justify rebuilding them at the present time.

At any rate, the *business decisions* that most of these five have made are not relevant to what you can expect from your Kaua'i vacation. Nearly everyone else has reopened long ago.

Unless otherwise noted, all hotel rooms described have air conditioning, an activity or travel desk, telephones, lanais (verandas), cable TV, and have cribs available upon request. None have room service unless otherwise noted.

All resorts with a ♿ indicate that there are wheelchair accessible rooms. Check with them further information.

North Shore Hotels

HANALEI BAY RESORT
(800) 827–4427 from Mainland, (800) 221–6061 from Hawai'i, or (808) 826–6522 on Kaua'i.

Until recently, Hanalei Bay Resort consisted of 120 hotel rooms and 75 condominiums. Now the condos are referred to as **EMBASSY SUITES KAUA'I** and will be described in the section on condominiums. All facilities and amenities are still applicable to both and the management has not changed for either. They have 8 tennis courts (4 of them lighted), a tennis pro shop, evening room service for light snacks, coffee makers, conference room, ocean gear available, cocktail lounge, restaurant (the Bali Hai), and a special wedding coordinator. Many have kitchens and VCRs. Hanalei Bay Resort is located in Princeville on 22 acres of beautiful, lush, and winding grounds. There are dashing waterfalls pouring into the pool and spa as well as a small, man-made keiki (kids) beach. The service is very personalized. Rooms are pleasant— nearly all have good views. One thing we noticed is that they are more conservative with their view designations than many others (i.e., Mountain View rooms often come with impressive ocean views as well). The Happy Talk Lounge has always been a fantastic place to have a

drink in the evening, and now they serve food. As we went to press, they had a firm reopening date of April 1994. Rooms are $130–$220. ♿ Credit cards.

PRINCEVILLE HOTEL
(800) 826–4400 or (808) 826–9644

252 rooms, 8 tennis courts (one lighted), VCRs, 3 restaurants, 24 hour room service, cocktail lounge, an in-the-pool bar, 6 shops, ballroom, child care

A Real Gem

service, conference room, free valet parking, pool with three spas and a keiki pool, free shuttle service to the Princeville Airport, and a 60 seat cinema. They will have a lu'au on Fridays starting sometime in mid 1994. About a third of the rooms have lanais, the rest have been removed to increase room size. If you had visited this hotel before their recent reopening, you would have experienced a formal (some might say stuffy) staff dressed in a coat and tie, classical music playing in the lobby, and people at the front door who might remind you that the hotel had a dress code so please don't wear your tank top in the lobby. Shorts and a T–shirt—well, only if you *insist*. You would never have heard the word aloha. In short, it was a Hawaiian resort that had everything; except Hawai'i. But *no more*. The owners of the Princeville, who seemed to have made a career out of pouring money into this hotel, have finally gotten it right. Now, the hotel *stresses* Hawai'i and its culture rather than denying it. The staff is dressed in aloha wear and encouraged to be aware of their Hawaiian environment. Casual luxuriance is now the overall feel. The hotel is still richly furnished with a fabulous lobby featuring 18,000 square feet of marble,

WHERE TO STAY

giant flower arrangements everywhere, marble fireplace, clamshell fountain, and a drop dead view of Hanalei Bay through the glass walls. The lobby is *so* richly furnished that it's easy to miss little things...like their $100,000 19th Century Erard piano near the Cafe Hanalei restaurant. The valet parking area has their trademark serene fountains. The rooms are expensively furnished and quite comfortable. They even have a feature unique on Kaua'i. The bathrooms have windows with liquid crystal panes. The result; instant opaqueness at the flip of a switch. Some of these windows overlook the outside, some overlook the main hotel room.

The hotel is designed in a series of tiers, stepping their way down a mountain. The payoff is great ocean views from most rooms. At the bottom is the pool area. The swimming pool is filled all the way to ground level without the usual lip. Have a beverage inside the pool from the in-the-pool bar, or walk across the pool bridge and take a few steps to Pu'u Poa Beach. The Princeville Hotel was named the eighth best tropical destination in the world in the *1993 Condé Nast Readers' Survey*. In comparing the Princeville Hotel to the Hyatt, the Hyatt has a more exotic, tropical feel, whereas the Princeville has a richer and more expensive feel. Both are outstanding, it just depends on what you're looking for. Rooms are $250–$410. Prince Jr. Suites are $450. Other suites range from $825 up to $2,350 for the Royal Suite. This price includes complimentary everything (as it *darn* well should). ♿ Credit cards.

East Shore Hotels

ASTON KAUA'I BEACHBOY HOTEL
(800) 922–7866 or (808) 822–3441
243 rooms, lighted tennis courts.

Beachfront location. Not a bad value for the money. Rooms are $88–$118. ♿ Credit cards.

COCO PALMS RESORT
(808) 822–4921
As we go to press, the historic **Coco Palms Resort** is closed and they have no plans regarding its reopening (See note above). Consequently, they have informed us that they will not be reopening until *at least* 1995.

GARDEN ISLAND INN
(800) 648–0154 OR (808) 245–7228
21 rooms. This inn, located in Nawiliwili, is a good, clean place to stay for those seeking merely a place to sleep. Located near Kalapaki Beach. Rooms are $50–$85. Credit cards.

HOTEL CORAL REEF
(800) 843–4659 or (808) 822–4481
26 rooms, no phones, no air conditioning. This is another one of those places to stay if you are only looking for a place to sleep. Good oceanfront location and reasonably clean rooms. Rooms are $80.

ISLANDER ON THE BEACH
(800) 847–7417 or (808) 822–7417
198 rooms, pool and spa, poolside bar. Plantation style setting adjacent to Wailua Beach. Open grounds. We recommend this place. A couple of years ago we would have *vigorously* recommended it but a change in management awhile back seems to have brought a more indifferent staff. Some staff are great but some are rude. Each building has a name. The Kaua'i and Ni'ihau Buildings are fairly close to the ocean allowing you to fall asleep to the sound of the surf. Rooms are $95–$125 *(these prices include a rental car)*. Credit cards.

KAUA'I COCONUT BEACH RESORT
(800) 222–5642 or (808) 822–3455
Formerly a Sheraton, they have 300 rooms, tennis courts, coffee makers, room service, restaurant, two conference rooms, lounge, pool and spa, and a lu'au on the premises. The only complaint we have is that the rooms are on the small side. Rooms are $90–$170 (ocean front rooms are a bit larger). Suites are $215. Ⅾ Credit cards.

KAUA'I RESORT HOTEL
(800) 367–5004 (Mainland), (800) 272–5275 (Hawai'i) or (808) 245–3931
Formerly Aston Kaua'i Resort Hotel, 228 rooms, lighted tennis courts, restaurant, lobby bar, pools and spa, 3 conference rooms, BBQs. Pleasant and neatly kept grounds. They are right across from Lydgate State Park, the safest place to swim on Kaua'i and a great place for kids to play in the ocean. In addition to the hotel they have cottages, some with kitchenettes. Their smallest cottages are $69 per night—a pretty good value if you can live without a lot of space. Cottages are $69–$159. Rooms are $99–159. Suites are $200. Credit cards.

KAUA'I SANDS HOTEL
(800) 367–7000 or (808) 822–4951
203 rooms, pool, conference room, restaurant (Al and Don's). Ocean front location and reasonable prices make this a very popular hotel with tour package promoters. Most of the visitors are senior citizens as the hotel has fairly generous senior discounts. Buildings are fairly old, but clean. Rooms are $75–$85 for studios, $90 for kitchenette. Add $15 and you get a car. Ⅾ Credit cards.

OUTRIGGER KAUA'I BEACH HOTEL
(800) 642–6262 or (808) 245–1955
350 rooms, lighted tennis courts, room service, restaurant (Jacaranda Terrace), cocktail lounge, shops, 8 conference rooms, valet parking, pool and spa, wedding coordinator, nightclub (Gilligan's). Formerly The Hilton, they have a wide variety of services available. This, coupled with an oceanfront location make it a reasonable choice for the money. Located between Lihu'e and Kapa'a, its only neighbors are the adjacent Aston Kaua'i Beach Villas. The beach offshore is not swimmable but a short walk northward brings you in front of the Wailua Golf Course and its beach. Rooms are $110–$160, 1 bedroom suites are $380. Ⅾ Credit cards.

TIP TOP MOTEL
(808) 245–2333

Solid Gold Value

Let's face it, the name Tip Top Motel doesn't exactly instill confidence. But if you are looking for a clean, simple place to stay, this is the place for you. They have 34 air conditioned units, some with TVs. The rooms are very basic and usually immaculate. Each room has two single beds. The restaurant downstairs is a great bargain (see review under **Dining**). Owned by the same family since 1916. Price per room is $45.70. Can't beat that. Located on Akahi Street on Lihu'e.

WESTIN KAUA'I RESORT
(800) 228–3000 or (808) 245–5050
The Westin Kaua'i is one of those five resorts we mention on page 174 that has not reopened, and won't until *at least* 1995 (maybe 1996). They have only recently resolved their ownership problem (the banks own it and are looking for buyers). When they do reopen, expect many changes including a name change. With their unimaginable opulence and Disneyland/Las Vegas atmosphere, they were never able to fully find

their niche. As the largest resort on the island, with 840 rooms spread over 800 acres, the Westin had a disproportionate influence on mainland travel agents' perception of Kaua'i. This influence is misdirected because the resort has *reportedly* been a money loser since its inception, and the Hurricane was only the *last* straw. In other words, don't blame its long closure entirely on the Hurricane. If the resort opened today, they would almost certainly be upstaged by the Hyatt in Po'ipu and the Princeville Hotel. Until it does reopen all of its restaurants, with the exception of The Terrace Restaurant, will stay closed. The golf courses on the premises are open and usually vacant since so many people think they are still closed. It is our hope that the Westin's new owners, whomever they turn out to be, will have great success. With its wonderful location and tremendous assets, it has the potential to be an incredible resort.

South Shore Hotels

HYATT REGENCY KAUA'I RESORT & SPA
(800) 233–1234 or (808) 742–1234

A Real Gem

600 rooms, 4 tennis courts with pro shop, golf course, VCRs, room service, 5 restaurants, cocktail lounges, Camp Hyatt child care service, 5 conference rooms, free valet parking, 3 pools and spas, health club, lu'aus by arrangement, nightclub (Kuhio's), and complete business services. It was hard for us to review this resort without sounding like a couple of drooling sycophants. But the reality of the Hyatt is that they did almost everything right. As you walk into the lobby and see the ocean framed by the entrance, you realize that here, they really sweated the details. The grounds are as exotic as any you will find in all the islands. The upper swimming pool seems to meander forever. It even has a slight current and hides such goodies as caves tucked behind small waterfalls (they're easy to miss). At the end of the upper pool, you can take the free waterslide to the bottom. There you will find what they call the action pool complete with a volleyball net, waterfalls, spas, and an area for children. One of our few complaints is that the sidewalk material they use around the pool is quite slippery when wet—and, of course, it's always wet. Across from the lower pool are several acres of saltwater lagoon. If you want saltwater without the waves, here it is. The "sand" is actually gravel imported from San Juan Capistrano. Inside the lagoon are several landscaped islands. The grounds are lush and very well maintained and feature a smashing waterfall below the Seaview Terrace Lounge. The resort is located on a beautiful beach known as Shipwreck Beach. They have covered cabana chairs on the beach. If you're lucky enough to be under one in the evening during a passing shower, it's something you will long remember. Large hammocks are scattered throughout the grounds. Their nine shops run the gamut from fine art to footwear. Their activity desk by the pool has lots of freebies such as kites, walkmans, croquet sets, etc. They have a wedding coordinator on site. If your intention is to come to Kaua'i and never leave the resort (which we hope you *won't* do), the Hyatt is the place to come. You'll never get bored here. This is a great place to bring the kids. Camp Hyatt provides extensive child care service and they even have a video arcade. Anara Spa is 25,000 square feet and the finest spa on the island. So, what's the catch? Well, amenities like this don't come cheap, but they are not as expen-

sive as we expected. Rooms are pleasant and not spartan like other big resorts can be. Rooms are $230–$370. Suites are $425–$1,800 (ouch!). ♿ Credit cards.

The other three Po'ipu hotels, **Sheraton Kaua'i Hotel** (800) 325–3535 or (808) 742–1661, **The Stouffer Wai'ohai Beach Resort,** and **The Po'ipu Beach Hotel** both at (800) 468–3571 or (808) 742–7214 are among the five we speak of on page 174 that will not be reopening until at least 1995. See that page for more information. The Sheraton Kaua'i actually consists of two hotels, the Sheraton Kaua'i Garden Hotel, and the Sheraton Kaua'i Beach Resort. The former has been reopened for a long time but they will not be providing regular services until the Sheraton Kaua'i Beach Resort is opened. And they haven't even *begun* that yet.

West Shore Hotels

There aren't any. See West Shore Condominiums.

CONDOMINIUMS

One of the confusing aspects to renting a condo, cottage, or house on Kaua'i is the fact that there's no central rental source to many individual properties. Most condo complexes, whether large or small, consist of individually owned condominiums. An individual owner has the prerogative of renting his or her unit through any rental agent they so choose. Consequently, a 50-unit condo resort might be represented by a dozen or more rental agents. Usually (but not always) prices for comparable units within a given resort are equivalent through different agents. When we describe a particular resort, we will often give the names or phone numbers of one or two rental agent companies that dominate the rental pool. But realize that this does not always do justice to the *entire* property. When we describe rates and credit cards accepted, it is for the larger rental agents. Different agents have different policies for the same complex.

Once you have decided where you want to stay, you can call the number we list for a given resort. You may also want to contact some of the rental agents we list at the end of this section to determine if they represent any units on the property you have chosen.

Also realize that condominium owners usually have complete autonomy in how they furnish their individual units. Consequently, a resort that we describe as a good deal might have individual units that are not as hot. (Notice how we neatly cover ourselves so that if you get a less-than-charming condo in a resort we recommend, we can always say you got one of the few duds there.)

Three bedroom/two bath units are described as 3/2, two bedroom/one bath units are described as 2/1, etc. Differentiation between half baths and full baths is not made. The price spread for rooms of a given size are due to different views, different locations within the resort, and occasional seasonal fluctuations. So when you see that a 2/2 unit rents for $110–$140, you should figure that $140 units have a better view or are closer to the water. The terms Ocean Front, Ocean View, and Garden View are used rather capriciously in Hawai'i so we have avoided them. **Unless otherwise noted, all rooms come with telephones, complete kitchens, coffee makers, lanais (verandas), cable TV, ceiling fans, and have cribs available upon request. None have air conditioning unless otherwise noted. (On Kaua'i, trade winds usually make A/C unnecessary and few opt for it.)**

North Shore Condominiums

ALI'I KAI II
(800) 826-7782 or (808) 826-7444
56 units, pool and spa. Units on the small side and not at all lavish. 2/2 units are $110–$125. Not a bargain.

THE CLIFFS
(800) 622-6219, or (808) 826-6219
194 units, tennis courts, pool and spa, activity desk. Nicely furnished interiors. 1/2 units are $120–$150, 1/2 units with loft (quasi second bedroom) are $155–$195. Bldgs 6–9 have the best views. Credit cards.

EMBASSY SUITES KAUA'I
(800) 827-4427 from Mainland, (800) 221-6061 from Hawai'i, or (808) 826-6522 on Kaua'i
Until recently, Hanalei Bay Resort consisted of 120 hotel rooms and 75 condominiums. Now the condos are referred to as Embassy Suites Kaua'i. The Hanalei Bay Resort hotel rooms are described in the section on **Hotels**. All facilities and amenities are still applicable to both and the management has not changed for either. They have 8 tennis courts (4 of them lighted), a tennis pro shop, evening room service for light snacks, conference room, air conditioning, ocean gear available, cocktail lounge (the Happy Talk Lounge), restaurant (the Bali Hai), and a special wedding coordinator. Many have VCRs. Free shuttle service to Princeville Airport. Additionally, they have free daily maid service, a rarity among condos. In fact, they are run more like a hotel than a condominium resort so expect more services than other condos. Located in Princeville on 22 acres of beautiful, lush, and winding grounds. There are dashing waterfalls pouring into the pool and spa as well as a small,

man-made keiki beach. The service is very personalized. Their Happy Talk Lounge is a north shore favorite for enjoying an evening drink. They have a shuttle to usher you around the grounds or down to the beach. Some units command excellent ocean bluff views. As we went to press, they had a firm reopening date of April 1994. 1/1 units are $240–$270, 2/2 units are $350–$460, and 3/3 units (which are over 2,000 square feet) are $650. They also have "Prestige Ocean Suites"— 1/1 units are $500, 2/2 units are $750, and 3/3 units are $1,000. These are expensively furnished with many extras. Credit cards.

HALE MOI
This 20 unit complex was trashed by the Hurricane. A year later nothing had been done and they have no concrete plans. This complex and adjacent **HANALEI BAY VILLAS** are the only eyesores you'll find in Princeville. If they ever come back on line, we hope you'll do your part and avoid them.

HANALEI COLONY RESORT
(800) 628-3004 or (808) 826-6235
52 units, pool and spa, BBQ, kitchens lack microwaves and dishwashers. No telephones or TV. Only beachfront resort on the north shore. *Some of their units are as close to the water as you will get on Kaua'i (25 feet).* Secluded and somewhat isolated. All units are two bedroom (although the bedrooms are not completely walled-off). Units G2 and G3 have *particularly good views* and are highly recommended. While not lavish, their location is outstanding. The lack of room telephones might make arranging your day slightly awkward. Adjacent to Charo's Restaurant. 2/1 units are $95–$190. Credit cards.

MAUNA KAI
(808) 826–6855
46 units, VCR, pool. 2/2 units are $90–$100, 3/2 units are $100–$110. No real views but large units for the price. 3 night minimum.

PALIULI COTTAGES
(800) 628–5533 or (808) 826–9229
8 units, fireplace, microscopic pool in each unit. Each unit is a stand alone condo, so you will get lots of privacy. Pleasant valley views and reasonably spacious split level interiors make this a decent bargain. The pools are a joke—probably looked good on paper. 2/2 units are $115.

PALI KE KUA
(800) 535–0085 OR (808) 826–9066
98 units, pool and spa. Nicely furnished units, private path to beach below cliffs. Many units have nice ocean views. Restaurant on premises (Beamreach). 1/1 units are $120–$160, 2/2 units are $125–185. As we go to press, they have a "firm" reopening date of April 1994.

Pu'u Poa
(800) 535–0085 (Mainland) or (800) 219–9700 (Hawai'i Only)
56 units, lighted tennis courts, pool, each unit has a separate atrium in addition to lanai. **A Real Gem** *Outstanding* ocean bluff views and nicely furnished interiors. Directly above Hideaways Beach (which, during calm summer seas, offers outstanding snorkeling). As with Pali Ke Kua, they have a "firm" reopening date of April 1994. 2/2 units are $185–$195; 2/2 suites are $205–$275. Credit cards.

SEALODGE
(808) 826–6751
86 units, pool. 1/1 units are $75–$85, 2/1 **Solid Gold Value** units are $90–$110. Great ocean bluff views at a very reasonable price. They were completing the last of their reconstruction as we went to press and will probably be open by the time you read this.

East Shore Condominiums

ASTON KAUA'I BEACH VILLAS
(800) 922–7866 or (808) 245–7711
150 units, air conditioning in bedrooms, pool and spa, tennis courts. Spartan accommodations, you can get a better oceanfront value next door at the Outrigger if you can do without the kitchen. 1/1 units are $140, 2/2 units are $195–$255. Not a very good value. Credit cards.

BANYAN HARBOR
(800) 422–6926 or (808) 245–7333
248 units, tennis court, pool. Adequate rooms, but unkempt and unpleasant grounds. Since most of the units are long term rentals, you might not feel like you're on vacation (i.e. people working on their cars next to your room). 2/2 units are $95–$105. Credit cards.

KAHA LANI
(800) 922–7866 or (808) 822–9331
74 units, lighted tennis court, pool, most of the units are nice inside, but the oceanfront units aren't that close to the ocean. Adjacent to Lydgate State Park. Not a bad value. 1/1 units are $117–$147, 2/2 units are $150–$185. ♿ Credit cards.

KAPA'A SANDS RESORT
(800) 222-4901 or (808) 822-4901

24 units, pool. This is probably the best bargain on the island. **Solid Gold Value** Their small oceanfront studios (some have a pull down Murphy bed—these are recommended for more living space) are very clean and cost $85. For this price you are as close as 30 feet from the water on a pretty beach. What a deal! Resident offshore turtles will keep you entertained at dusk. Quiet and private. 3 night minimum. Studios are $75–$85, 2/2 units are $99–$109. Credit cards.

KAPA'A SHORE
(800) 827-3922 or (808) 822-3055

81 units, tennis court, pool and spa. Located on a pretty but unswimmable beach, this complex also houses many long term rentals. Average grounds, you can do better elsewhere. 1/1 units are $90–$120, 2/2 units are $110–$140.

LAE NANI
(800) 777-1700 or (808) 822-4938

84 units, lighted tennis court, pool. Pleasant grounds, very helpful staff and nice oceanfront location. They have a heiau on the premises as well as a wonderful boulder–enclosed ocean pond for the keikis (kids). Building 5 has ocean front units. The place has a nice ambiance. 1/2 units are $150–$205, 2/2 units are $200–$275. Credit cards.

LANIKAI
(800) 755-2824 or (808) 822-7700

18 units, pool. Small but lush manicured grounds, high quality rooms and lots of living space (1,460 sq. ft.) 2/2 units are $225. 1 week minimum. Credit cards.

PLANTATION HALE
(800) 462-6262 or (808) 822-4941

160 units, air conditioned, three pools. Sounds good on paper but the place is worn and not real clean. Indifferent staff. Popular with packaged tours so if you stay, you'd better get a cheaper price than their RACK rate. 1/1 units are $105–$120. Credit cards.

PONO KAI
(800) 388-3800 or (808) 822-9831

217 units, 2 lighted tennis courts, VCRs, pool and spa, 2 saunas. 2 bedroom units have exceptionally large master bedrooms. Reasonable accommodations but slightly worn. 1/1 units are $115–$145, 2/2 units are $145–175. Credit cards.

WAILUA BAY VIEW
(800) 767-4707 or (808) 245-4711

45 units, pool, VCRs in most. For the money they are nicely **Solid Gold Value** furnished inside, clean and command good elevated ocean views. 1/1 units are $110.

South Shore Condominiums

ALIHI LANI
(800) 742-2260 or (808) 742-2233

4 units, pool. Units have an expensive, spacious feel. Great ocean view. 5 night minimum; quiet, peaceful and essentially ocean front (separated by a road). Nice place for the money. 2/2 units are $210.

GARDEN ISLE COTTAGES
(808) 742-6717

9 units, partial and complete kitchens, no phones. Each unit is different. The oceanside units command good views of an

ocean inlet. The deluxe unit has lots of windows and a very large living space but is spartan. $73–$135 for two persons.

KAHILI MOUNTAIN PARK CABINS
(808) 742–9921

29 units, no phones or televisions. These cab-  **Solid Gold Value** ins are rent- ed to visitors to help subsidize the adjacent private school. Run by the Seventh Day Adventists, these cabins are a heck of a bargain. They are simple but *incredibly clean* and the grounds are as quiet as any you will find on Kaua'i; there is even a small waterfall nearby to sit by and ponder. Bear in mind that as cabins, you won't get valet parking, a golf course, and room service. You *will* get an inexpensive, stand alone unit at the same price they charged ten years ago. Cabinettes are $25 per night but you share a bath with other units. Cabins are $35—kitchenette, bathroom and several beds. Shower outdoors. New cabins are $50, everything is inside. Located off Highway 50, past 7 mile mark.

KIAHUNA PLANTATION RESORT
(800) 367–7052 or (808) 742–6411

K i a h u n a P l a n t a t i o n Resort is the only resort that falls in the gray area regarding **A Real Gem** r e o p e n i n g.  Unlike the five resorts we speak of on page 174 which won't be open until 1995, and most of the rest that are already open, Kiahuna plans to reopen in July or August of 1994, and their reopening date is reasonably firm. Construction is ongoing. No pool on the premises, but they have a great beach.

Plantation Gardens Restaurant is being sold and will probably have a new name as well. 333 units. Spread out on 35 beautiful acres in Po'ipu, this resort is popular with package tours. With their renowned gardens and lush, well-tended grounds, Kiahuna is popular with repeat guests. Expect more color on the grounds with more flowering trees than they had before. Banana trees are liberally strewn throughout the grounds. The cactus garden is the same as ever. Also expect the resort to stress Hawai'i and its culture more than they did in the past. Employees are being properly "educated" to enhance the Hawaiian theme. There is a larger than usual spread in room prices depending on proximity to, and view of the ocean without any substantial differences in the quality of rooms, but the oceanfront rooms *really are* oceanfront. 1/1 units are $150–$385. 2/2 units are $275–$435. Credit cards.

KUHIO SHORES
(800) 367–5025 or (808) 245–8841

They are located right at the waters edge in Po'ipu. And that was their problem when the Hurricane hit. Although some units are available now, expect construction noises to fill the air here until 1995.

NIHI KAI VILLAS
(800) 325–5701 or (808) 742–1412

70 units, tennis court, pool and keiki pool. Well maintained grounds—wish we could say the same about the units. Hit or miss on rooms, not much continuity. Cleaning staff needs a pep talk. Small bedrooms. In general, you can do better than this for the money. 2/2 units are $85–$170, 2/2 units with dens are $144–$220. &

THE POINTE AT PO'IPU

217 units, air conditioning, 2 conference rooms, health club, pool and keiki

pool (as well as a sand bottom pool), and spas. This fabulous new resort is located next door to the Hyatt. With 22 acres of neatly groomed grounds, beautiful stair-step lily ponds and lots of nice touches, The Pointe is positioning itself to be the new *in* place on Kaua'i. The units are very nice inside with expensive furnishings and fittings. Master bathrooms have separate showers and bathtubs. 1/1 units are $195–$255. 2/2 units are $235–$295. ♿ As a *brand new* resort, they are scheduled to have their grand opening in April 1994. As we go to press, they have not chosen their telephone number, so you will have to call information (Area Code 808).

PO'IPU CRATER RESORT
(800) 367–8020 or (808) 742–7400
30 units, pool, saunas, tennis court. Located in the bottom of a small crater, the grounds are pleasant and well maintained but there is no view (technically speaking, you're in a hole). When the trade winds aren't blowing it can get pretty hot in there. 2/2 units are $98–$117.

PO'IPU KAI RESORT
(800) 367–8020 or (808) 742–7400;
(800) 777–1700 or (808) 742–6464
350 units, 8 tennis courts with pro shop, 6 pools and spas, ocean gear available. This sprawling 110 acre resort sports lots of open ground, widely varied units and close proximity to the Hyatt and its restaurants and shops. Although many rental agents represent Po'ipu Kai, **Suite Paradise** and **Colony** have the most units. **Suite Paradise** has the better rooms and at lower prices, but **Colony** deals with most of the tour package companies who get good rates for you. If you book it yourself, do it through **Suite Paradise** (theirs are the first two numbers listed). The resort is broken into 5 regions with the Po'ipu

Sands region having the best beach access (Building 5 is particularly good). In some of the ocean view units, the ocean is only visible if you break your neck in two places and hang it out the window. **House of Seafood** is the on site restaurant and is a winner. Prices are all over the place. In general, **Suite Paradise** 1/1 units are $96–$174, 2/2 units are $109–$204, 3/2 units are $144–$201, 4/4 units are $208–$248 (no oceanfronts for 3/2 or 4/4). **Colony** 1/1 units are $150–$200, 2/2 units are $210–$325, 3/2 units are $285–$345. **Grantham Resorts at (800) 325–5701** also has many units at Po'ipu Kai and at good prices.

PO'IPU KAPILI
(800) 443–7714 or (808) 742–6449

A Real Gem

60 units, lighted tennis courts, VCR, pool. Pleasant grounds, very large rooms, professional staff and a second home atmosphere. Resident turtles offshore. They take special pains to accommodate SCUBA divers (Sheraton Caves, a popular boat diving spot is directly offshore and is swimmable if you *really* want to). 1/2 units are $119–$165, 2/3 units are $162–$235 (plus $50 extra at Christmas). Credit cards.

PO'IPU MAKAI
(800) 367–5025 or (808) 245–8841
15 units, *very* small pool. Located next to the water, grounds are a bit cramped. 2/2 units are $140–$170, 5 night minimum.

PO'IPU PLANTATION
(800) 733–1632 or (808) 742–6757
9 units, air conditioned, spa, BBQ. Not really a condo, nor a hotel, nor a B&B.

More like a plantation (hence the name). Family owned, family feel, and nice folks. The "main house" is available for weddings. 1/1 units are $80–$95, 2/2 units are $105–$115. Credit cards.

PRINCE KUHIO
(800) 722–1409 or (808) 742–1409

60 units, pool. Located across the road from the ocean, this used to be a hotel and was converted to condos, so expect a hotel type layout. Studios are $69, 1/1 units are $79–$89. 1 week minimum.

SUNSET KAHILI
(800) 827–6478 or (808) 742–7434

36 units, pool. Built in 1969 (you'd swear it was the '50s) it has an old, worn feel to it. All units have nice ocean views, with the fifth floor being particularly good. Their staff is professional. You get what you pay for here. 1/1 units are $80–$85, 2/2 units are $110–$116. Credit cards.

WAIKOMO STREAM VILLAS
(800) 325–5701 or (808) 742–7220

33 units, tennis court, pool. Pretty grounds and large rooms (all garden views). Nice privacy, real good value. 1/1 units are  **Solid Gold Value** $70–$120, 2/2 units are $80–$130.

WHALERS COVE
(800) 367–7052 or (808) 742–7571

38 units, pool and spa. Expensively furnished interiors (you know it's expensive when there is koa floor trim in the closet), tastefully decorated and small but manicured grounds. Adjacent to Koloa Landing (a popular beginner SCUBA spot), this is a good place to watch the sunset. Expect more personalized service than you will find else-where. (They will even do your grocery shopping before you arrive and stock your refrigerator.) 1/2 units are $225–$275 (these actually have two bedrooms but you are limited to 2 people and charged as if it were 1/2), 2/2 units are $270–$375. Credit cards.

West Shore Condominiums

KOKE'E LODGE
(808) 335–6061

12 units, wood stove (wood is extra). Rustic is the operative term here. These cabins, located 4,000 feet up in the Koke'e State Park are controlled by the State. Don't expect nightly turndown service or a mint on your pillow. This is roughing it Kaua'i style and these cabins are in big demand. A third of the guests are locals who come here because it is cheap, chilly at night, and beautiful. Rooms usually come with several cheap beds. This is a particularly good place to stay if you are going to be doing some heavy hiking in Koke'e. The Lodge Restaurant is a good place to get some Koke'e chili and cornbread for lunch. Dinner isn't usually available so arrange your own. Reservations should be obtained 4–6 months in advance. Duplex cabins are $35 per night. Single cabins (the best value of the two types) are $45 per night. 5 night *maximum* stay. Reservations require a deposit by check. Credit cards for actual payment.

WAIMEA PLANTATION COTTAGES
(800) 992–4632 or (808) 338–1625

48 units, tennis court (smaller than regulation size), stereos, pool and keiki pool, conference room. These cottages were once plantation workers' homes. Each has been refurbished with modern amenities but they retain the old style feel inside, usually without feeling old and worn. Their attempt to display Kaua'i as

it was in the old days is successful. Each unit is different. Located on an old plantation property, peace and privacy are yours—the tradeoff is relative isolation given the location on the extreme west side. There is much feeling of 'ohana (family) here and you will definitely experience the aloha spirit. With their location so close to the mouth of the very reddish Waimea River, swimming in the murky ocean water is less than ideal. The coconut grove and banyan trees add to the charm of this property and this is a good place to watch the sunset over the private island of Ni'ihau. On site restaurant is the Grove Dining Room. Units vary tremendously from $100 for some 1/1 cottages, to $225 for a four bedroom cottage. Contact them for a complete list. Credit cards

Rental Agents

Nearly all the rental agents on the list below represent private home vacation rentals as well as condominiums in various resorts. Contact them in advance to obtain lists of rentals available. Many great bargains can be found this way.

Bed and Breakfast

B&Bs are a very popular around the world and Kaua'i is no exception. They come in all shapes and sizes. Many people love the intimate feeling one gets at a B&B. Of course, what you gain in intimacy you sometimes lose in privacy. Accommodations can run the gamut from a spare room in someone's house to a full fledge B&B inn. Since every person's needs are different and since it is not feasible to rate all of Kaua'i's B&Bs, we have selected a few that stood out from the rest for one reason or another. But bear in mind that there are many other B&Bs here that can surely give you what you want. Therefore, we also provide a list of B&B services. They will determine your

'Anini Beach Vacation Rentals	(800) 448-6333 or (808) 826-4400
Aston Hotels and Resorts	(800) 922-7866
Blue Water Vacation Rentals	(800) 628-5533 or (808) 826-9229
Colony Hotels and Resorts	(800) 777-1700
Garden Island Rentals	(800) 247-5599 or (808) 742-9537
Grantham Resorts	(800) 325-5701 or (808) 742-7220
Ha'ena Lanui Rentals	(808) 826-6239
Hanalei North Shore Properties	(800) 488-3336 or (808) 826-9622
Hanalei Aloha Rental	(800) 487-9833 or (808) 826-9833
Harrington Paradise Properties	(808) 826-9655
Hawaiian Islands Resorts	(800) 367-7042 or (808) 531-7595
Kaua'i Paradise Vacations	(800) 826-7782 or (808) 826-7444
Kaua'i Vacation Rentals	(800) 367-5025 or (808) 245-8841
Marc Resorts Hawai'i	(800) 535-0085 or (808) 922-9700
Na Pali Properties	(808) 826-7272
Oceanfront Realty	(808) 826-6585
Prosser Realty	(800) 767-4707 or (808) 245-4711
Po'ipu Connection	(800) 742-2260 or (808) 742-2233
Realty and Rentals	(800) 367-8022 or (808) 742-7555
Suite Paradise	(800) 367-8020 or (808) 742-7400
Village Resorts	(800) 367-7052

needs and find either a B&B or vacation home for you. We only list those with (800) numbers, so the call's on them.

Bed and Breakfast Services

BED AND BREAKFAST WAILUA
(800) 822-1176 or (808) 822-1177
Liz Hey knows the ins and outs to B&Bs on Kaua'i and can fix you up anywhere on the island. Tell her your needs and let her do the rest.
BED AND BREAKFAST HAWAI'I
(800) 733-1632 or (808) 822-7771
Run by longtime B&B expert Evie Warner. She even has a book called *Bed and Breakfast goes Hawaiian.*
ALL ISLANDS B&B
(800) 542-0344 or (808) 263-2342
BED & BREAKFAST HONOLULU
(800) 288-4666 or (808) 595-7533
HAWAIIAN ISLANDS B&B
(800) 258-7895 or (808) 261-7895
PACIFIC HAWAI'I B&B
(800) 999-6026 or (808) 262-6026

Selected B&Bs

TASSAHANALEI (808) 826-7298
Located on Wainiha Powerhouse Road in Ha'ena, this secluded B&B is nestled next to the Wainiha Stream. The rooms are about 50 feet from the stream and the sound of its tiny waterfall fills each of the three rooms. They have created a pool in the stream for swimming. 2 hour massages available for $50. There is a spa next to the stream. This is a great place to get away from it all and utterly relax. Lush jungle, peaceful surroundings, and a great price make this a B&B to recommend. Rooms are very clean and have private entrances. $75 for the smaller rooms (which have small but usable kitchen areas). $95 for the largest room which has full kitchen. Additional price for more than two people. Two

caveats; jungle setting makes mosquitoes a bit more prevalent, and the two smaller rooms share a quaint detached outdoor bathroom. Breakfasts are gourmet continental. No minimum stay required.

MAHINA KAI (808) 822-9451
Located in Anahola on Kaua'i's northeast side, this B&B has four units. They have beautiful, well tailored grounds, a spa and a swimming pool (unusual for a B&B). Staying here is like staying on a Japanese plantation, complete with bamboo floor mats, shoji doors, and a tea house. Lots of abstract original art. The place was designed as a B&B. A bit pricey but distinctive. Rooms start at $95 for one person, $115 for two. Others go for $150.

NANI IKENA (808) 822-5723
Located 5 miles up Kuamo'o Road on a quiet cul-de-sac in Wailua, they have 2 self-contained apartments complete with small but useable kitchens. With gorgeous mountain views and an unbeatable price, you won't find a better place to stay on Kaua'i for $50.

BLACK BAMBOO GUEST HOUSE (800) 527-7789
In Kalaheo a few miles from the ocean, they have four units with a large lanai around the upstairs (where the guests stay) in the traditional plantation style. They too have a swimming pool as well as a spa and BBQ. Units without kitchens are $60–$75, those with kitchens are $70–$85. No children. 2 night minimum. Expanded continental breakfast.

CLASSIC VACATION COTTAGES (808) 332-9201
Three self-contained units in Kalaheo offer independence at a reasonable price. All rooms have kitchens, some have phones. $58–$65 without continental breakfast, otherwise add $5.

Index

For those interested in reading more about Kaua'i, try these books:

Kaua'i Tales, by Frederick B. Wichman, Bamboo Ridge Press.

Polihale & Other Kaua'i Legends, by Frederick B. Wichman, Bamboo Ridge Press.

Kaua'i, The Separate Kingdom, by Edward Joesting, University of Hawai'i Press and Kaua'i Museum Association Limited.

Feathered Gods and Fishhooks, An Introduction to Hawaiian Archeology, by Patrick Vinton Kirch, University of Hawai'i Press.

Beaches of Kaua'i and Ni'ihau, by John R. K. Clark, University of Hawai'i Press.

Kaua'i Trails: Walks, Strolls and Treks on the Garden Island, by Kathy Morey, Wilderness Press.

Paddling Hawai'i, by Audrey Sutherland, The Mountaineers.

● ●

If you would like to order additional copies of this book for yourself or as a gift, send $10.95 for each copy, plus $3.00 shipping and handling to:

Wizard Publications
P.O. Box 991
Lihu'e, Hawai'i 96766–0991

$3.00 shipping and handling charge covers up to ten copies.